D0935149

A publication in
The Adult Education Association
Handbook Series in Adult Education

Examining
Controversies
in Adult Education

*Burton W. Kreitlow
and Associates*

Examining
Controversies
in Adult Education

Jossey-Bass Publishers

San Francisco • Washington • London • 1981

EXAMINING CONTROVERSIES IN ADULT EDUCATION
by Burton W. Kreitlow and Associates

Copyright © 1981 by: Adult Education Association
of the United States of America
810 Eighteenth Street, N.W.
Washington, D.C.   20006

Jossey-Bass Inc., Publishers
433 California Street
San Francisco, California   94104

Jossey-Bass Limited
28 Banner Street
London EC1Y 8QE

Library of Congress Cataloging in Publication Data
Main entry under title:

Examining controversies in adult education.

  (AEA handbook series in adult education)
  Bibliography: p. 257
  Includes index.
   1.   Adult education—United States—Addresses,
essays, lectures.   I.   Kreitlow, Burton W.   II.   Series:
Adult Education Association.   Adult Education Associa-
tion handbook series in adult education.
LC5251.E9   374'.973   80-27058
ISBN 0-87589-489-5

Manufactured in the United States of America

JACKET DESIGN BY WILLI BAUM

FIRST EDITION

Code 8103

THE JOSSEY-BASS SERIES IN HIGHER EDUCATION

The AEA Handbook Series in Adult Education

WILLIAM S. GRIFFITH
University of British Columbia

HOWARD Y. McCLUSKY
University of Michigan

General Editors

Edgar J. Boone
Ronald W. Shearon
Estelle E. White
and Associates
Serving Personal and
Community Needs Through
Adult Education

April 1980

John M. Peters
and Associates
Building an Effective
Adult Education
Enterprise

April 1980

Huey B. Long
Roger Hiemstra
and Associates
Changing Approaches
to Studying Adult
Education
April 1980

Robert D. Boyd
Jerold W. Apps
and Associates
Redefining
the Discipline
of Adult Education
October 1980

Alan B. Knox
and Associates
Developing, Administering,
and Evaluating
Adult Education
October 1980

Burton W. Kreitlow
and Associates
Examining Controversies
in Adult Education
March 1981

Foreword

Adult education as a field of study and of practice is not well understood by many literate and intelligent American adults whose exposure to the field has been limited to one or a few aspects of its apparently bewildering mosaic. Since 1926, when the American Association for Adult Education (AAAE) was founded, the leaders of that organization and its successor, the Adult Education Association of the U.S.A. (AEA), have striven to communicate both to the neophytes in the field and to the adult public an understanding of its diverse and complex enterprises. A major vehicle for accomplishing this communication has been a sequence of handbooks of adult education, issued periodically to convey a broad view of the mosaic. In 1934, 1936, and 1948 the AAAE published the first three handbooks. Although the Association had intended to issue a handbook every two years, that plan was not carried out for a number of reasons, including the outbreak of World War II and the termination of support by the Carnegie Corporation. Within three years of the publication of the 1948 handbook the Association dissolved itself in order to establish the AEA, which included the former members of both the AAAE and the Department of Adult Education of the National Education Association. It was nine years before the AEA was able to publish its first handbook, the fourth in the sequence, followed a decade later by the fifth version.

In the early 1970s both the Publications Committee of AEA and the Commission of the Professors of Adult Education (an affiliated organization of the AEA) explored the kinds of handbooks that could be designed to serve the changing nature and needs of the field. They found that different parts of the field were developing at different rates—in some areas information was becoming outdated rapidly, whereas in others a decennial handbook would be adequate to maintain currency. Moreover, the growing literature and the many developments in policies and programs led them to conclude that a single volume of traditional size would not be sufficient to treat the expanding knowledge base, the changing policies and practices, and the controversial topics in adult education. Accordingly, the Publications Committee decided that the next handbook would consist of several volumes, allowing the presentation of an increased amount of information on each of eight selected parts of the field and preparing the way for subsequent revisions of each volume independently on a schedule reflecting the pace of change in each area. The result is The AEA Handbook Series in Adult Education, which is being developed by the general editors with the guidance and assistance of the Publications Committee.

Examining Controversies in Adult Education was intended to reflect the vigor and commitment of the junior members of the profession, those who had completed their doctoral studies and who were committed to opposing, yet well-thought-out, positions on topics that are known to arouse strong feelings among practicing adult educators. The other seven volumes deal with Changing Approaches to Studying Adult Education; Serving Personal and Community Needs through Adult Education; Building an Effective Adult Education Enterprise; Developing, Administering, and Evaluating Adult Education; Redefining the Discipline of Adult Education; Comparing Adult Education Worldwide; and Training for Leadership for Adult Education.

Preparation of the series required the cooperation and dedicated efforts of scores of chapter authors, Publications Committee chairmen and members, and successive executive committees of the AEA. In bringing together the insights and perceptions of adult education scholars, the series is a major contribution of the Association to the advancement of an understanding of adult education as a field of study and of practice.

February 1981   WILLIAM S. GRIFFITH

                                                             HOWARD Y. McCLUSKY

                                                             General Editors

Preface

Adult education is often mistakenly perceived as being a fairly traditional conservative activity dealing with unexceptional subject matter of a professional, vocational, remedial, or hobby nature. The content of adult education programs is usually noncontroversial, avoiding sensitive issues and steering clear of disputations about values. Not surprisingly, observers of practice and programs in this field frequently get the impression that adult educators are people who never get involved in disputes, men and women who adroitly avoid arguments as they seek community approbation for their programs and institutions. In fact, adult educators are a quite contentious lot who spend a great deal of time embroiled in arguments among themselves about purposes, methods, audiences, and procedures. *Examining Controversies in Adult Education* was planned to reveal to neophytes in the field, and to all other educators as well, just what kinds of topics are being debated.

Twenty authors have contributed their views on ten questions that confront practicing adult educators. For each topic two authors present their views, which may be diametrically opposed or may provide contrasting or in some cases complementary perspectives on a given issue. This pairing of authors was done intentionally to ensure that the various perspectives would be presented. In some cases readers who have not been following the journals and magazines that abound in adult education may be surprised to learn that certain topics are still in dispute. In other cases they can expect to gain an appreciation of the reasons why a topic that may have appeared noncontroversial is being actively disputed among adult educators.

In the introductory chapter, "Philosophies at Issue," the author sets out an ideal procedure for the examination and presentation of competing, or at least contrasting, philosophies. The approach he recommends is demanding, so much so that few of the earnest debaters who have contributed their thoughts to this book are able to follow it completely. Nevertheless, he writes convincingly of the need to address controversial issues in a rigorous manner if the field is to have a defensible sense of direction.

Chapter Two addresses the question "What Should Be the Major Focus of Adult Education?" Instead of adopting the stance that adult education should be primarily focused on vocational or professional education, a position that would be supportive of most governments' funding policies, the authors argue that helping individuals lead fulfilled lives and that freeing the individual from all forms of mental and physical bondage are the focuses of greatest worth. These ultimate focuses are offered as the most desirable ends all adult educators should promote—and accordingly all teaching and curriculum development ought to be designed to serve them.

Chapter Three asks "Should the Adult Educator Be Involved in Social Intervention?" and while both authors believe adult educators have a responsibility in this area the nature of that responsibility is perceived quite differently. In the first case the argument is developed that while adult educators have a responsibility for social reconstruction, they do so most effectively not by manning the barricades but instead by educating the oppressed to recognize their condition and to acquire the skills essential to changing the system. In the second case it is argued that whatever responsibility for social reconstruction an adult educator may have, that responsibility does not flow from any characteristics of his professional role but rather arises from his obligation as a citizen.

Chapter Four tackles a question of concern to all members

of professional associations, "Should Continuing Professional Education Be Mandatory?" In one argument the element of compulsion is embraced, based on the assumption that such educational involvement does lead to increased competence or at least delayed obsolescence. In contrast the argument against mandatory continuing education is based on a set of assumptions about the nature and obligations of professionals as well as the responsibilities of professional associations. Possibly no other topic in this book is of more immediate practical concern to all professionals.

Chapter Five looks inward at adult educators themselves and asks "Should Professional Certification Be Developed for Adult Educators?" Inasmuch as adult educators are involved in preventing obsolescence and in bringing the skills of individuals in other professions up to date, it is reasonable to inquire what they are doing to ensure their own competence and that of their colleagues. Although the first position taken provides compelling arguments for certification, enumerating the benefits that could be anticipated to result from it, the opposing viewpoint brands the suggestion as both unfeasible and unnecessary. Because of the different kinds of expertise required for effective practice as an adult education teacher, administrator, researcher, or any of the myriad other roles adult educators perform, the nature of the competencies appropriate for each position varies so widely that no single standard for certification appears feasible. Nevertheless the issue persists and readers will find the arguments quite instructive.

Chapter Six asks "Should Government-Funded Programs Meet Established Standards of Performance?" Although it is possible to argue that "whoever pays the piper gets to call the tune," the issue is far too complex to be settled so simplistically. After considering the implications of different approaches to the setting or attainment of objectives, the argument is advanced that cooperative goal setting and program planning is essential to effective adult education. The discussion exposes previously ignored facets of the question and should help each reader clarify his own position.

Chapter Seven raises the question "Should Adult Education Be Competency Based?" In the first paper the author demonstrates her belief in the effectiveness of the entire behavioral objectives approach, involving the reader in a sequence of tests that address the nature and advantages of competency-based education. The author of the rejoinder assumes that the main argument in favor of using competency-based education is its utility in ensuring accountability, an argument he considers spurious. Given the current enthusiasm for competency-based education, this rejoinder cuts to the core of the issue and asks the reader to participate in this surgery.

Chapter Eight inquires "Should Colleges Grant Credit for Life Experiences?" and answers the query with contrasting but yet conservative positions. In the first paper the author endorses the idea but expresses reservations concerning how best to make wise decisions in determining which life experiences are sufficiently educative to warrant the granting of specific amounts of credit. Even so the practice is seen as having so much value that the effort required to improve the process is fully justified. Arguing from an array of assumptions, the contrasting paper concludes that on balance the effort required to develop and manage the system so as to prevent fraud is so great as to outweigh the potential benefits.

Chapter Nine examines what may be the most persistent issue in the history of the field: "Should Adult Education Require Self-Support from Learner Fees?" In this case the authors clearly take opposing viewpoints, presenting possibly the fullest treatment of the issue that has appeared in the literature of adult education. The positions are argued well, a fact that will prevent the readers' reaching an easy decision about which view they support.

Chapter Ten opens up the issue of local control by discussing "Should Adult Education Program Goals Be Established at the Local Level?" In these two papers the authors thoughtfully assess the contributions that local communities are best prepared to make in adult education programming. But in the first case the author concludes that the advantages are so overwhelming that the question can only be answered in the affirmative. In the second case the author analytically explores the contributions that can be made by individuals, groups, associations and departments serving a larger geographic area and concludes that while full control of local programming should in no case be relinquished to external agents, efforts directed to obtaining outside advice and perspectives pay off in superior programming.

Chapter Eleven assesses leadership responsibilities for the field, paying particular attention to the place of the national government in the pattern of sponsors and program providers. In raising the question "Should the Federal Government Assume a Major Leadership Role in Adult Education?" the authors present both pragmatic and philosophical arguments. In the first paper the answer is affirmative, justified on many grounds but primarily because no other group or association is capable of performing the combination of functions required of active leadership. In the second paper the author acknowledges the importance of various levels of government in the provision of financial support for adult education but argues that in the long-term best interests of the field and of the public the professional adult educators must organize themselves to perform the major leadership role.

Chapter Twelve, the final chapter, turns from the pattern of presenting contrasting, conflicting, or complementary views on a single controversial issue and sets out through a series of scenarios reaching into the twenty-first century to identify what are likely to be the issues that will arouse adult educators and spark debates. In accordance with the growing interest in futurism and the large membership of organizations established to explore the future, this chapter shows adult educators and observers of the field how a futurist imagines the future of adult education.

Throughout, these authors provide a thoughtful examination of controversial issues, each one of which is a major concern of a sizable number of adult educators. The reader who seeks closure will be disappointed for the issues addressed are such that conclusive resolution is exceedingly difficult. Nevertheless, having examined contrasting position statements of articulate, professionally trained adult educators on these issues, the reader will not only have a clearer notion of the nature of these persistent controversial issues, he may also be led to examine his own positions on them and to arrive at a more integrated view of the evolving adult education field.

Madison, Wisconsin   BURTON W. KREITLOW
January 1981

Contents

The Authors

HAROLD W. BEDER, assistant professor of adult education, Rutgers University

DAVID L. BOGGS, assistant professor of adult education, Ohio State University

ROGER W. BOSHIER, associate professor of adult education, University of British Columbia, Canada

CATHERINE ROSENKRANZ CAMERON, visiting lecturer, University Federal de Santa Maria, Brazil

NOREEN M. CLARK, director of public health education, assistant professor of health administration, Columbia University

J. DAVID DESHLER, assistant professor of adult education, Cornell University

MARY JANE EVEN, assistant professor of adult and continuing education, University of Nebraska-Lincoln

ROBERT A. FELLENZ, associate professor of adult and extension education, Texas A & M University

LAVERNE B. FOREST, associate professor of continuing and vocational education, University of Wisconsin-Madison

MARGOT KEITH GREEN, evaluation consultant, Indiana Department of Public Instruction

HERSCHEL N. HADLEY, associate director, Evaluation and Research,

Commonwealth of Massachusetts Center for High Technology and Education

GRACE M. HEALY, associate professor of adult education, Syracuse University

WAYNNE B. JAMES, assistant professor of occupational and adult education, Oklahoma State University

BURTON W. KREITLOW, professor of continuing and vocational education, University of Wisconsin-Madison

LEO McGEE, assistant dean of extended services, Tennessee Technological University

PAUL ST. CLAIR McGINNIS, program director, Canada World Youth, Montreal

KENNETH J. MATTRAN, assistant professor of adult and continuing education, University of Nebraska-Lincoln

ALLEN B. MOORE, assistant professor of adult education, University of Georgia

FLOYD C. PENNINGTON, director, Office of Continuing Medical Education, University of Michigan

KATHLEEN ROCKHILL, assistant professor of adult education, University of California-Los Angeles

JOHN C. SNIDER, director, Center for Continuing Education, Colorado State University

HAROLD W. STUBBLEFIELD, associate professor of adult and continuing education, Virginia Polytechnic Institute and State University

HOWARD A. SULKIN, vice-president for planning, De Paul University

Examining
Controversies
in Adult Education

Chapter One

Philosophies at Issue

David L. Boggs

To become an issue in adult education, a phenomenon, trend, or practice must be significant enough to affect present and future practice, and individuals must hold differing views on the best course of action in its regard. A reasoned discourse on any issue in adult education, whatever its origin, will include four kinds of normative statements. These statements are the substance of any traditional philosophical exposition as outlined by Frankena (1974). They need not follow any particular order. First, an author will state what he believes adult educators should or should not do with respect to an issue. Second, the author will provide analyses of the terms, concepts, arguments, slogans, or statements that others have used to express opinions on an issue. Third, whenever possible, the author will buttress his position by empirical facts, hypotheses about their explanation, experimental findings, and predictions. Finally, a complete discourse on any given issue will go one step further and describe how to accomplish the desired objective, providing evidence and arguments to justify the process.

In response to such a discourse, two forms of behavior, both of which are inherently philosophical, are expected of the reader. He must first be analytical, locating and examining assumptions and meanings of words employed by an author. The analytical reader searches for internal consistency in the beliefs, commitments, and criteria stated by the author. This is fundamentally a proactive process, one which we attempt to foster among adult learners. "It is the process of posing meaningful questions and seeking intelligent response to those questions—questions that deal primarily with the nature of reality, the criteria of knowledge, and problems of value" (Brauner and Burns, 1965, p. 21). Second, the reader can augment his analysis of the positions and argument of the authors with his own conclusions to guide professional practice. Such conclusions themselves take the form of normative statements to be analyzed by others in turn.

But do we have a body of thought, an agreed-on corpus of

normative propositions concerning the scope, ends, and means of adult education that are internally consistent and composed of the responses made to questions raised in the process of philosophizing? The pluralistic nature of adult education seems to preclude such a possibility. Yet those who deal with the teaching and learning of adults frequently feel considerable pressure to provide and to justify a theory of adult education based on sound philosophical processes. The argument can be made that adult education needs a unifying theory because it consists of a hodge-podge of facts and theories derived from other disciplines, as indeed does all of education. Understandably, there are those who caution against devising any unifying theory: "All of us are prone from time to time to indulge in the unwarranted faith that the academic mind at its best is equal to the task of providing a system of philosophy that will prove itself adequate to the complex exigencies of fact. And the systematic academic mind is understandably susceptible of this persuasion whenever reforming zeal runs high. Conversely, the creative and dedicated scholar is uniquely impervious to this profane presumption himself and always suspicious of it in the many varied forms it takes in others" (Kirchner, 1974, p. 23).

Strategies of Thought Regarding Adulthood

With the caveat of "profane presumption" firmly in mind, let us explore whether there is a distinctive way of thinking about the nature of adulthood; that is, a strategy of thought that can contribute to our understanding of the field we call adult education.

Beck (1974, p. 285) identifies some typical features of philosophy as it contributes to a strategy of thought concerning adulthood. First, "Philosophy is typically concerned with problems that cannot be settled by straightforward and immediate observation. The philosopher typically concerns himself with problems at some remove from the realm of observation." Moreover, the philosopher "will typically get data by drawing upon research carried out by nonphilosophers whom he has judged by some criterion to be reliable." In this regard, data for the study of adulthood are abundant and varied, but the archives for such study wait to be created. According to Graubard (1976, p. v), "Whether the data are psychoanalytic, medical, literary, or religious, . . . the problem is to develop analytical procedures that will make the study of 'adulthood' as common as the study of childhood."

Another feature of philosophy noted by Beck is that it clarifies meaning, develops concepts, establishes frames of reference, and, in general, provides the intellectual tools for the thought and observation involved in answering substantive questions. Philosophy has always fulfilled this role in regard to education, and adult education has fulfilled this purpose for mature learners. It has provided the means whereby adults could not only get information but also interpret it, organize it, and use it in making decisions and in taking action. Hence, adult educators not only deliver information but also assist adults in the analysis, evaluation, and employment of it.

Historically, philosophers have had great impact on educational theory and practice. All educational theories or systems are based on some view of man, and the philosophers have examined man's nature. Every educator has at least an implicit philosophical anthropology. Educational systems are but reflected images of philosophical creeds. What the philosophers said yesterday about man, educators are saying today. It seems reasonable to conclude, then, that the philosophy of adult education should have as its basis some clear notions about adulthood. That is, it should grow out of and reflect not merely what it means to be human but what it means to be adult. A clear understanding of adulthood then becomes the basis for formulating criteria for judging the worth or value of educational efforts for adults. This understanding is more fundamental than knowing the aims and objectives of adult education, or the role of teachers and learners in the instructional process, or the content of adult education activities.

As might be expected, however, philosophers' deliberations on the nature of man have more immediately influenced the development of educational theory and practice with children than they have influenced the field of adult education. At times the philosophers themselves made applications of their theories to education. For instance, John Amos Comenius, Jean Jacques

Rousseau, and Johann Pestalozzi all believed that to perceive things directly is to know them, so that the senses are the gateway to knowledge. Their positions gave impetus to the now well-accepted educational principle that children best learn the nature of material things by first-hand sense experience with them. A logical extension of this principle in adult education is to make learning problem centered rather than subject centered, since problems are always concrete. Adults do not lack an experiential base; their need is to make sense of the experiences that bombard them.

In some cases, applications of a philosopher's teachings to the field of education were made by his followers or contemporary philosophers of education. Immanuel Kant, for example, enunciated the notion of a "categorical imperative," a sense of duty which is the essence of all morality. In doing one's duty, one never regards others as means to an end; rather, one respects the intrinsic worth of every human being. Kant's teaching is used by Brown (1966, p. 203) to identify two distinct senses of duty in the realm of education for children: "A teacher may feel that he is doing his duty when he strives to do what is officially expected of him by a superior, even though on occasions he may feel that what he does is not in the best interests of children. . . . His sense of duty is to 'higher officers'—to what is expected of him. The morally strong teacher or administrator who sees children only as ends and refuses to have them treated as means may act out of quite a different sense of duty, a sense of moral obligation." For adult educators, Kant's categorical imperative means that learners should be involved in needs assessment and in the entire educational process. The adult educator's sense of moral obligation might be described as loyalty to the learner over all other considerations.

It is not surprising that philosophers have failed to differentiate between children and adults in their treatise on man's nature or that applications of their teachings to education have typically been made with only children in mind. The time lag between the generation of philosophical propositions and their application to practical disciplines such as education is generally about 200 years, whereas the concept of adulthood in the sense we use it today is of relatively recent origin. According to the *Oxford English Dictionary*

(OED), the word *adultness* came into use only a century ago. The term *adult* is, of course, considerably older, but nonetheless a relatively recent acquisition. It derives from the past participle of the Latin *adolescere*, "to grow up," which implies a process rather than the possession of a particular status. The word was used infrequently in eighteenth- and even nineteenth-century America. Only in recent years has it taken on the burden of freight it carries in such phrases as "adult education" and "adult films" or "adults only."

Furthermore, even though "adult" and "adulthood" are in common usage in contemporary society, they usually designate merely a catch-all category for everything that happens to the individual human being after attaining the statutory age of majority. They have none of the concreteness that attaches to terms such as *childhood* or *adolescence*, because adults in contemporary society are generally viewed in an undifferentiated manner, the perception being that adulthood is a static condition. According to Graubard (1976, p. v), "All too little thought is given to the way they [adults] differ from one another or from children. Despite the growth of interest in the human life cycle, we still know far too little about the 'stages' of adult life, not nearly enough about the transition from adolescence to adulthood, and surprisingly little about middle age, let alone senescence."

Recently, however, more and more writers are recognizing adulthood as a time when significant personal changes occur. The advent of books such as *Passages* (Sheehy, 1976) and *Making It from 40 to 50* (Davitz and Davitz, 1976), past and promised issues of *Daedalus* devoted to the meaning of adulthood, and the attention being given to middle and old age as distinct topics in texts of psychiatry lend substance to the hope that we may indeed be entering the "century of the adult." It is left to contemporary scholars and practitioners of adult education to make applications of principles derived from studies on the nature of adulthood and the adult life cycle to their fields of study and practice.

Recurring Themes

A careful review of the meanings assigned to being adult by various religions and cultures, as well as an examination of pertinent works of contemporary scholars—a process similar to that recommended by Beck (1974, p. 284) as entirely appropriate to philosophy—can enrich the perspective of adult educators and contribute significantly to our philosophical base. The sources for this review are abundant and varied. Our purpose is not to review their substance here but rather to identify the common thread which appears consistently throughout: that growth and change are endemic to adulthood.

Religious Views. The essential element in the Christian idea of adulthood is a capacity for growth. The Christian is not to evade the challenges of life but, rather, to venture out, even at the risk of making mistakes, for the sake of growth. The worst thing for a person to do is to cease growing and remain fixed at any point in life. Immaturity is the refusal to grow.

The Muslim tradition, too, provides a notion of what the fully matured person should do. Allowing for the diverseness of the Islam tradition, Lapidus (1976, p. 96) explains that it lays heavy stress on matters of this world and on the moral, ethical, and psychological nature of man. Legal rules and moral standards are important, but inner growth through emotional awareness also is stressed. In coping with contradictory truths of the heart, the Muslim is to develop the emotional stability and maturity that make ethically correct behavior possible. Maturity has as much to do with emotion as with intellect.

The Chinese perception of adulthood as embodied in the Confucian tradition is not that of a condition attained but of a process unfolding. Without self-cultivation as a continuous effort to realize one's humanity, biological growth becomes meaningless. Adulthood, then, is "to become a person." In Confucian literature, the Way is a root metaphor for the idea of adulthood, which is a way of "becoming." An often-quoted dictum from Confucius is "If you can renovate yourself one day, then you can do so every day, and keep doing so day after day." Implicit in the Confucian tradition is that each person is to realize humanity or adulthood in himself. There is no one correct standard or model. Adulthood, then, can be recognized, but it can never be defined.

According to Tu Wei-Ming (1976, p. 114), respect for the old is based on the assumption that, in the long and unavoidable journey of self-improvement, an old person ought to have forged way ahead in furnishing his life with inspiring contents.

Rohlen (1976) contends that the Japanese view of aging centers on personal growth, demands considerable effort and application, looks to a release from "the self" rather than to its satisfaction, and stands as a most important yardstick of personal achievement and the life well led. The Japanese, too, view being an adult as a process of becoming human through intentional effort at personal cultivation. The process is not automatic and is not limited to a set period of life.

Erikson's Analysis of Stages of Adulthood. Erik Erikson's analysis of growing into adulthood through successive life stages has a universal quality to its interpretation. Each stage is defined by a phase-specific task and follows a general chronology without being linked to specific age limits. Erikson's own focus of interest has been shifting to the last three stages: young adulthood, maturity, and old age. The phase-specific task for each stage is defined in terms of the polar opposites of successful outcome or failure. Erikson provided two terms which are virtually antonyms as descriptions for his life stages. One is the word for failure and the other for success in a particular development. Erikson also identifies a virtue or dynamic quality corresponding to each phase-specific task, the cultivation of which is required for its successful resolution.

Two distinct elements of growth having implications for adult education can be noted within Erikson's scheme. First, the virtues themselves are capable of being augmented and developed. For example, the virtue associated with the phase-specific task of generativity versus self-absorption, characteristic of the middle years of adulthood or maturity, is care. Care, as defined by Erikson (1976, p. 24), is "the widening concern for what has been generated by love, necessity, or accident; it overcomes the ambivalence arising from irreversible obligation." Adults can learn to understand and express this caring in ever more effective ways through activities that enhance their functions as parent, spouse, mentor, and leader in professional organizations. Adult education, then, is predicated on the philosophical assumption that adult intelligence, behavior, and inner dynamic strength are malleable and responsive to systematic learning activities. The second element is that each life stage, passage, crisis, or developmental period has its own inherent learning needs and forces for growth and change. Adult education has the capacity to meet those needs and assist and inspire that growth process.

Other Contemporary Themes. Three themes, each with its own important and unresolved issues, recur most often in the philosophical literature on adult education: aims and objectives, roles of teacher and learner in the instructional process, and content. For example, Powell and Benne (1960) have reviewed two major American theories of adult education. The rationalist camp stresses continuity with past cultural traditions, as found in liberal arts, reading-discussion, great books, and humanities. The developmental camp emphasizes the application of problem-solving intelligence to present needs. White (1970) considers the questions of who is to teach and who is to learn, what is to be learned and how, as the ingredients basic to formulating a philosophical base to adult education. Bergevin (1967) and Schwertman (1958) dwell primarily on the goals and purposes entertained by participants as the principal focus for such a theory. Elias and Merriam (1980) have recently described the relationship of six philosophical positions to the planning of adult education.

Adult Education and the Enhancement of Growth

What has been learned and what will be discovered about adulthood should contribute significantly to the philosophical base undergirding the practice of education for adults. Since being an adult is a function of growing and expanding that ends only with the termination of life itself, educational experiences designed to assist adults in accommodating to the changes within and around themselves must of necessity be life-giving experiences. Adult education is life giving or enhances growth to the extent that it (1) enables a person to develop latent skills and a viable self-concept; (2) helps to dissolve fears, prejudices, errors, and half-truths and releases one from allegiance to slogans, myths, propaganda, and stereotypes; (3) supports creative capacity in literature and the arts; (4) supports the individual's dreams of achievement and progress toward a significant goal; (5) enlarges a person's capacity for tolerance, generosity, sensitivity, understanding, and judgment; (6)

provides access to greater opportunity; (7) reanimates our national promise of the realization of each citizen's full potential; and (8) contributes to revitalizing our cultural and humanistic traditions.

Adult education is not life giving, however, when a learner (1) is given certitude when controversy and doubt remain; (2) is led to premature closure when issues are still unresolvable by reliable methods of knowledge; (3) is given answers rather than reaching them independently; (4) is not challenged to exceed previous levels of attainment; and (5) accumulates information but is not helped to interpret, organize, evaluate, and use that information in taking action.

The question of what is life giving and what is stifling and defeating in the realm of adult education and the issues that confront it is open to serious debate. The debate should proceed from the premise that adult education must above all be a vehicle for enhancing adultness. Hence, the issue is never merely whether adult education should be compulsory or whether college credit should be given for life experience. Rather, in addition to meeting the criteria for a substantial philosophical exposition as outlined earlier in the chapter, each position taken on an issue should be thoughtfully examined for the contribution it makes to adult education as a life-giving enterprise and for the extent to which it reflects the complex nature of adulthood. Perhaps through such examination we can arrive at what is normative for adult education.

Chapter Two

What Should Be the Major Focus of Adult Education?

The Focus Should Be on Life Fulfillment

Harold W. Stubblefield

The field of adult education does not have a major focus, and this lack should not be surprising. Adult education is usually defined to encompass all organized learning activities in which adults engage, including vocational education. Moreover, adult education is a function of many social institutions and not of a designated agency such as the public schools or the higher education system. Even these supposedly monolithic institutions have difficulty in defining their adult education roles. In adult education no single agency, either public or private, has authority to compel the various sponsoring agencies to agree on a common purpose or even to discuss it. In those areas where national policy has been formulated, adult education is directed toward such groups as the disadvantaged. Finally, adult education can and does serve many purposes. It can be used to increase productivity in a factory, to indoctrinate persons, to raise the consciousness of oppressed groups, and to help persons become more competent learners.

Anyone who advocates that one major focus for adult education should be adopted as the integrating idea for the field enters a thicket of controversy. If it is argued that the major focus should be on life fulfillment, the controversy is assured. In proposing that adult education should have a major focus and that that focus should be on life fulfillment, one must address several concerns. An obvious concern is whether there is even a need to agree on a major focus. Is it indeed possible for one dominant purpose, an undergirding philosophical assumption, an integrating idea, to serve as a focal point for activity in this amorphous field? And if so, how can such a focus be realized? If the concept of life fulfillment is adopted as the major focus, how can this concept be described in operational terms, and how will the field be affected?

The term *life fulfillment* is like a Rorschach inkblot in that individuals impose their own meanings on it. In this paper, adult education for life fulfillment refers to the life needs and aspirations of adults. It centers on individuals and the ways in which they find meaning and fulfillment in life. Life fulfillment is not a condition or state for which one can be educated. It is, in a sense, a by-product, attained when one finds satisfaction and meaning in what one does. Adult education that focuses on life fulfillment builds on a model of human beings as purposive and self-directed, choosing and acting according to their own goals and needs in relation to personal values, significant others, and the larger social order.

A distinction is drawn here between adult education for life fulfillment as a form of education and adult education for life fulfillment as an integrating idea for the field. In descriptive analyses of adult education, writers have classified continuing education for fulfillment as one type of adult education. Liveright's 1968 study is a well-known example. In this study he classifies adult education into four types: (1) education for occupational, vocational, and professional competence; (2) education for personal or family competence; (3) education for social and civic competence; and (4) education for self-realization. Education for self-realization includes education for leisure and retirement and fulfillment of a person's potential as an individual; that is, "education for its own sake." Similar classification schemes are common in the literature (see, for instance, United States Department of Health, Education and Welfare, 1972).

Life fulfillment provides a metagoal for educators of adults. If the goal of life fulfillment were taken seriously, every educational activity would be judged not only by the degree to which the learning objectives were attained but also by the ways in which the activity enhanced skills in self-directed inquiry and promoted the qualities of maturity. A focus on fulfillment compels a holistic view of the adult, who is more than a worker, more than a family member, more than a buyer of goods. Instead, he is a complex person, enmeshed in a network of relationships and seeking competence in various areas—most basically, the competence of learning.

Historical Perspectives

When the belief that the major focus of adult education should be on life fulfillment is examined historically, it becomes clear that such an idea is not a new development in adult education thought or a peripheral concern of leaders in the field. Although historically the term *life fulfillment* itself was not used, the long-standing belief that adult education should foster individual growth for a social end clearly implies life fulfillment. In the formative years of the adult education movement, 1926–1929, this belief that adult education should be the means of individual growth within a social medium for a social end emerged as the core tradition (Stubblefield, 1976).

In 1926, in the earliest formulation of this core tradition of adult education, Lindeman argued that the purposes of adult education should be derived from what adults want. He saw adult education as an instrument for helping adults understand their experiences and thereby find meaning in their lives. In his view, persons who engage in adult education are striving to improve themselves; that is, to gain intelligence, power, self-expression, freedom, creativity, appreciation, enjoyment, and fellowship. Lindeman's basic thesis was that adults do not have to be forced to learn. Adults learn what is meaningful to them, what helps them to understand their experiences and to respond creatively to their life situations. If adults refuse to participate in educational activities, the problem cannot be attributed to their lack of either ability or motivation. The problem lies with educators who do not know how to create the conditions that permit adults to be active participants in their own learning. Adults do not want to be schooled; they want to learn.

But adult learners seek more than self-improvement, Lindeman maintained. They also want to change the social order, to create a social environment that permits personalities to grow. Beyond self-improvement, adult education has a further purpose of helping adults understand the nature of their associational life, the collectivism of urban, industrialized society, and approaches to the problems created by collective life.

To these purposes Lindeman added a third: to equip adults to manage the threats to democracy. The rise of specialized domains of knowledge had produced experts who threatened to eclipse the decision-making role of the citizens. Adult education, he argued, should provide adults with skills to determine the ends they want to pursue and then arrange for access to experts to help them achieve those ends.

The interpreters of the adult education movement who followed Lindeman stressed one theme or another from the ideas comprising this core tradition. One of the themes centered on the individual and his growth toward maturity. Overstreet (1949, p. 41) emphasized the maturity concept in adult education and formulated its most thorough expression: "The business of man is to mature: to mature psychologically as well as physically, to mature along the lines of what is unique in him and what he healthily shares with all his fellows, and to continue the maturing process throughout his life." According to Blakely (1960, p. 6), adult education should foster "the development of individuals who will fulfill themselves and freely serve the society which values individuals." Bergevin (1967, p. 5) advocated as the principal task of adult education the "development of free, creative, and responsible persons in order to advance the human maturation process." To him the term *maturity* meant the growth and development of persons toward wholeness for the purpose of achieving constructive spiritual, vocational, physical, political, and cultural goals.

A second theme touched on the characteristics of society and the personal competencies and social mechanisms required to cope with changing social conditions. From an analysis of the characteristics of the modern world, Hallenbeck (1960) derived five social functions for adult education: expanding communication skills, developing flexibility, improving human relations, facilitating participation and involvement in politics and organizations, and expediting personal growth. Benne (1967) focused his analysis more sharply on the need to build mechanisms for resolving conflicts between persons and between groups at every level of social organization.

A third theme, stressing adult civic life, appeared less frequently; for many interpreters assumed that a mature adult would, as a matter of course, participate in the larger social order. Lindeman (Smith and Lindeman, 1951) and Benne (1967), in particular, examined the behavioral requirements of democracy and the implications for adult education. Lindeman called these behavioral requirements "the democratic disciplines" and Benne "the arts of democratic citizenship." But both stressed the need for skills of conflict resolution, of understanding the opinions of others, and of discussion so that various points of view could be presented and examined and decisions made about a course of action.

In these attempts to provide a central focus for adult education, the adult is portrayed as a growing, developing person whose primary motivation for learning springs from the quest for personal maturity and the desire to manage constructively the requirements of a changing society and a democratic political and value system. Hallenbeck (1964, p. 13) acknowledged that adult education has many functions, but he argued that there should be a common denominator to guide the activities of persons in the field: "The role of adult education in American society is twofold: to keep the social, political, and economic machinery of its dynamic civilization in operation; to inspire, induce, guide, and teach adults in all phases of personal development and enrichment so that each individual can work out his own way of living, and of finding meaning in life, his own approach to realizing himself as an individual."

Significance, Present Status, and Alternatives

That the field of adult education should have a central purpose seems important, but such a purpose appears to be of crucial significance now. The field of adult education is in a state of flux similar to the situation in the 1920s, when the first coordinating organization was formed. New currents move in the field, and new social, economic, and political forces are at work. Even the term *adult education*, which once described the field, is being replaced by such terms as *continuing education, recurrent education, lifelong education,* and *human resource development.*

Adult education has become the frontier of education and is its largest potential for growth. Adults in increasingly larger numbers participate in educational activities sponsored by core and peripheral institutions and in self-planned, self-initiated, and self-directed learning projects. Higher education institutions are beginning to modify their operations to make higher education more accessible to adults. Community colleges offer an array of educational opportunities to adults, and public schools are enlarging their programs within the community education movement. Social institutions of all kinds now promote adult education for their staffs or for the publics which they serve. A system, or series of systems, for the continuing education of adults is emerging. Such a structure should not be built without clarification of its philosophical assumptions about the nature and purpose of the education which it offers.

In the late 1960s and 1970s, several authors addressed the problem of a dominant purpose for adult education. Blakely and Lappin (1969) concluded that adult education should focus on some of the large "action objectives" that concern the American people—for example, the concern for human development or for controlling the consequences of applied sciences. Either of these, in their view, would provide an integrating idea around which the work of various persons in the field could be focused. Recognizing that the applications of adult education are multiform, Houle (1972) doubted that adult education can be focused around a major goal. Several credos, he pointed out, have attempted to provide unity to the field, but none has proved comprehensive or compelling enough to do so. Using the several philosophies of education as a starting point, Apps (1973) derived from each a dominant purpose for adult education. Though a useful analysis, Apps's effort did not result in a rationale for selecting one dominant purpose. More recently Elias and Merriam (1980) have described six competing philosophies, but they hold out no hope for eventual unification.

Though he was not concerned with identifying a unifying purpose for adult education, Jensen (1970) examined the characteristics of adult education that would promote self-fulfillment. Taking as the basic assumption that education for self-fulfillment seeks to help individuals meet their individual needs and become all that they are capable of becoming, Jensen proposed several kinds of educational experiences that adults should have. These experiences, he felt, should (1) help adults understand their own values and attitudes and communicate with groups other than their own reference group; (2) enable adults to learn how to learn; (3) provide knowledge and skills about the social aspects of living; and (4) provide help in learning problem-solving skills.

Life fulfillment is, of course, not the only possible major focus for adult education. An alternative view is that all adult education contributes to life fulfillment. Educational activities that help an individual upgrade job skills so that both satisfaction and income are increased promote life fulfillment, as do activities that help persons achieve personal satisfaction in activities such as playing the banjo or decorating a cake.

A second alternative view is that adult education needs a major focus but that that focus should be on something other than life fulfillment. Some, for instance, believe that educational accessibility, rather than life fulfillment, should be emphasized. At the heart of this position lies the belief that education is a social good and that educational opportunities provided for children, youth, and young adults should be extended to adults, usually through the same institutions. Such a concern can be seen in the movement for nontraditional study, recurrent education, lifelong education, and the learning society. Such a movement has arisen at this time for many complex reasons, among them the need of adults for credentialing, the need of higher education institutions for students, and the recognition that learning must be extended into adulthood to meet changing social and technological conditions. Others would emphasize economic education: education for work and the consumer role. Activities in this area include (1) remedial education, such as adult basic education; (2) consumer education; (3) job-related training activities for job updating, retraining, and entry-level skills; and (4) career education. This type of education is recognized as socially legitimate and warranting national policy action. Special attention is directed by legislative mandate toward the socially and economically disadvantaged, the physically and mentally handicapped, and the elderly. Still others would emphasize civic education. In a democracy the importance of this emphasis cannot be denied, and as an integrating idea it transcends the special interests of diverse groups. It has never proved effective, however, as a focal point.

A Personal Position

The point of view presented here is that life fulfillment should be the major focus of adult education. Among the forces promoting interest in the continuing education of adults, at least two present persuasive reasons why adult education should be focused on life fulfillment. One is the impact of social and

technological change. A rapidly changing society requires many
persons to update their job skills or to train for new careers periodically; it also influences the nonvocational life of adults in such
areas as transportation, communication, and medicine. Adults
need to continue learning not only to adapt to change but also to
control its effects and to initiate change projects themselves. The
second force is the recognition that learning is a natural and pervasive human activity by which individuals adjust to change and
enhance their own potential. This force should compel, more than
it does now, the attention of policymakers, adult education practitioners, and those who study adult education.

Adult education that focuses on life fulfillment derives its
rationale from the learning motivation of adults: their desire for
self-actualization and for the control of their social environment.
Within this frame of reference, the goals of education are seen
from the learner's, rather than the educator's, point of view.

Such a position derives from several assumptions about
adult education. The first assumption is that the continuing education of adults, in its most fundamental definition, refers to a
process of problem solving related to the continuously evolving
interests and needs of adults. Continuing education is "proces-
sional" in that it is a way of gaining new information about, and
awareness of, one's environment and of gaining competencies to
act on that environment. As Leagans (1972) puts it, adult education
is a process of learning to fulfill individual aspirations and to develop individual potentialities for meeting demands of a changing
environment. Adult education is not just schooling extended to
adults of all ages. Adult education must be based on a developmental perspective that combines both a psychology and a sociology of
adulthood; that is, it must be built on knowledge about the patterns
of adult growth and the structure and demands of the society
in which adults live. Adults pass through age stages, each with
dominant concerns or tasks to which they must attend (Havighurst,
1976; Houle, 1974; Huberman, 1974). Unlike students in formal
systems of education with predetermined curricula, adults use education to meet the demands and aspirations of their particular
periods of life. "Learning is anchored firmly to the changing
nature of the individual" (Houle, 1974, p. 443). The interests

that adults have for particular categories of educational programs change with age.

The second assumption is that the most important human competence to be cultivated through education is the competence of learning; for learning enables us to "acquire the skills to interpret and modify our experience through new and more satisfactory courses of action" (Ziegler, 1976, p. 255). The human organism adapts itself to its environment through learning. This basic human competence—the ability to change the self and the environment—is refined through systematic learning; that is, education. The highest order of systematic learning is competence in learning and in directing one's self in using that competence. Self-directed learning requires basic skills in planning, selecting resources, acquiring information, interpreting that information, and acting on it. But self-directed learning is more than learning without a teacher; it engages the whole person. Learning is a form of action in which one diagnoses the situation and its demands. The self-directed learner—or the autonomous learner, as he might be called—is aware of the process of learning and out of this process creates useful knowledge. Blakely (1971, pp. 77–78) has described the essential skills of the adult learner: "Human learning is a dynamic process. As a process, learning is a set of attitudes, values, and methods. Self-initiated, self-directed learning must be powered by inner motives, guided by goals, and controlled by skills. The most general skill is the ability to diagnose the educational needs implied in the demands that others make upon one's self and the aspirations that one holds for one's self, and to meet those needs by undertaking appropriate experiences of systematic learning. A component of such skill is knowing when and how to seek the help one needs in diagnosis, design, and execution."

The third assumption is that adult education derives its purpose from the values inherent in the political and social system in which it is embedded. In a government based on a democratic political and social philosophy, the people—the citizens—themselves determine the ends which they want to pursue and the means by which these ends should be attained. Within this system, education for adults seeks to accomplish two primary purposes. First, it enhances the learning competencies of adults so that they are free to pursue their own ends. Second, it enhances the competencies of adults to engage in collaborative decision making, problem solving, and action taking. In the absence of these competencies, democracy cannot survive. In a democracy, adults to a large extent govern themselves through participation in such voluntary associations as political parties, labor unions, chambers of commerce, churches, and civic clubs. Adult education for life fulfillment encompasses both education for self-actualization and education for governance.

Conclusion

To make life fulfillment the major focus of adult education will not be easy. But a number of efforts can be made to promote this goal.

First of all, the thesis presented here—that the major focus of adult education should be on life fulfillment—should become the subject of serious debate and reflection among adult educationists, adult education practitioners, and policymakers. Such an undertaking would address the questions of what the term *life fulfillment* means, how adult education contributes to life fulfillment, and what characteristics of adult education promote life fulfillment. Each sponsoring agency should examine its efforts in view of this encompassing purpose. At the very least, serious consideration of this thesis should produce the beginnings of a social philosophy of adult learning.

In such a sustained study, the purpose would not be to reduce the varied adult education activities into a single mold. Adult education has many functions to perform, and particular social, cultural, economic, and political circumstances compel concentrated attention to one function or another. But adult education does have a tradition of fostering diversity. Consideration of life fulfillment as the major focus of the field may be the means of clarifying a common purpose.

A second aspect of a sustained effort to promote life fulfillment as the major focus should be directed toward the study of adult education history. A descriptive and analytical historical study of adult education activities might produce useful information about the reasons why and the conditions under which adults engage in learning to further their own interests and the interests of the larger society.

A third part of this effort calls for empirical research on the learning behavior of adults: the motivation for learning and the uses that adults make of their learning. Houle (1961), Tough (1971), and others have begun this task. Any widespread and massive attempt to meet the learning needs of adults through any delivery system or series of delivery systems ought to be built on a body of knowledge about the learning modes of adults. Adults should be assisted to learn in ways that are most natural to them and not only in ways that are most convenient for the sponsoring institutions.

A fourth part of this effort centers on the development and diffusion of a methodology of adult learning which permits adults to control their own learning, which enhances their competencies in self-directed inquiry, and which promotes their maturity. Such a methodology has already been partly developed, and significant work is presently under way to refine and extend its applicability to a variety of learning situations.

The adoption of life fulfillment as the major focus has numerous implications for the field of adult education.

1. Given life fulfillment as the major focus, more attention would be addressed to action-oriented learning: learning directed toward the attainment of individual, organizational, and social goals. An indispensable competence for every adult would be skill in conducting learning projects and in collaborating with others in learning, problem solving, and decision making. Each person would become his own educator.

2. Such a focus accentuates the diagnostic and consultative functions of the adult educator in working with various client systems: individuals, groups, organizations, and communities. The adult educator gives primary attention to diagnosing the situation of his client to identify problems and desired goals. His task is developmental in that he attempts to enhance the competencies of his client to function more effectively through learning activities. His posture is consultative in that he assists the client to identify educa-

tional needs and to design educational interventions to meet those
needs.

   3. Every learning activity in which adults engage is an experience leading toward maturity or immaturity, toward wholeness
or fractionation, toward competence or incompetence in learning.
Adult education which promotes life fulfillment furthers the quest
for maturity, wholeness, and learning competence.

The Focus Should Be on Human Liberation

Paul St. Clair McGinnis

"The great thing about adult education is that it is a morass, un-definable, it's . . . it's beautiful!" This statement by an adult educator illustrates the scattered, tentacled nature of adult education. Some adult educators argue that their field should remain a morass to ensure that they and their colleagues are unable to exercise control over adult learning to the same degree as youth-oriented educators dominate the traditional educational system. Education conducive to personal growth and development is next to impossible in an environment dominated (as is the traditional educational system) by rules, restrictions, and compulsion. The field of adult education is drifting, unfortunately, toward a more structured educational format similar to youth-oriented schooling. This concern forces me, ironically, to propose a focus for adult education in the hope of arresting and turning the tide of traditionalism and conservatism which threatens to engulf the field. This focus, if adopted, would create the potential for adult education to become a dynamic movement with little opportunity for control by professional adult educators.

A Personal Position

The goal of human liberation should become the guiding force behind the work of adult educators. Human liberation, for the purposes of this discussion, is the process of man's continuous efforts to create a society in which all people feel themselves to be and are in fact free from all forms of oppression. Thus, individuals moving toward this goal perceive themselves to be increasingly in control of themselves and in harmony with their total environment. They realize their importance in solidarity with others in the struggle to eliminate human exploitation. They understand also the need to think critically about their own role in society before becoming involved in issues of social concern. In the process of developing and acting on their humanistic caring for others, they begin to experience, almost as a by-product, an increasing sense of personal freedom, independence, and authenticity.

Perhaps the two most internationally renowned proponents of education for liberation are Freire (1970) and Illich (1970). It is no coincidence that the concepts of these seminal thinkers were formulated in the Third World, where the ravages of exploitation and oppression are etched most graphically. Some adult educators, however, sense the applicability of their ideas for industrialized nations such as Canada and the United States. Cultural action for liberation may be seen as the "praxis" of those who are seeking to become creative participants in their own history by overcoming their own alienation and the constraints to which they have been subjected. This conception of human liberation centers on the point at which personal development and societal change merge and reinforce each other. Apps (1973, p. 38) concluded after reading Freire that "the polarity between individual growth and societal change is a false issue." This perspective suggests that the very act of working toward social change can offer the individual a sense of personal growth and liberation.

Some adult educators in Canada and the United States are studying the implications of Freire's work. London (1973b, p. 54), for example, draws on the theme of liberation: "A central problem for adult education is to undertake programming that will raise the consciousness of the American people so that they can become aware of the variety of forces—economic, political, social, and psychological—that are affecting their lives. . . . The awakening of consciousness is necessary so that people can not only critically analyze their world and thus attain freedom but also become aware of their own dignity as human beings." Freire (1970) contends that education must either "liberate" or "domesticate." Turner and Williams (1971, p. 76) discuss the application of this concept for international education: "We insist that international education will either create part of the social basis for change—the sympathy, the skill, and the commitment—or it will lead directly to more intensive and sophisticated mystification and exploitation." Thus, some adult educators have begun the process of applying Freire's ideas in the context of industrialized nations.

   Illich (1970) attacks directly what he perceives to be the repressive nature of the whole educational enterprise. Human liberation, in his view, is stifled by compulsory learning. Thus, "deschooling society" has become the focus of his attack on the educational system. Illich proposes "learning webs" or "networks" in lieu of schools. These networks would include reference services to educational objects and educators-at-large, peer matching, and skill exchanges. Each citizen would pay for these services with state-supplied "educredits," which could be "cashed in" at any time throughout life. Ohliger (1975) in the United States and Carlson (1975) in Canada have employed Illich's critique, at least in part, to question what they feel is a trend toward compulsory adult education. Ohliger (1974a, pp. 37–39), for example, lists a rather large number of groups—such as traffic offenders, nurses, civil servants, and military personnel—who are now subject to mandatory continuing education in the United States and Canada; and he observes with alarm the views of his colleagues regarding compulsory adult education: "When I first pointed to the growing number of courses which adults were required to take by law, regulation, or pressure, I was told by my colleagues, 'Don't waste your time! There's no trend toward compulsory adult education; this is a voluntary field. At the most you're premature, too early.' Now with the trend glaringly obvious those same colleagues say 'Don't waste your time! It's too late to stop it. Climb aboard the bandwagon and help make the required courses as good as possible" (1974b, pp. 47–48). Thus, the element of voluntary participation, an important feature of adult education, may be modified in the direction of replicating the compulsory, restrictive features of the present schooling system—a system that Illich and others find repressive.

It is important to understand the philosophical foundation of adult education for human liberation. Apps (1976, pp. 22–23) identifies several beliefs that adult educators might hold regarding their profession. He poses the following five questions to clarify the role of adult education in society: (1) Is continuing education the handmaiden of society? (In other words, should continuing education pass on culture and help disadvantaged people into the "mainstream" of society?) (2) Is continuing education's purpose to help reform society? (3) Is the purpose of continuing education to seek major changes in societal structures? (4) Is the purpose of continuing education to help individuals achieve maximum personal growth? (5) Is the purpose of continuing education some combination of the above purposes? Adult educators concerned about human liberation would focus their attention on personal growth and make major changes in societal structures.

Conclusion

Concerned adult educators, if they hope to shift the field in the direction of human liberation, must make their impact felt within their own institutions and in their community. Ohliger (1974b, p. 55) envisions three forms in which "true" adult education should be practiced. He suggests the need to loosen controls within "standard-brand institutions," to work outside the establishment with individuals and groups who are acting against some form of oppression, and to assist counterculture groups in their search for community and an improved society for the future. The most crucial ingredient for success is the commitment of a reasonable number of adult educators. They will discover ways and means of creating learning situations and environments conducive to human liberation.

Work within "standard-brand institutions" will probably involve at least two major components. First, adult educators can attempt to generate dialogue on the goals and value orientations of their own profession. More research of a historical, philosophical, and sociological nature might be initiated to explore the convergence of politics and culture with adult education. Graduate students of adult education should be encouraged to discuss and question the assumptions and program directions of the profession they are about to enter. Conferences might be organized with the purpose of reexamining the values underlying the work of professional adult educators. Second, discussions and action can be launched with the support of sympathetic colleagues to loosen restrictive economic and bureaucratic controls. The support of administrative personnel and students can also be enlisted in this particular struggle. Adult educators, from their bases within institutions, can attempt to shift the focus of their profession and their own institutions in the direction of human liberation.

Few adult educators in Canada or the United States seem to be engaged outside the establishment in endeavors geared to political, economic, or cultural liberation. London (1973a, p. 68) has decried this state of affairs: "We need more innovative and radical programming to help adults confront the issues and problems of rapid change occurring in the decade of the 1970s, and a conservative response to the need for change, often coming from the formal system of education, will be of little help to us as we approach 1984." Ulmer, Blakely, and Kuhn (1975, p. 35) are disturbed by a trend in which "adult educators are suggesting that we devise new tools for continuing education which might well exacerbate the current inequities in the social structure." Freire (1970) offers, at a theoretical level, some guidelines for tackling major societal problems. Adult educators with his frame of reference could initiate action programs in their own community or help strengthen the efforts of ongoing public interest groups. In Canada, for example, such groups concern themselves with issues like the Third World, racism and multiculturalism, the struggles of native peoples, poverty, the role of women, and the environment. Counterculture individuals and groups may be in the forefront of cultural or life-style changes which will become the norm in the future. The participation of adult educators with such individuals and groups could take the form of support, involvement, and research. Adult educators committed to the goal of human liberation will discover meaningful roles for themselves both within and outside their institutions.

Adult educators in Canada and the United States who focus their efforts on human liberation will never become fully acceptable within the "mainstream" of educational institutions. Penfield (1975, p. 40) observes that "marginality can be a great benefit in promoting program responsiveness; yet operating pressures are such that any good administrator will seek to maximize security for the purposes of program stability." Adult educators committed to human liberation need to walk a very tight line between program responsiveness and stability. It is even conceivable that adult educators could draw battle lines in a similar fashion to the process that ensued in the 1940s and 1950s in the wake of the growing influence of the group dynamics movement on adult education. Strong opposition to this alleged effort to capture the field quickly grew up, with the result that opinion became polarized. Some of the wounds inflicted in the ensuing battles have still not healed. Thus, debate between adult educators who favor a focus on human liberation and those championing another focus or no focus at all could embroil the field in conflict and controversy. Whether all this turmoil would generate growth and creativity or bitterness and resentment is an unanswered question.

To the extent to which adult education for human liberation is accepted, an increase in programs of an exploratory, experimental, participatory nature would be developed. The philosophy underlying such educational experiences precludes exact predictions about the direction in which the movement might flow. It is likely, however, that the educational institutions' grip on adult learners would be loosened. Tough (1971), for example, has suggested such innovations as a reduction in the number of years of compulsory schooling and the emphasis on credit, changes in grading to a pass/fail distinction, increasing institutional flexibility to enable students to learn wherever they judge themselves to be best served, and a large reduction in the amount of course work which must be taken on campus to qualify for a university degree. Extension departments in universities and other postsecondary institutions may focus more of their attention on reaching individuals and groups who have not been taking traditional courses from such institutions. Thus, within educational institutions we might expect a number of creative attempts in the direction of "deschooling" the learning environment for adults.

Work outside the traditional educational system would

change with the ongoing needs of the learners and the situational constraints they face. The nonestablishment nature of these educational endeavors could thrust involved adult educators into a position of insecurity and vulnerability. If they could help develop meaningful programs, their precarious position might become somewhat more stable. They might feel themselves part of a process of making a solid contribution to human liberation.

Whether inside or outside the system, programs and activities that generate increased human liberation will, by their very nature, be responsive, dynamic, and creative. New theories for the field might emerge from these experiences. The experimental nature of such programs offers the potential of personal enrichment for all the participants, including the adult educators. Above all, the future of the field of adult education would remain unpredictable and thus exciting, challenging, and . . . beautiful.

Chapter Three

Should the Adult Educator Be Involved in Social Intervention?

Adult Educators Should Help Citizens Become Involved in Social Reconstruction

Grace M. Healy

It is no exaggeration to describe the last quarter of the twentieth century as a time-place where the unanticipated consequences of a life style of personal and social irresponsibility abound. These can be seen in wasted resources and in weakened support systems for human beings. Many life forms on earth suffer increasing deprivation. There are continuing and seemingly irreconcilable struggles among various ethnic groups and between groups of haves and have-nots. Members of this society are confronted with problems of the quality of life in mental institutions, in prisons, and old-age homes; problems of intergenerational conflict; problems of changes in sexual mores and in male-female self-concepts; problems concerning health care and schooling.

Which persons are to handle these problems? Statesmen? Politicians? Specialists? Technocrats? The Elite? Planners? Educators? Certainly, all of these, but not only they. Issues of environmental decay or incarceration of the elderly, for example, are not just matters of common concern and action for all members of a society. What is being suggested here is that all persons in a society ought to take responsibility for active membership in that society; specifically, all persons should learn to question their experiences and to analyze them critically, so that the questioning and analyzing will lead to increased awareness and to subsequent action. Reconstruction of society, rather than adaptation to it, is what is demanded of Americans in the next decades.

In a reconstructed society, the numerous problems of the society will no longer be seen as amenable only to national policy interventions, which themselves effectively deprive persons of their sense of potency. Social and expert roles, which are governed by levels of economic and educational attainment, will be replaced by the agency (the concern and actions) of persons working together as citizens within a given society.

An initial response by adult educators to the question of whether or not they have a responsibility to engage in social intervention in order to bring about a reconstructed society would undoubtedly be positive. Certainly, adult educators ought to take action for social improvement! Is that not, after all, the point of education? Many teachers, learners, and others outside the educational system share a belief that what goes on within the system can and will have a salutary effect upon society; that a better-educated population will mean a better society. Hence, it might be suspected that the affirmative answer of adult educators is given in terms of what they are currently doing. This is their intervention. Anything additional is considered to be outside of their expertise or at best a private matter. In the following pages, I want to raise some issues and questions related to intervention because I believe that currently held beliefs and practices need to be reexamined.

Recent Social Interventions and Their Effects

Interventions by government agencies at local, state, national, and international levels have escalated enormously over the last two decades in the form of recommendations, legislation, funding, and provision of human and additional material resources. Government actions have affected individuals through changes in educational systems, in business and industry, and in the delivery of social services and economic support. In addition, government itself has precipitated social interventions by educational institutions and other agencies. Major new programs were enacted as a result of the Higher Education Act of 1965 and the Elementary and Secondary Education Act of 1965. Health care systems (deliverers and recipients) were affected as Medicare and Medicaid came into existence. From 1960 to 1970, for example, the Health, Education and Welfare budget nearly tripled, while the Office of Economic Opportunity grew to an agency with an annual budget of one and a half billion dollars.

Interventions of whatever kind were undertaken in the belief that they would produce social improvements. This was true of the federal intervention that provided for the Peace Corps and Vista. It was true of academicians who entered into the arena of social action in the 1960s, directing their energies toward peace efforts, the civil rights movement, and the problems of the haves and the have-nots. But what can be said of the results of most interventions intended for improvement of the human condition?

The emerging picture of professional intervention, we are told by evaluators, is far from clear (Mullen, 1972). The data do not definitely indicate whether such interventions are effective or ineffective, since the evaluators appear to be unable to separate intended outcomes from unintended consequences. In some instances, actions and programs brought about no apparent overall improvement but prevented conditions from worsening for individuals and groups. In other instances, the intervention did not accomplish its intended goal but did provide glimpses of alternatives to present structures and possibilities for the future. It is often claimed—especially by persons who have worked through institutions of higher education (Franklin and Franklin, 1976)—that the interventions in themselves are of merit, despite the lack of measurable long-range, system-wide impacts.

Regardless of whether interventions tend toward the successful or toward the unsuccessful end of the range, evaluators agree that too often interventionists have inadequately considered questions such as those raised by Rivlin (1971, pp. 6–7):

1. How do we define the problems and how are they distributed? Who is poor or sick or inadequately educated?
2. Who would be helped by specific social action programs and how much?
3. What would do the most good? How do the benefits of different kinds of programs compare?
4. How can particular kinds of social services be produced more effectively?

Lack of clarity on answers to such questions, evaluators claim, has led not only to vaguely stated goals but also to erroneous conclusions about cause-and-effect correlations and about the relationships of means to ends. Economists, statisticians, and other analysts have worked on the problems they perceive to be associated with social intervention. They have concluded that considerable progress has been made in identifying and measuring the social problems and the initial costs and benefits of social action programs that have been used as instruments of intervention. They admit, however, that little progress has been made either in comparing the benefits of different programs or in knowing how to produce more effective services.

One way to remedy these shortcomings, in Rivlin's view, is to conduct experiments with the delivery of social services in such ways that their effectiveness can be judged by reliable performance measures. The process of developing new methods, trying them out, evaluating them, and trying again would be continuous.

Issues of Expertise

While the preceding suggestions are appropriate, they have been made within the context of expert findings, and it is within this context that I believe a certain weakness lies. The use of expertise, although a necessary condition, is far from sufficient for the solution of human problems in this society. Despite enormous expenditures on adult basic education, for example, there has been no significant decrease in the illiteracy levels of millions of Americans who were the target groups of such programs. More teachers with a given expertise, or teachers with greater expertise, or better delivery or evaluation methods may make a difference. In my opinion, however, the use of expertise will not have a lasting effect until the members of the "target population" define with the teachers and the experts not only the problems, the needs, and the expectations but also the intentions for the future. The assumption of common intentions between deliverers and recipients of social services, between consultants and clients, between teachers and students, when there may indeed be none, is, perhaps more than any other factor, responsible for an apparent lack of success of many social interventions.

Unfortunately, rather than looking to themselves, persons in this society have come to depend more and more on organizational interventions for solutions to their problems. This is, perhaps, a tribute to a particularly successful intervention on the part of the government. With the training of persons in the hard sciences and the development of bigger and better hardware has come the pervasiveness of the mechanistic metaphor; mechanism has penetrated the unconsciousness of our entire culture (Weizenbaum, 1976), and computer-assisted systems have become a prime moving force. Overlooked in this movement is the fact that computers are able to answer only the can questions—in other words, can a thing be done? The ought questions, the ones basic to the solution of human problems, are beyond their scope. Information, expertise, and rules, while necessary, are not sufficient. To speak only with the authority of science is to neglect the questions of justice; it is to rely on the expert to take care of the problems that expertise creates. All problems are then reduced to logic; that is, to objective, measurable criteria. Dependence on mechanistic models and their organizational forms has led to the impotency of people and to their dehumanization. It has also led to people who are lacking in a sense of responsibility. The ethical questions, the questions of ought, can only be addressed by persons who take on their responsibility as members of society to analyze their experiences critically, to engage in inquiry about the concrete aspects of a just society, and to engage in collective action to make possible a society's development.

Is there a particular contribution to this development, an intervention to be made by those who call themselves adult educators? Ziegler (1976) has proposed that our unique contribution is to revitalize the willingness and ability of citizens, as learners, to reengage with their public life, to reestablish their civic potency in their concrete intimate action settings, and to deliberate together about their common issues, experiences, frustrations, and goals. What Ziegler is claiming is that the vitality of public life and the commitment to learning cannot be separated. In other words, those who call themselves educators of adults are being told that they have a particular intervention to make; namely, that of bringing those whom they would teach to the realization that whatever persons study, whatever specialized roles they aspire to, must ultimately be placed in the service of their responsibilities as citizens, members of a given society.

Adult Education as Reconstruction

Education has, through the centuries, been defined in many ways and has been charged with tasks ranging from the most limited and pedantic to the most exalted and utopian. Generally, however, most conceptions and expectations have fallen into the following categories:

1. Education for transmission of culture (including the development of understanding of the culture and of skills for adaptation to it).
2. Education for expertise (including the development of specialist knowledge and skills and generalist views and understandings to be used in the service of societal organizations and institutions).
3. Education for the renewal of organizational forms and for the restructuring of societal groups in order to deal better with the problems of a given society.

Any and all of the preceding have been and may continue to be taken as goals for adult educators and may set the limits to their interventions for social improvement. What is proposed here, however, as necessary in the latter half of the twentieth century is

4. Education of persons for the reconstruction of a society and for the development of communities of persons who are adequate to the tasks of reeducation and invention.

By communities of persons is meant associations of people who, in their involvement with each other, are aware of the human effects of their actions on those within and beyond the associations and who are committed to being responsible for the effects of their actions (Benne, 1973).

What is suggested, then, is that adult educators intervene in the educational system in such a manner that reconstruction of society and development of communities of persons adequate to this task become the goal of education.

With educational purposes such as these, persons will be

brought to the realization and conviction that they, as members of
the human community, should be and can be active and creative
citizens reconstructing their society; in addition, persons will be
enabled to develop the competencies necessary for the tasks of
reeducation and reconstruction. Plans will no longer be made by
experts to meet the needs they define for the people to be affected
by those plans. Nor will needs, plans, and interventions be defined
solely by relevant technical and economic conditions and requirements. The teaching and learning activities in which adult educators engage will be dialogic (Ziegler, Healy, and Ellsworth, 1976).
It will become the learner's responsibility to (1) define the goals and
the tasks of a given activity, and (2) evaluate the success or failure
of an activity.

In short, educators of adults will be developing in themselves and in those whom they teach a willingness and an ability to
perform the following activities (Ziegler, 1974):

1. Engage in intentional action as members of a society for its
   reconstruction.
2. Create teaching and learning situations that will enable all persons, regardless of their educational or economic backgrounds,
   to engage in intentional action as members of the society.
3. Create and support institutions based on differing conceptions
   of social improvement to educate learners with divergent views
   of society and varying attitudes toward approaches to producing social change.
4. Discover through collaborative action what are and what should
   be matters of common concern among members of the society.
5. Extend and redefine the limits to collaborative inquiry and action among members of the society.

Conclusion

Whether or not there are problems within our society has
not been considered to be at issue. Whether or not society needs
reconstruction has not been considered at issue. Both of these are
assumed. What is at issue is: Who does the reconstruction—the
experts alone or all members of the society? In my view, it is

the responsibility of all members of society. If this position is accepted, the issue becomes: What skills are required of persons in the reconstruction of a society, and how will these be developed?

Both of the issues have been addressed, and some responsibility has been laid on those who call themselves adult educators. Specifically, theirs is the responsibility of intervening within the educational system so that intervention for social improvement becomes the task of all members of a society.

Adult educators may choose not to make this intervention. They may consider it inappropriate or leave it to others within the system. My contention remains the same: The need for societal reconstruction is there; it will be undertaken—undoubtedly by those who are educators of adults. These persons, however, may turn out not to be adult educators.

Adult Educators Should Not Necessarily Be Involved in Social Intervention

Mary Jane Even

As adult educators search the troubled social milieu of our times for clarity and understanding and try to differentiate their roles, two assumptions emerge. First, there is the assumption that adult learners seek out educational experiences to meet their felt needs and look to adult educators to assist them in that process. The adult learners should in the process become more astute and self-reliant and take more dynamic roles as members of our society. The second assumption is that the enterprise of adult education has the potential to make all things right in the world. I believe that the first of these assumptions should dictate the major social role of adult educators today. If the second were considered primary, the professional intent of adult educators would be seriously altered. In addition, the forced change implied by such a plan would be in opposition to the current educational, social, and political climate. The current trends in our society include an increasing recognition of and support for change which comes from the people rather than from bureaucratic units. Today the energy for change is coming from the adults who are served by adult educators. Can we do less than assist each adult to become a dynamic part of social change? Can we do more—effectively?

Although adult educators have varying views of the goals of adult education and the "use to which the learning situation should be put" (Powell and Benne, 1960, pp. 49–50), they have a common commitment to the adult individual they serve. Historically, the determination to provide effective learning opportunities for all adults to achieve their potential and to take an active and responsible role in our society is the basis for the commitment of adult educators to their work.

Placed in a position to assert whether all persons who call themselves adult educators should engage in intervention for social improvement, one must first examine the varying roles in which adult educators practice their profession.

Aspects of Diversity

Instructors, planners, administrators, or consultants who have as their primary, secondary, subordinate, or coordinate function the education of adults are called adult educators. In recognition of this diversity of roles, the field has sought a way to classify these leaders. As early as 1960, Houle suggested that these leaders be identified by the way in which they are trained. Individuals who obtained their adult education training primarily through graduate schools are referred to as professionals. Those who are not trained in adult education and do not call themselves adult educators but who engage in adult educator roles are called paraprofessionals. (Many full-time paid adult educators have had no formal training in this field. Their background is entirely in some other discipline.) Volunteers are untrained and usually unpaid persons acting in adult educator roles (Hiemstra, 1976, pp. 57–59). Many persons, however, do not fit these specifications. Some volunteers do undergo training in adult education but they are distinctly a minority. Others, for instance, have adult education roles in community development, urban renewal, and neighborhood centers, where "the flexibility that is required to serve the people's needs is restricted by the pressure upon the developer to support the sponsoring institution and to follow its program prescriptions" (Biddle and Biddle, 1965, p. 261). It is unrealistic, therefore, to suggest that all adult educators can or should engage in societal intervention.

As the diverse roles of the educators cause concern for identity, so also does the diversity of social-planning models and program-planning models they use. At least two models of social planning and derivatives of these models could be employed: (1) the abstract–rational process model, where plans are abstracted from the realities of the social setting; and (2) the concrete–social process model, where planning emphasizes the social process and social action (Warren, 1971). The first model is incongruous with adult education's philosophy, for it fails to recognize the limits of human nature and is deterministic in view. The second model views the problems in a broad perspective, is present oriented, uses pluralistic decision making, and recognizes planning as a continuous process toward truth. The intent here is to advocate the second model for planning.

A third aspect of diversity deals with the goals of the field. This diversity exists because some believe that primary emphasis should be given to meeting individual needs, whereas others emphasize societal needs. Educators who believe that individual needs should be served justify their position by saying that the needs of individuals are the same as the needs of society, since the society consists of and exists for individuals. Those who emphasize the needs of society believe that people do not exist apart from groups and society and that out of people's relationships comes an array of needs for adult education to meet (Schroeder, 1970, p. 33). Persons advocating the first theme believe that the adult educator should meet the needs of individual learners without reference to any larger societal purposes. Those who advocate the second theme believe that the goals of the particular program should clearly indicate the end toward which the particular learning experience is directed in relation to societal purposes (Knowles and Klevins, 1972, p. 13).

Since adult educators serve in many capacities with a variety of clientele in numerous settings for adult learning, they must decide for themselves whether the purpose of their educational work is primarily to meet the felt needs of the learner or the ascribed needs of society.

Intervention as Professional or as Citizen

The question is not whether an individual adult educator should engage in intervention for social action. Of course he should and does. The question raised here is whether the adult educator's role within the field of adult education should be defined to include the added dimension of intervention for social improvement. The position taken here is this: When adult educators engage in social change activities, they do so simply as responsible citizens and not as professional adult educators. Adult educators in leadership positions should engage in social intervention only when they are directed to do so by their constituency. This intervention, instigated by the organization rather than the adult educator, is undertaken to meet the needs of the organization's members; the adult educator does not intervene as an agent of social change on his own initiative.

Adult educators should not assume that they as a group can make decisions regarding the proper purpose of education. Rather, they should encourage citizens to engage in social action by (1) demonstrating their own interest and involvement to the citizens or (2) acting as leaders or consultants to groups concerned with a social action problem. If adult educators attempted to use the processes of social intervention in all their programs, they would be exceeding their educational role. This process would lead to the spawning of activist groups directed by self-appointed adult education authorities. It would also indicate that the adult educator had abdicated his leadership in all education intended to achieve other goals. Adult educators should not participate in social intervention except to meet client goals as the client perceives them. The goals of adult education are not defined solely in relation to societal goals. The learners have their own felt needs to be met.

Adults need to adapt to the pressures of social change. It is the responsibility of adult educators to provide leadership skills to persons who wish to work for social action in response to these pressures. For adult educators to commit themselves exclusively to these efforts would seriously limit their functions and contributions.

Conclusion

Adult educators function in a variety of leadership capacities. If one of these leadership capacities enables them to function as an advocate for social intervention in relation to specific issues, it is the responsibility of educators, as with other citizens, to engage themselves in that process. Leadership responsibilities are basic to any adult educator role but need not be construed as authority. Indeed, it is most inappropriate to suggest that all adult educators should engage in social intervention. Social intervention ought to be selective and appropriate, not mandatory and inclusive.

Chapter Four

Should Continuing Professional Education Be Mandatory?

Mandatory Education Increases Professional Competence

Kenneth J. Mattran

The position taken here is that mandatory professional continuing education is not of and by itself the negative and harmful practice some consider it to be; that, indeed, mandating professional up-grading is not an infringement on individual freedom; and that the cause of increased professional competence can be well served through mandatory educational involvement—provided important but reasonable requisites are met. Much of the problem, it seems, derives from the usual pejorative connotation attached to the word *mandatory* in a libertarian society. This pejoration need not be if the word is examined in the light of the context in which it is used. Certainly the idea of mandatory mass continuing education is dis-tasteful, as is mandatory military service or a mandatory curfew and the like, whereby the mandate is imposed on an individual or group by another individual or group which does not share even a shred of commonality of identity except, perhaps, in the broadest sense of nationhood or humankind. Consider, however, a situation where a mandate is imposed on an individual independently for personal or professional reasons, or where a group of people shar-ing a common identity accept a self-imposed mandate after delib-eration and consensus. Here the word *mandate* loses much of its negative impact and refers instead to an admirable form of self-discipline. In short, it is not the fact of a mandate that is so repul-sive so much as the source from whence it comes.

When a person decides to pursue a professional career in a field that has traditionally required licensure, that person also de-cides to abide by the canons of the chosen profession. This is true in medicine, law, education, dentistry, and all the others; and when the individual accepts the mantle of the discipline, the person also tacitly accepts the responsibilities attendant to that acceptance. Ac-quiescence is voluntary in nature, but subsequent professional be-havior is largely mandated by the chosen discipline, which thereby attempts to assure that standards of practice are high and that the thread of professional commonality remains secure.

Since the professions are not static but dynamic, individual members of the professions cannot retain their integrity if they themselves remain static. Thus, the question of mandated continuing education's violating individual freedom is not really an issue. A profession and the public it serves have the right and, indeed, the duty to impose standards on practitioners, as long as the standards are not arbitrarily and capriciously ordained.

Assuming, then, that *mandatory* does not, by definition, necessarily refer to an inherently malevolent state and that, in certain well-defined circumstances, mandatory continuing education is not an infringement on individual freedom, a discussion of its appropriateness is in order.

Kathleen Rockhill, in the following article, acknowledges that licensure to enter the practice of a profession is granted by government after a candidate for the license serves an institutionalized educational apprenticeship. She also reports that by 1974 continuing education was required in thirty-eight states for health or other professional groups and that continuing education participation is increasingly being tied to relicensure, the states' granting permission for an individual to continue practicing within the discipline. She opposes this practice for a variety of reasons, many of them sound and hardly contestable.

The real question, however, is not whether mandatory continuing education for relicensure becomes widespread and legally institutionalized. Instead, it is the manner through which it is institutionalized and sustained. If, on the one hand, a government legislates continuing education for professional relicensure into existence as an exercise in control of professional activity, that is not only reprehensible but indeed dangerous, for the state is then assuming power that it does not rightfully possess, even if the stated intention is to use the power to protect the general public. On the other hand, if the state, in response to the desire of a professional body to improve through continuing education the services offered to the public, uses its power of licensure to ordain into law standards and procedures recommended by the professional body, the state's authority is legitimate. One of the philosophical premises of this republic is that "governments are instituted among men deriving their just powers from the consent of the governed." In the case of licensure, those who are licensed to practice a profession tacitly consent to be governed in a certain way simply by becoming members of the profession. They also, upon acceptance into the profession, assume the responsibility of assuring the maintenance of high standards of ethical practice, and one of the ways that they do this is through encouraging legislation such as that governing mandatory continuing education.

This method of ensuring the competence of professional practice is acknowledged throughout the relevant literature. It is the professions themselves—not government, not the public, but the practitioners—that seek to require continuing education for relicensure. And there is no convincing evidence that where a professional group has called for mandatory continuing education, the decision to do so was arrived at casually or in haste.

This, then, is a major point of this apologetic: If the mandate for continuing professional education derives from those who must live with the mandate and if certain conditions are met, it violates none of the principles of adult continuing education articulated by Rockhill or stated elsewhere in the slim corpus of adult education literature. It is, in fact, an act of educational volunteerism on the part of people with a common identity who wish somehow to improve practice within their ranks.

Granted, education is not an omnipotent force that by itself confers on its consumers the competence that assures excellence in practice. At best it promotes, as Rockhill asserts, competence and knowledge; at the very least, it exposes the uninterested to information that they otherwise would not encounter on their own.

Conditions for Effective Compulsory Continuing Professional Education

In order for compulsory continuing professional education to exercise a powerful influence on promoting competence, important conditions must be met. These have been alluded to previously and are described below.

First, in order to approach if not fully realize the ideal of volunteerism, any endeavor to circumscribe continuing professional education must originate from within the profession. That is to say, an area of educational need should be ascertained by members of the profession through some rational procedure for determining needs. This must be accomplished not only with respect to specific educational activities but in the larger sense of the need for inaugurating a continuous programmatic structure in which to house the specifics—institutionalization, if you will. Institutionalizing, the establishment of a permanent vehicle for professional continuing education, must express the will of the group in relation to its observed and felt needs and desires to encourage competence among its individual members.

Second, in order that mandatory continuing education can effectively contribute to the maintenance and improvement of professional competence, the design for education must derive not only from the will of the corporate profession but also from the day-to-day realities affecting the ability of individuals to engage in a process of education. That is, when a group has decided to accept the injunction for continuing education, it must offer the widest range of educational alternatives to the membership, so that individuals can participate with minimal disruption of their professional and private lives.

Third, it is not enough simply to require that education be accessible and that it derive from the will of the professional group. It must, in addition, present means whereby the offerings of the program are made more attractive in content and format than the forms that were previously available to the practitioner, assuming, of course, that one of the reasons for adopting a mandated program was the amorphous nature of the offerings that had been available—if, indeed, there were any. A professional person—a physician, attorney, architect, nurse, dentist, educator—is a busy, frequently preoccupied, often distracted individual. The pressures of meeting the daily exigencies of clients, patients, and students occupy huge chunks of the person's time and energy, and even the most well intentioned put aside intrinsically recognized obligations to maintain currency with advances in the fields. The requirement for the pursuit of continuing education obviously mitigates procrastination, but that is of no practical value unless the mandate is part of a program that creates a strong desire to participate among practitioners. Accordingly, learning will only occur optimally if attractive programs are mounted which encourage active learning as well as physical attendance at such programs.

The Adult Educator's Contributions

The adult educator putatively possesses relevant talents that can be employed by the professions in developing programs that address the implicit objectives of mandatory continuing professional education. At the same time, the adult educator occupies a fairly modest position on the periphery of the other professions—a position that is consultative rather than suasive, responsive rather than generative. Once a discretely defined professional group such as medicine or law has decided for itself to require of its practitioners participation in continuing education, it is not within the professional purview of adult educators to try to dissuade that organization from its intent. It is, however, appropriate that adult educators lend their talents to the organization and delivery of continuing education services of quality. The skills of the adult educator need not be iterated here in their entirety, but some small discussion of adult educators' talents relevant to professional continuing education is in order.

It can be guardedly assumed that, because of their necessary preoccupation with the details of their work, few members of the professions under discussion have developed the andragogical competence that is crucial to effective continuing education. However, the adult educator does know about designing forms suitable for adult learning. For example, he realizes as perhaps few other educators do the singular importance of assessing learning needs and desires and the appropriateness of scheduling to meet the convenience of learners. And the adult educator knows how to do this rationally and systematically as an essential step in program design.

That is just one example of the myriad forms of expertise adult educators have to offer the other professions. Because of their education, training, and professional experience, adult educators are conversant with the processes that encourage adult learning and the alternative ways that the processes can best be implemented in given circumstances. This special knowledge can be employed advantageously in assisting the professions to build into their programs the quality which, if not an absolute guarantee of efficacy, can help significantly to reduce the statistical risk taken by a consumer when the necessity arises to call on the professional services of, say, a physician or an attorney.

Conclusion

Mandatory continuing education for the professions is now a fact. Whether it should exist or not is no longer debatable. Whether it is effective or not will always depend on the central issues of control—government or professional body—and quality. Adult and continuing education as a professional arena of practice can and should speak to the issue of quality in professional continuing education. It cannot, with authority, decide whether such education should exist. That decision is at present in the hands of the professional associations, as well it should be. The proper concern of adult educators is the quality of programming within the framework mandated by the professions, for it is here that the field of adult education can make its most legitimate contribution to the improvement of professional practice.

Professional Education Should Not Be Mandatory

Kathleen Rockhill

Continuing education as a basis for relicensure is being mandated in response to growing public demand for greater professional accountability. It is part of the larger accountability movement of the last decade, in which the public has insisted that its interests be protected and that public monies be spent responsively and responsibly. While Ralph Nader has been instrumental in catalyzing public concern, the roots of dissatisfaction go beyond the influence of one individual. The accountability movement is the public's attempt to regain control of services in areas now dominated by professionals. The paradox inherent in the highly specialized, service-oriented postindustrial society is that, as individual accumulation of knowledge increases, so does one's dependence on the knowledge of others. Some of the educated are dependent on others among the educated for many services that the former could handle for themselves had they the time, inclination, and specialized knowledge. And good services are demanded—the latest that science has to offer, delivered with respect for human dignity and uniqueness as well. The demand for professional accountability may reflect not so much a decline in professional performance as the rising expectations of an educated and vocal public.

To control professional competence, a stop is being put to the automatic renewal of licenses. Professionals are being asked to demonstrate that they are still competent to practice, and participation in continuing education is being regarded as evidence of continuing competence. As has often happened in our history, education is being used to resolve a political and social problem. Viewed historically, the practice of requiring participation in educational activities as a basis for relicensure may be the most significant educational event since the Servicemen's Readjustment Act of 1944, which brought with it the transformation of higher education into a massive extension of the schooling system. So, too, mandatory continuing professional education carries with it the potential of a further extension of schooling beyond higher education into a massive system of continuing education.

The issue under debate among professionals, including some educators, is whether continuing education should be mandatory or voluntary. The distinction between mandatory and voluntary policies is a crucial one; the purpose of a mandatory program is to control, and control entails requirements and sanctions. Proponents of mandatory continuing professional education see it as a necessary mechanism of social control to assure the public of continuing professional competence or, conversely, to protect it from incompetence. Mandatory educational requirements for practicing professionals allow for the possibility of sanctions where there seem to be few alternatives. In the absence of academic or competence standards, sanctions now come primarily in the form of denying the right to practice to those who do not participate in a prescribed amount of continuing education activity. The only mandated performance criterion is participation. Continuing education can claim to serve as a guardian of competence, however, only if individuals who do not successfully complete prescribed learning objectives are failed. Once failure mechanisms are instituted, adult education will be fully captured by the inappropriate impediments of formal schooling. The policy of mandating continuing professional education to respond to the public demand for professional accountability rests on the two fundamental assumptions: (1) that performance depends on knowledge and (2) that the necessary knowledge can be delivered by mandating continuing education. Mandatory continuing professional education then rests on the following simple equation: Education = Competence = Accountability. That education may only partially contribute to competence, and that competence may be only one component in accountability, does not matter; a mandatory educational policy assumes that accountability is dependent on education. We may know that this assumption is false. If we *act* as though it is true, however, we operate from the same false premise that underlies the use of formal schooling as a selection device for the world of work. Rather than a means to competence, education becomes the end; alternative ways of developing competence and accountability are looked to less and less. Whereas initially education may have been considered a desirable activity, by mandate it becomes a necessary one and de facto becomes the sufficient condition for assuring competence.

Consider how this happens. Most would agree that education does not assure anything; at best, education promotes competence, and with competence comes greater accountability. The catch is that sanctions hinge on the logic of absolute relationships. The mandating of a particular behavior rests on the premise that the behavior is essential to a desired outcome. In the case under consideration, continuing education is taken as essential to continuing competence. The threat is: "If you don't participate, you will no longer be permitted to practice." Denying the right to practice one's life's work is no small matter; it rests on the assumption that participation in prescribed educational activities is critical to protect the public's interest. To allow for alternative means of protection would be a challenge to the underlying assumptions that through education one acquires competence and that the competent professional will be an accountable one.

It is true that education is not the only means of professional control. Other review mechanisms, both by professionals and the public, do exist. But these are very limited in their scope and in the past have been used to control only extremely deviant cases, not as a general accountability measure. A look at Professional Standards Review Organizations (PSROs), an important effort in the health fields to provide for more general accountability to the public, demonstrates the dilemma of developing competence criteria and enforcing sanctions. PSROs were mandated by the Social Security Act of 1972 to control the quality of care received by the recipients of Medicare, Medicaid, maternal, and child health funds. After a long struggle by the members of the public to play a meaningful role in the review process, it finally appears that the PSROs will utilize peer review procedures which involve a considerable amount of informal teaching and learning. The public has acquiesced to the mystique of professional expertise—that only experts are competent to judge experts—which is a major reason why professionals stay firmly in control of their activity. Because it is consistent with the mystique of professional expertise, education is the only acceptable control mechanism. Even though it may not work, it is trusted by everyone concerned not to harm.

Accountability and even competence are not reducible to educational intervention, though education may play a part or many parts in promoting desired change. If we focus on the problem context, the possibility of alternative educational strategies opens up. For example, education may have a vital role to play in increasing the competence not only of professionals but of the public as well. Nonprofessionals then might overcome their need for external protection because their ability to protect themselves has been increased. For example, programs that might provide the public with knowledge like that presented in the best-selling women's book *Our Bodies, Our Selves* would give individuals the knowledge they need to make more informed decisions in professional areas, thereby providing a check necessary for professional accountability and promoting consumer self-reliance.

Precedents for Mandatory Continuing Professional Education

Why use education to assure continuing professional competence? The precedents for using education as a means of social control are already well established. To extend its use to that of assuring continuing competence simply requires plugging into an existing system of controls. Thus, three major reasons can be given for the use of education to assure competence: (1) Through the credentialing system, education has been established as a necessary and sufficient condition for determining who has the right to practice. (2) The meaning of education has been expanded to signify performance competence as well as subject matter and technical expertise. (3) In light of few alternatives, education is a pragmatic solution, acceptable to organized interest groups. These observations are developed below.

The Credentialing System. Although not an explicit component, education is integral to the three-pronged credential system, an interlocking system of controls which includes mechanisms for certification, accreditation, and licensure. Today the distinction between certification and licensure has become blurred, with the states often granting certificates rather than licenses. Originally, however, certification was used by professional associations to signify expertise in their field of specialization. The only sanction available to professional associations was denial of membership to the uncertified. As they sought to establish a monopoly over a field of practice, professional associations lobbied for legislation which would legitimize their claims of expertise as manifest in certificates awarded. They succeeded, and licensure was the result. In granting licenses, states typically endorse certification standards lobbied for by professional associations, and hence the confusion, particularly since some licenses are called certificates.

Most states do not have a written statute authorizing licensure; instead, that authority is usually an extension of the state's policy power to protect the public health, safety, and welfare (Geake, 1976). This authority was established in the case of *Dent* v. *West Virginia* in 1889, when the U.S. Supreme Court ruled that the power of the state to provide for the general welfare of its people authorizes it to prescribe all such regulations as, in its judgment, will secure or tend to secure them against the consequences of ignorance and incapacity as well as deception and fraud.

Whose ignorance and incapacity? The professionals' obviously. But the need for public protection derives from public ignorance and incapacity as well. Am I not more likely to be a victim of someone else's ignorance if I am ignorant? State effort has been directed at combating professional incapacity to the total exclusion of overcoming public ignorance. Surely the same logic used in the *Dent* case could be used to provide for the education of the public so that individuals can protect themselves from professional incapacity. If an important aspect of the problem is public ignorance, why limit educational programs to the learned professionals— thereby widening the gap between the haves and have-nots with respect to professional knowledge?

Professional associations have been the primary movers in institutionalizing the massive credentialing system that now defines much of our work and education. As occupations sought professional status, they exerted pressure on state licensing authorities to give them control over a field of practice on the premise that their specialized knowledge was essential to performance. Whereas originally licensing was a voluntary means of letting the public know who had presented evidence of meeting professional standards, it has become compulsory and is used to restrict practice to a designated group. As restriction became the goal for an increasing number of occupations, participation in formal education was used as the mechanism to control occupational entry, and it replaced examinations as the criterion for awarding licenses. Through the institution of admissions requirements, standard and often rigid educational requirements, and a system of grades and failure mechanisms, education was able to perform the necessary sorting-out function for the professions.

Theoretically in the public interest, in fact licensing serves to further professional interests. Except for an occasional public member, state regulatory boards have been composed entirely of professional practitioners (Angel, 1970). Thus, licensure has not checked the absolute authority of professionals. The hegemony of professionals over licensure practices has become a target of reformers, and it will be important to study the effects of legislation which dramatically increases lay representation on licensure boards.

Educational requirements have become increasingly important as the means of establishing and implementing standards for certification and licensure. Accreditation is the process by which educational programs are standardized, so that, on the award of the appropriate degree or credential, individuals can be certified or licensed to practice. With the exception of law, all major professions require that a student complete accredited programs before sitting for examinations, and law is now following the trend. Completion of approved programs has now become the necessary and sufficient condition for certification and licensure in most professional and occupational categories. Educators have emerged as an important interest group in establishing certification standards; a consequence has been the standardization of educa-

tion as the willing handmaiden of professional interests. Eager to
serve those interests, continuing educators developed the Continuing Education Unit, the unit measure necessary for standardization, and the National University Extension Association (NUEA)
appointed a task force on accreditation.

From Expertise to Continuing Competence. Institutionally organized continuing professional education is a relatively recent
phenomenon. It was under the Engineering, Science, Management
War Training (ESMWT) Act of World War II that the benefits of
continuing professional training became apparent. Following the
war, some of the more progressive university extension divisions
continued and extended the training begun during the war years
(Penfield, 1972). Business, industry, universities, and the government joined in providing opportunities for professional education,
usually in the form of part-time graduate study, certificate programs, conferences, and short courses.

During the last ten years, continuing education has developed in unheralded proportions. The post–World War II transition from the production of goods to the provision of services as
the primary economic base for society has brought with it new
professional groups (for example, occupational therapists) and
new specializations within old professions such as law, medicine,
and engineering. Three important factors in accelerating the demand for continuing education have been (1) the proliferation of
degree and certificate requirements for entry into increasing numbers of occupational categories, (2) the use of continuing education
to certify specialization after initial entry, and (3) the need to keep
abreast of new developments in one's field. While it is true that the
knowledge explosion has had its impact, the demand for certificates has been the primary force in the growth of continuing professional education.

With the accountability movement, another force is ascend-
ing: the use of education to promote continuing competence. It is
this demand that has the most serious implications for continuing
education. The idea of continuing competence represents a significant shift in thinking about certification. It suggests that entry
certification will no longer be accepted as evidence that one is qualified to practice for the duration of one's career. More subtly, it

reflects a significant transition in the meaning of certification and the social function it is being asked to serve. Whereas certification has historically been used as evidence of expertise, it is now being used as evidence of competence to practice. In the past, expertise has meant that one had developed the command of a body of scientific knowledge in a given area, and that knowledge was taken as sufficient evidence that one was qualified to practice. Professional claims to autonomy and self-control are rooted in the notion that only the members of a profession are the masters of a given body of knowledge which is deemed essential to effective practice. Consider that it was during the progressive era in America, from the 1890s to 1910, that professional associations, licensing boards, and certification standards emerged. A hallmark of the progressive era was the ascendance of science and, with it, the use of expertise as a basis for making social decisions.

Though it may have been recognized that more than book learning was needed to perform effectively, it was assumed that other traits were either a matter of character, which could be controlled by entry criteria or socialization, or technical competencies, which could be learned on the job. As education became the necessary and sufficient condition for practice, claims were made that it could develop the general competencies as well as the expert knowledge deemed necessary for effective performance, and certificates were taken as evidence of performance competence. Education could overcome not only ignorance but incapacity as well. Only recently has the accountability movement in education challenged the assumption that competencies were being developed automatically. The outcome has been a rush toward designing competency-based education programs.

The transition from expertise, defined as scientific knowledge, to continuing competence, defined as the ability to practice effectively, has brought with it the use of continuing education for professional control as well as development. Whereas once the distinction between competence and expertise was unimportant, now it is important for understanding the new requirements being placed on education. A knowledge of much more than facts is needed to perform effectively; the depersonalization of services has necessitated institutionalized checks on competence. This transition is all the more significant because it reflects a diminution in the absolute authority of professional associations. As the service society grows, and the private professional is replaced by the employed professional, countervailing interest groups are coalescing and insisting on a voice in the credentialing process. The most obvious interest group is the public or consumer with its demand for professional accountability. Less noticeable, but very influential, are governing officials, insurance companies, employers, and educators. Consequently, to the use of certification by professional associations as a basis for signifying entry-level expertise and restricting entry has been added its use by nonprofessionals as a means of quality control for practicing professionals. Along with developing expertise through knowledge-updating courses, continuing education is being asked to develop and check professional competence (Cohen and Miike, 1973).

The turning point in the use of certification to control quality beyond entry-level requirements came in 1967, when the report of the National Advisory Commission on Health Manpower recommended, as a matter of public policy, periodic relicensure based on examination or "acceptable performance" in continuing education programs. Another significant step in extending the use of certification as a means of assuring greater public accountability came in 1971, when New Mexico required continuing education as a basis for relicensure for doctors; by 1974, thirty-eight states had passed similar legislation for health or other professional groups (Strother and Swinford, 1975). Another landmark appeared in 1972, when, as a basis of eligibility for public medical funds, the Social Security Act required demonstration of proficiency and Professional Standards Review Organizations (PSROs) were instituted in the health field (Cohen and Miike, 1973). As has been indicated, continuing education is being used by PSROs to enforce standards.

The Pragmatic Response. Proponents of mandatory continuing education recognize that education will not guarantee competence, but alternative controls are difficult to come by. Competence measures and performance evaluation are preferred; but competence measures are difficult to develop, and performance evaluation is difficult to administer. Until a better alternative is developed, mandatory education seems the only option. For example, in their study of health manpower licensure, Cohen and Miike (1973) point out that, limited though it is, continuing education is easy to formulate and can be administered on a wide scale. From the adult education perspective, Knox (1976) lists many disadvantages to compulsory continuing education but suggests that it is acceptable as an interim measure.

Except for engineers, mandatory continuing education requirements have not met with rigorous opposition from professional associations. Most see it as the lesser of a number of possible evils. Practicing professionals clearly prefer continuing education to an examination requirement. Furthermore, tax incentives for professional study in a variety of luxurious conference settings make the continuing education pill palatable to those in the more lucrative professions. Those in the lower-status professions, such as nursing, may be relegated to taking less glamorous courses at their local educational institutions, but faith in education and rising professional status offset this disadvantage. Moreover, professional associations have considerable control over continuing education and are even delivering their own educational programs (Frandson, 1976).

Educators also have a vested interest in continuing education, particularly if it is mandatory. For institutions of higher education, it provides a source of students in an era of declining enrollments. For adult educators working in continuing professional education, mandatory education brings not only money but a stable supply of students, overcoming the difficulties of planning for a fluctuating student population. With a regular clientele and resources to promote programs, adult educators can move from the periphery into the mainstream of educational activities. Moreover, serving the interests of affluent and influential professionals is particularly attractive to those adult educators who have long bemoaned their low status—or marginality—among educators.

Educating professionals is also consistent with a national educational policy that promotes programs to develop ever higher levels of trained manpower. There is no policy tradition of promoting the general knowledge level of the public—only to promote degrees and certificates for those who have failed at the first go around or for the already educated (Penfield, 1975). Despite complaints, a mystique about professional expertise and the power of knowledge continues to dominate public action. Thus, only peers are deemed capable of reviewing professionals, and the more degrees one has acquired, the more competent one is assumed to be. Finally, education is certainly harmless—so why not require it of everyone?

Negative Effects of Mandatory Continuing Professional Education

While it may be true that everyone has something to gain from exposure to knowledge, it does not follow that mandatory continuing education is harmless as a national policy to promote professional accountability. The dilemma is that its negative effects are not so blatantly harmful as to deter those who see it as a potential good. Will people really be hurt by giving up a little freedom, by becoming a little more dependent on specialists, by being told what they have to learn and how, or by being denied the right to practice if they have not conformed to a public mandate which in itself is not so objectionable? This is precisely the problem; because the policy appears reasonable, we are willing to let it slip by. Perhaps a look at the full array of negative side effects will prompt some to reconsider. Mandatory continuing professional education should be opposed because it (1) limits individual freedom, (2) puts efficiency before ethical considerations, (3) limits learning, (4) has negative effects for adult education, (5) has negative social consequences, (6) will not solve the problem, (7) may exacerbate the problem, (8) deters problem resolution, and (9) perpetuates the use of education for social control rather than the maximization of learning.

That compulsory education limits individual freedom is clear. However many options are provided for fulfilling the requirements, the mandate remains. While it is true that subtle forms of social and cultural pressure to participate in further education are a fact of modern life, political compulsion is a serious step. True, some freedom must be sacrificed in the interests of the greater common good, but only when essential. Can it be demonstrated that mandatory education is essential to effective performance? Is a compulsory approach, one based on sanctions, more effective than one based on voluntary participation for intrinsic reward?

The argument has been made that compulsory participation in even meaningless activities can have the desirable outcome of promoting compliant behavior and socialization to group norms. In his research on professions, Moore (1970) points to the persistent possibility of failure as an important ingredient in continuing occupational commitment: "Persons who get into positions of absolute security, with no need to expose themselves to risk and uncertainty, in fact become occupationally unproductive." Challenge and controls, not learning deficits, seem to be the issue. Continuing education can provide the necessary check if it mimics the failure system of schooling institutions by providing a series of hurdles to be overcome. Rather than challenging adults to be creative and take the initiative and responsibility for their own education through personalized review procedures, mandatory education treats them as children and forces compliance to a series of regulations that may have little to do with improving individual performance. The test is participation—the behavior mandated as appropriate—not how well one does or whether one's performance improves.

Because values of efficiency dominate ethical concerns, mandatory continuing professional education is legitimized as a pragmatic solution without the requisite evidence that it works or is necessary. It is more efficient to mandate the same behavior of everyone than it is to develop responses that are tailored to a multitude of unique problem situations. Promoting genuine learning and competence apparently is not valued as highly as responding quickly and at minimal cost, for inadequate programs are being mounted as absolute answers, and the necessary resources for the development of alternatives are not allocated. To establish programs of mandatory education as interim measures is a grave error. Once established, institutions become permanent fixtures with a vested interest in self-preservation. The supposedly efficient solution is absurdly inefficient if it does not work.

Mandatory continuing education may actually limit learning. It is generally believed that individuals learn more when intrinsically motivated than when extrinsically motivated. For learning to be maximized, the locus of control should be in the individual. However humanely it may be implemented, compulsion takes the locus of control away from the individual. At best, compulsion can contribute to extrinsic motivation, but there is good reason to believe that it may contribute instead to learner alienation and entrenched resistance to learning. Mandatory educational requirements can lead to the deterioration of the learning situation. Specifically, (1) teachers must work with students motivated by the need to "get by" a hurdle rather than by the desire to further their personal development through new learning; (2) with a captive clientele, less effort is made to develop challenging and exciting educational experiences (Penfield, 1975); (3) resources are put into meeting the general needs of the mass at the expense of meeting the unique needs or interests of various subgroups (Knox, 1976). Mediocrity has been the by-product of mass educational requirements, and it stubbornly remains despite the heroic attempts of reformers. Witness current disenchantment with the formal educational system and attempts at its reform.

The deterioration of the learning situation is one way in which mandatory continuing education will have negative effects for adult education. Related negative effects are the institutionalization and standardization of adult education as it is defined by external regulations. Once certification defines legitimate learning, and adult education is called on to cull out the undesirables and develop the necessary failure mechanisms, it will become another form of schooling. Finally, mandatory continuing professional education perpetuates a limited public policy toward the education of adults which recognizes only work-related learning needs—and only of the most highly educated at that. Thus, resources are diverted from meeting the general learning needs of the populace.

The negative social consequences of mandatory continuing professional education are similar to those of the rest of the schooling system. Unless barriers to participation are removed for all, with differential social and economic costs taken into account, offerings are bound to discriminate against those for whom the costs are greater. Unless requirements can be demonstrated as essential to performance, the requirement itself becomes a barrier and limits equal access to jobs, advancement, and the right to work at one's profession. Unnecessary requirements per se have not yet been declared illegal, though a major step in this direction was taken in 1971 by the U.S. Supreme Court in the case of *Griggs* v. *Duke Power Company*. In that decision the Court ruled that it is illegal to use selection devices which are discriminatory in their effect unless they can be demonstrated as essential to effective job performance. That the discriminatory effect is difficult to prove does not take away from the ethical issue decided by the *Griggs* case. In announcing the decision, Chief Justice Burger delivered the following opinion: "The facts of this case demonstrate the inadequacy of broad and general testing devices, as well as the infirmity of using diplomas or degrees as fixed measures of capability. History is filled with examples of men and women who rendered highly effective performance without the conventional badges of accomplishment in terms of certificates, diplomas, or degrees. Diplomas and tests are useful servants, but Congress has mandated the commonsense proposition that they are not to become the masters of reality" (quoted in Huff, 1976, p. 46).

Continuing professional education will become a master of reality if it is massively mandated rather than individually prescribed. Other negative social consequences are that mandatory continuing professional education furthers the overspecialization of society, perpetuates and promotes the monopoly of professionals over a body of knowledge, and furthers the dependence of the public on professionals and the judgments of others. A different policy might disseminate knowledge to promote public self-reliance and the ability to make judgments about professional expertise.

The crux of the matter is that mandatory continuing professional education alone will not solve the problem of professional accountability. As a case in point, medical education demonstrates the inadequacy of the proposed solution. It has been estimated that there are 16,000 incompetent physicians in the United States, and many more practicing substandard medicine (Geake, 1976). Existing procedures revoke licenses from less than .5 percent of these. Using nonparticipation in mandatory continuing education as a basis for revoking licenses, New Mexico suspended the licenses of

127 of its 2,500 registered physicians at the end of the first reporting period. Of these, ninety resided out of the state and fourteen
were retired, leaving twenty-three, the majority of whom were over
65. Aside from age and residential discrimination, what has the
legislation accomplished? The secretary-treasurer of the New Mexico Examining Board does not report whether the twenty-three
who chose not to participate were incompetent; he states only that
they chose not to comply and that the loudest protests came from
the octogenarians (Derbyshire, 1976).

It is highly unlikely that mandating education will stop incompetent doctors from practicing. The more realistic hope is that
it will raise the general level of practice, but here too the relationship is tenuous at best. Houle (1980) has concluded, with very
limited data, that lifelong professional education seems to improve
practice. As yet, it is only an article of faith that the addition of
compulsion does much to reduce the likelihood of incompetent
professional practice.

The addition of compulsion may exacerbate the problem
by adding to overspecialization and further establishing the
hegemony of professionals over their fields. Professional autonomy
is rooted in the mystique of professional expertise and the sanctity
of the knowledge on which it is based. The power of knowledge is
the power of controlled knowledge. Though it is recognized that
competence requires more than esoteric knowledge, that recognition has not resulted in the conclusion that consumers may have a
very critical role to perform in evaluating professionals. Instead,
further education is mandated and the myth of professional in-
violability perpetuated.

An incorrect solution deters problem resolution and the
public is misled into thinking that its interests are protected. Reliable accountability checks are needed. Despite all the rhetoric,
competency-based education continues to be elusive; effective ways
of defining performance criteria, evaluating performance, and determining whether given experiences can improve performance
need much more development before an effective program to promote accountability through education can be launched. Ways
must also be found to stimulate learning, self-assessment, and self-
direction, as well as to provide the best in organized programming.
To fall back on periodic testing of the type represented by the

American Bar Examination seems as inadequate a solution as does mandating education. That more effective measures have not been developed testifies to the paralyzing effect of partial solutions. Other approaches might be explored with the cooperation of new interest groups (for example, employers and the public) and sufficient resources for research, experimentation, and development.

Finally, mandatory continuing professional education perpetuates the use of education for social control rather than for the maximization of learning. The consequence is the abuse of education in its subjugation to other ends. One of the underlying assumptions of adult education has been that it is free of just this control: it is a voluntary field of activity chosen by individuals who desire to learn something for their personal growth. Definitions of the field and andragogical principles rest on the assumption of voluntarism (Knowles, 1970). In witnessing the bandwagon response to mandatory education, one wonders whether voluntarism came about as a chosen principle of the field or by default. When mandatory educational programs have been called for in the past— for example, in Americanization programs—few adult educators have expressed concern (Carlson, 1976; Ohliger, 1974b). Eager to move out of the periphery into the core (Moses, 1971), adult educators are only too willing to ignore their heritage of voluntarism, giving challenge to the assumption that either voluntarism or its corollary, learner-oriented education, has truly been the guiding principle of the field.

Toward a Policy of Voluntary Learning

Given our lack of knowledge about the effectiveness of mandating continuing education, and given our assumptions about its likely negative consequences, a moratorium should be placed on further mandates until research can be completed that will reveal the effects of mandating continuing education. With or without a moratorium, research is critical if an intelligent public policy is to be developed. Following are some of the pressing questions:

1. What have been the politics and processes that resulted in the establishment of mandatory continuing professional education? How pervasive is the practice?

2. How have mandatory continuing education requirements affected practitioners and practice?
3. Is more learning achieved under voluntary or compulsory educational policies? What are the optimal conditions for maximizing such learning?
4. How can the natural learning of practitioners be modified to make it possible for them to keep up to date and to improve their competence? Is modification necessary?
5. How can lay persons develop the expertise necessary to make professionals more directly accountable to them?
6. What are the limits of learning and education in improving professional practice?
7. Can participatory learning processes be developed which would be consistent with the humanistic tradition of adult education, avoid the pitfalls of schooling, and promote competence?

To say that continuing professional education has only two approaches, mandatory or voluntary, is accurate and yet an oversimplification. The logic of absolute relationships on which a mandatory policy is based leaves little choice but opposition; mandatory cannot be a halfway measure. Still, four alternative policy positions can be identified: (1) political compulsion, (2) social compulsion, (3) voluntary learning policy, and (4) private responsibility. The first position is to mandate continuing professional education as the basis for relicensure; the second is to provide more subtle forms of compulsion in order to promote participation (for example, maintenance of professional standing, job advancement, salary incentives, good advanced certificates); the third is to promote voluntary continuing education through public policy; the fourth is a laissez-faire approach with continuing education as a private responsibility, not to be promoted at public expense.

My position is the third one. Continuing education for professionals should be developed as a matter of public policy, but as a voluntary, open learning policy. This would call for voluntary, decentralized learning experiences in a wide variety of settings, maximum learner control, a comprehensive approach to personal as well as professional learning needs, accessibility for all, applicability to individual situations, and participatory planning in designing learning experiences which are wanted and needed by the intended recipients. No small order, it would require excellence in programming, which would result in desired, rather than mandated, learning. Continuing education would be individualized, building on the natural learning configurations used by learners and worked out through a cooperative process of performance and self-evaluation. Depending on individual style, the individual may or may not choose to participate in organized learning experiences, although the decision not to participate should be a matter of choice, not constrained by a lack of resources. The key link is a learning facilitator whose job would not be to teach but to catalyze, advocate, and encourage the design and execution of learning plans on the part of individuals and groups.

Education would be used to develop expertise primarily, and competence insofar as it can. Education would not be used to measure competence, but only to provide the opportunity for its development. Accountability would be promoted through personalized review procedures, with individualized learning contracts and performance assessment where necessary and possible. Accountability can also be promoted through programs of popular education which follow the principles named above. Through adult education, individuals who choose can be enabled to learn to make better judgments in areas of dependence on professionals.

The limits of education must be fully recognized and a policy of public disclaimers embarked on where the public insists on mandating education against the advice of educators. That education cannot assure competence must be made clear. Adult educators can take an active stance in opposition to mandatory education and turn back its development, while promoting individualized and group opportunities for voluntary learning. Given the lack of evidence that mandatory education can work, the issue is ultimately one of ethics: adult educators had best consider whether they really want to become part of the schooling establishment; if not, alternative principles for policy implementation, such as those listed above, must be developed and adhered to.

We are at a historic point in the history of adult education. The passage of the Lifelong Learning Act was an important event because it demonstrated that Congress recognized the need for a uniquely adult approach to education. The response to the mandate for continuing professional education can serve as the necessary prototype for a lifelong learning policy which is adult oriented and voluntarily chosen.

Chapter Five

Should Professional Certification Be Developed for Adult Educators?

Certification Should Be Established

Catherine Rosenkranz Cameron

Adult education has been termed an "emerging profession" long enough. It is time to establish standards and processes for professional definition—namely, certification that adult educators do indeed possess unique competencies in their educational practice.

Adult education is an established profession with a historic tradition (Grattan, 1959). Philosophers and religious leaders of all civilizations have been teachers of adults, not of children. In the United States, the education of adults has long been advocated—as evidenced by Cotton Mather's discussion groups of the colonial era; the establishment of public libraries; the development of education programs for apprentices and immigrants; the Chautauquas, which brought cultural enlightenment to the prairies; and a host of contemporary programs meeting a wide range of adult learning needs.

Self-identification of adult educators began on a national scale in the 1920s. The first national association for adult educators, the American Association for Adult Education, adopted its constitution in 1926. It was succeeded by the Adult Education Association of the U.S.A. in 1951. Membership in the association was open; there are no qualifications, either of educational background or professional involvement.

Postgraduate programs in adult education are also of recent origin. The first doctorate in adult education was awarded by Teachers College, Columbia University, in 1935. The number of universities and colleges offering courses and degrees in adult education has expanded dramatically in the years since then. By the end of 1978, 2,239 people had earned doctorates in adult education from United States and Canadian institutions (Ford and Houle, 1980, p. 123). This spectacular growth indicates that many individuals who are, or plan to be, engaged in teaching adults feel a need for educational experiences offered in graduate programs. A corollary assumption is that those people who complete such programs acquire information and skills which distinguish them from people in other disciplines.

Opinions on certification range from no certification to establishment of state-administered and state-enforced licensing for adult educators. Some oppose credentialing in adult education because they oppose the basic concept of credentials: "It should be against the law to require scholastic credentials or tests as a condition of having any job. A person's ability to perform a job should be decided by his or her co-workers" (Jensen, 1974, p. 166). Still others would maintain the status quo, although numerous problems of capricious or exclusionary employment requirements exist under it. In the field of adult basic education, for example, different institutions have different certification requirements for the same type of teaching responsibility. In some instances, certification requirements more appropriate to elementary teachers or social workers may close jobs in this field to some university-trained adult educators. Perhaps as a reaction to apparent discrimination against adult educators, another group would open up jobs or even reserve job markets for those formally trained in adult education. This would inevitably lead to formal credentialing and pressure for state licensing of adult educators, just as it is required for elementary and secondary school teachers, nurses, and numerous other professionally employed persons regulated through state agencies.

In coming to terms with the ideas represented by differing groups in the matter of credentialing, one may philosophically espouse the ideal of "deschooling society." As a practical matter, however, professional credentialing appears highly desirable. Consumers have the right to be provided with information about the services they purchase. Just as consumers may choose whether to employ a bookkeeper or a certified public accountant, whether to seek advice from a retail clerk at a paint store or a member of the American Society of Interior Design, or whether to consult a licensed physician and surgeon or a board-certified surgical specialist, so too the adult education consumer should be provided with information which designates the individual who has training and experience in working with adult students and who has undertaken activities to acquire skills as an adult educator.

Certification of adult educators should be voluntary and

should assure us of high-quality professional practitioners. Certification requirements and those standards and processes necessary to ensure quality should be determined and established by the profession for the profession.

A Rationale for Professional Training and Certification

A profession growing as rapidly as adult education must assess the needs of the present and look to those of the future in a policymaking decision as important as certification. Today's changing educational task and tomorrow's continuing need for creativity and expansion of knowledge mandate a trained and qualified group of professional practitioners. In recognition of these needs, in 1976 both the Commission of Professors of Adult Education and the National Association for Public Continuing and Adult Education created task forces studying issues related to certification.

Changing Nature of Educational Tasks

Lowe (1975, p. 107) delineates the worldwide need for increased training of adult educators: "In proportion as adult education becomes more closely associated with social and economic goals and especially with vocational training, there is a consequent demand for a higher degree of professionalism in the definition of objectives, program and course design, materials design, and program and methods evaluation." A legitimate impetus toward certification arises from the changing nature of educational tasks facing adult educators. Education at all levels has been profoundly affected by the needs of a complex urban society. There are more people to serve, and education is expected to serve an increasing percentage of the population. In addition, the changing social consciousness of the nation has given new roles to education—for instance, in fighting wars on poverty and unemployment and in helping veterans readjust to society (Institute for Educational Leadership, 1976).

The scope of adult education activities financed or provided by the federal government, by industry, and by other public and voluntary agencies is one indication of the diversity of adult education activities in the United States. Adult educators are now engaged in helping more people learn more things in more settings than at any time in the past. The 1976 edition of the Office of Management and Budget's *Catalog of Federal Domestic Assistance* lists some 275 educational and training programs serving individuals past compulsory school age. These programs range from continuing professional education to basic education, from museum education programs to minority businessmen's training. In addition, there are large commitments of funds to provide educational opportunities for both military and civilian governmental employees (Christoffel, 1976).

In some programs one finds people with learning needs resulting from changes in society or within their personal circumstances. For example, an individual may find that a minimum wage job does not provide enough income to meet growing financial responsibilities. This person may turn to a program funded under the Comprehensive Employment and Training Act or some other available postsecondary educational program for assistance. Teachers, program planners, and counselors need special skills to provide relevant educational opportunities for these part-time students.

An ever growing emphasis on continuing professional education is an additional impetus to participation in adult education. Many professions are now requiring members to show a minimum amount of recognized educational activity to remain eligible for licensure or professional recognition (Grogan, 1974).

There is ample evidence that education is no longer a single "front-loaded" enterprise—an activity for those years between age 5 and completion of a career program. New jobs, new interests, changing social roles, and need for personal growth are valid reasons for participation in adult education.

Need for Increased Professional Skills

Let us consider a few ways in which the adult educator's role has changed in the past few decades. First, let us look at an important group of new clients in adult education. These clients might be classified as reluctant learners, educationally handicapped or educationally disadvantaged. They may be forced into an educational program or enticed into one through financial remuneration or the promise of help in overcoming educational limitations. Their learning environment may be a correctional institution or a variety of vocational, prevocational, and adult basic education programs. The reluctant student often lacks skills that would enable him to learn by traditional methods. He is usually also handicapped by other psychological and sociological barriers to learning. Teachers, program planners, and curriculum designers all need specialized information, skills, and attitudes to provide successful educational programs for these students.

In addition to the challenges of a new clientele, the pressures of minimum class time, program budgets, and sheer numbers of students have brought about the need for changes in educational methods. From Socrates to the early agricultural agent, a basically tutorial model has been used. The teacher was in direct contact with a few students, and instruction could be individualized to meet student learning through direct dialogues. So, too, the apprenticeship model, whether father to son or through guild or trade union, has depended on an individual approach—the apprentice observing and doing, the journeyman guiding and supervising. In some cases, such as extending innovations in agriculture, the initial tutoring was extended through peer tutoring as other farmers came to observe, evaluate, and learn from the innovator (Rogers, 1962). While still an effective model for disseminating information, the tutorial approach has been made obsolete for many purposes by technological advances. To use the county agent as an example again, introduction of powerful chemicals into modern agriculture has made efficient large-group instruction and mass media approaches imperative. Trial-and-error evidence and person-to-person dissemination are too slow and inefficient when information is a matter of life or death to hundreds of people.

People preparing for a wide variety of occupations must be involved in training programs that can teach essential information and skills quickly and preferably at minimal expense. Instructional activities therefore require highly skilled educators who can motivate individuals to learn, facilitate learning of both information and skills through well-designed instructional materials and activities, and convince the learners that the new behavior is entirely consistent with the best professional practice so that the new behavior will be exhibited in appropriate situations. Effective development of instructional materials and strategies is crucial when large numbers of people must be taught the same thing or when the nature of instruction is difficult or technical.

Although there is diversity in needs of adult education students, there are strong similarities in the skills, attitudes, and information needs across programs. The adult educator must have general information about the special needs of adult learners. In addition, the adult educator must have skills that enable him to design and deliver an effective program; he must be an effective manager of resources, personnel, time (both his own and that of his students), and the instructional media and methods he uses.

Special Competencies Needed by Adult Educators

Adult education is an interdisciplinary field. It is also a field that encompasses a body of knowledge, has sets of skills that enhance the functioning of its practitioners, and rests on a philosophical base that sets it apart from other professions. Therefore, professional certification must be developed to define the core body of knowledge and skills for the categories of professionals in the field, especially teachers, program administrators, and related specialists. In addition, Lowe (1975) lists a dozen other relevant job titles—among them, counselors, producers of instructional materials, extension workers, and planners. These people need all or some of the core curriculum of an adult education program in addition to the special skills of their particular discipline. In some programs, persons already trained in a subject matter area may need to take a core of adult education courses for increasing educational skills. For example, an elementary reading teacher may seek part-time employment in an adult program, or a nurse must both develop and provide in-service education in a small hospital or nursing home.

A review of graduate programs in adult education in the United States indicates that most require a core curriculum of courses in the philosophy, psychology, and methodology of adult instruction. Additional course work is available to permit subspecialization in fields such as basic education, program development, gerontology, research, and administration. Teachers and trainers in adult education generally work with a more diverse group of students, receive less supervision, and have fewer instructional resources at their disposal than their counterparts in elementary school. Therefore, they need to know more about curriculum design, instructional strategies, and even recruiting of students and marketing of programs. Although many of these skills can be acquired by trial, error, and study on the job, formal training programs appear to be a quicker and surer way to acquire some or all of the competencies needed by adult educators—competencies discussed in the following sections.

Knowledge of Principles of Adult Learning. Understanding the psychology of adult learning influences what one teaches, how one teaches, and how one organizes the instructional program. A large body of research relevant to adult educators is now available on learning, motivation, and attitude change. For example, Gagné (1962a) alerts one to the need to analyze the skills the learner must possess before he can master the skills or information being taught. Social learning theories explored by Bandura (1969) and others have wide implications for appropriate teaching strategies. Skinner (1968) and the behaviorists point out the need for feedback and reinforcement. Humanists such as Rogers (1969) speak to the need for involving students in setting goals. Maslow's (1954) hierarchy of needs helps the teacher understand the requisites that precede the student's need to learn. McClusky's (1971) theory of margin contributes to understanding why some groups fail to participate in adult learning activities.

Although some believe that many of an adult's learning tasks are not significantly different from learning tasks of children, careful reading of research and thought on adult development, such as the writings of Erikson (1968), Bühler (1968), Neugarten (1968), and Sheehy (1976), reveals a number of differences even within the adult life span. Other researchers have investigated a variety of hypotheses related to cross-cultural differences in learning and communication patterns, cognitive learning styles, and other factors which differentiate adults from children and one group of adults from other groups.

Knowledge of the Use of Methods and Materials for Adult Education. To properly evaluate and use techniques and materials, a firm background of the principles of adult learning is required. Information and skills related to using and developing different techniques and multimedia approaches are becoming increasingly important to adult educators. Writing on the need for increased use of educational technology, Lowe (1975, p. 11) says: "The truth is that new learning aids are used only by those who are trained and conditioned to use them. The impact of educational technology will remain slight even in highly industrialized countries unless administrators and teachers are specially trained to take advantage of them and unless there is general curriculum reform." Proper use of such materials as Lowe describes is needed at the micro level (to increase an individual student's learning options) and at the macro level (to increase the number of people being reached).

The variety of commercially available instructional materials in adult education is increasing quantitatively and qualitatively. These instructional materials vary from simple learning games to simulations and games requiring several days to complete. Materials range from the free or relatively inexpensive to computer-assisted instructional programs highly expensive both to develop and utilize. Materials often are highly sophisticated applications of a number of research-based learning approaches. An example is PLATO, a computerized approach to teaching, used in industrial training programs and in some pilot applications in education. PLATO uses task analysis, feedback, relevance to student interest, and a variety of practices and reinforcement activities derived from motivational techniques.

Knowledge of Program Development: Issues and Methods. Developing programs in adult education requires information, skills, and a professional rationale for decision making. This is true whether the program is based in an educational institution or in business or a governmental agency; whether it is formal, resulting in a diploma or the awarding of credit, or informal, to meet a specific personal learning need of a specialized group—for example, a group of expectant mothers.

The decision-making skill involves the wider knowledge base of a qualified practitioner. For example, take the decision of whether to use an income test for admitting participants into a categorically funded program. Knowledge of who wants to participate and the political realities of the community may indicate that an income limit should not be applied. However, data on participation patterns show that the relatively affluent characteristically take advantage of these programs and the poor do not, thereby actually widening the income gap rather than promoting equalization of opportunity as envisioned by program goals (Best and Stern, 1976, p. 57). Another example of the nexus of research findings and program decisions can be seen in the growing popularity of competency-based adult high school programs in response to findings of studies such as the University of Texas Adult Performance Level Study.

Program planners need to be able to choose between competing program goals, to implement needs assessment procedures, to utilize existing demographic data and regional forecasts, to obtain and manage resources, and to evaluate program effectiveness. In addition, they need general managerial skills common to other administrative positions but with even more need for the interpersonal skills enabling them to relate effectively with the various publics they serve. These attributes could be acquired without formal training in adult education. However, educational intervention would provide a wider informational and theoretical base for decision making and would be particularly useful in developing specialized skills in areas such as needs assessment and program evaluation.

Certification Procedures and Implications

Certification of adult educators should be voluntary, should designate quality, and should be accomplished by the profession itself.

Certification standards should be developed by those professional organizations involved in a wide variety of adult education activities. Practitioners, employers, and those who train or educate adult educators should also be involved. Certification should establish minimum qualifications, which can be obtained either through experience or through successful completion of recognized courses or programs.

Administration of the certification program could probably be most efficiently accomplished by granting certificates through professionally recognized programs of adult education. This process might involve a related activity of institutional recognition by a body such as the Commission of Professors of Adult Education.

Professional certification could begin with the organization of a consortium to establish the qualifications and to set the minimum criteria used to judge whether voluntary applicants for certification are qualified. The professional organizations making up the consortium should be voluntary, but the consortium will not be effective unless the major organizations participate. This consortium could be begun by any of a number of organizations—for instance, the Adult Education Association, the National Association for Public Continuing and Adult Education, the National University Education Association, the American Vocational Association— or it could be spearheaded by the United States Department of Education.

Since the purpose of certification is to enhance quality, not simply to restrict professional entry, certification should be based on qualifications rather than simply on acquisition of credits in adult education. Alternative means of assessing competencies are being developed in many content areas through examination, demonstration of skills, or preparation of portfolios for evaluation. These techniques could be utilized in evaluating the certifiability of practitioners who have had little or no formal adult education background but who have developed skills, acquired information, and demonstrated a professional attitude as practitioners in the field of adult education. In addition, a number of avenues—such as internships, continuing professional education activities, and access to credit courses—must be kept open for mastering skills required for certification.

Adoption of certification would have implications for those who train adult educators, for adult educators themselves, and for the adults they teach.

Activities related to development of certification standards should upgrade weak professional development programs by setting up standards of student competencies. In some instances, certification may enhance the professional prestige of the adult education program within the institution.

Certification would provide incentives for many practitioners to engage in continuing professional training to upgrade or extend skills and knowledge about adult learning and teaching. Professionalization could be expected to enhance professional pride, even for those working with clients who are not highly regarded by society as a whole.

Most crucially, the adult student would benefit from professional certification. In far too many instances, teaching assignments are given to people not equal to the task. The teacher may know the subject matter but lack teaching skills; the teacher may understand the student but lack information on content; the teacher may be highly successful with full-time, well-prepared, and highly motivated students but unable to adapt to part-time adult learners with special learning needs. Certification standards will serve to acquaint employers with the kinds of competencies which the profession believes are essential for teachers of adults.

The professional definition provided by certification may also meet a variety of individual needs—such as opening up new markets to graduates of adult education programs, because employers will be aware of the profession and the types of skills adult educators possess. It may enable others to challenge restrictive licensing policies which militate against employment of adult educators in settings such as some public school adult programs.

Conclusion

A definable body of knowledge, a unique set of challenging tasks, and a firm philosophical base give teaching in adult education every right to recognition as an established profession. Postgraduate adult education, though recent, shows spectacular growth, indicating that there is strong recognition among adult educators of the need for professional training in the field. A corollary assumption is that those completing such professional training have knowledge and skills which differentiate their expertise from that of teachers in other levels of education.

The tasks of adult educators today are interwoven with the social and economic stability of our society and those of developing nations. Government programs, industrial programs, and programs of volunteer agencies are engaged in helping more people learn more things in more settings than at any time in the past. Lifelong learning is no longer a dream; it is a reality. These expanding tasks have increased the need for professional skills in teachers of adults. New groups to be taught, expanding numbers of students, and budget limitations have made new methods and materials mandatory, have made program planning more complex, and have made responsible administration a necessity.

While diversity in students and programs are facts of life in adult education, the special core or body of knowledge of adult learning serves as a basic need for all practitioners in the field. Additional course work is needed for specialized areas in adult education.

Certification standards must be determined by the profession itself and must be based on experience in the field or completion of recognized preparatory programs. Certification will provide impetus to individual development and to the upgrading of programs of training institutions. It will also benefit the great numbers of students in myriad programs everywhere, and it will give the professional practitioner access to greater opportunity in the field.

Certification Is Unfeasible and Unnecessary

Waynne B. James

Certification has become an issue of concern as adult educators seek to establish themselves as members of a legitimate field of study. The stigma and humiliation associated with such statements as "Adult Education! . . . That means second-rate courses taught by second-rate teachers to second-rate students" (Harrington, 1977, p. 7) can be substantially reduced through certification, some adult educators believe. They feel that certification will provide effective ammunition to combat such negative prejudices.

Exactly what are advocates of certification proposing as an answer to many of the problems of adult education? Cameron, Rockhill, and Wright (1976, p. 4) define certification as "the formal recognition of an individual as a bona fide and competent practitioner by a professional association or its surrogate." The certification discussed here, then, will be some officially recognized form of evidence of competence in, or qualification for, the teaching of adults.

The supporters of certification are divided into two camps with respect to the form such recognition must take if it is to be effective. Some say that it will be practical only if it is voluntary; others say that it will be meaningful only if it is mandatory. Cameron, in arguing for professional certification, assumes that adult educators will voluntarily set standards and strive to achieve them. She expects the adult educator's sense of professionalism to provide the motivation to ensure participation as well as to lead to an upgrading of training programs. Accordingly, she sees no need for legal compulsion to assure participation. Research such as that by Tough (1971) indicates that adults in general are highly motivated to acquire necessary work-related skills.

Another possibility is to require certification of all adult educators. This would be similar to the conventions of the medical and legal professions, in which a degree is evidence only of completed course work. Before practice in the profession can begin, each individual must also pass a legally mandated test. This testing seems to have added prestige and status to the fields.

Both of these positions, voluntary and mandatory, have supporters among the advocates of certification. Each has aspects that merit consideration. But it is my contention that certification in any form is simply not a practical answer to the problems currently facing adult education.

In their zeal to counter destructive beliefs about adult education, proponents of certification often fail to consider the difficulties and pitfalls connected with the concept of certification itself. Note, for example, the requirements that must be met if certification is to be effective: "[It] should be based on qualifications (not necessarily degrees) and should distinguish between competent professionals and all others. It should employ reliable means of assessing competencies and should be able to validate the certified competencies by criterion measures reflecting valued outcomes of practice. Most important, if adult education is to establish certification for its practitioners, the effort must be justified on the basis of a demonstrable public good—the provision of a valued service by bona fide and competent practitioners" (Cameron, Rockhill, and Wright, 1976, p. 10).

Assumptions of Certification Advocates

Advocates of certification believe that it can be made to fulfill these requirements. They base this belief on the following assumptions: (1) there is a core of knowledge and skills that can be identified as unique to adult education; (2) the level of competence to be required for certification can be established; (3) a process and an entity to review and evaluate individuals can be designed; (4) certification can offer recognition and protection to adult education as a profession; and (5) a correlation between certification and teacher effectiveness can be demonstrated.

Each of these five assumptions will be considered in turn, and this examination will suggest that, at present, certification is merely an empty promise. Certification may indeed provide a way to eliminate incompetent teachers, but the complications associated with it are overwhelming. Other steps need to be taken first.

A Unique Core of Knowledge and Skills Can Be Specified. Houle (1970, p. 10) writes that no one institutional form exists for adult education and that to study adult education one must "examine the career patterns of people at work in many institutions whose basic similarities are often obscured by their great variation of scope and purpose." He goes on to say that it is difficult to make any generalizations about the basic concerns of the total field. Schroeder (1970, p. 39) states that because "adult education is based in a multiplicity of instructions and agencies, the need for a classification system is obvious." He has presented a four-part typology (based on the work of Knowles, 1964, p. 42) in an effort to classify institutions offering adult education programs according to institutional goals. More recently, he has modified his classification system, producing sixteen patterns of decision control orientations (Schroeder, 1980, pp. 64–69).

Given this diversity and variety, do teachers in all types of agencies need to be certified? A demand for certified teachers in all these types of institutions would create grave problems. And what about adult educators who are not actually teaching? Administrative positions in these types of agencies would also fall under the auspices of adult education.

Adult education associations—one of the entities most likely to develop certification—exert little control over private agencies. In the view of these independent organizations, a teacher needs to be qualified in the subject area first; teaching methodology for adults is of secondary importance. Community and junior colleges also demand mastery of subject matter first. And as with many universities, knowledge of subject matter, publications, and competence in research techniques are the major criteria for tenure;

teaching ability is rarely a main consideration. Usually the only certificate necessary for employment is an advanced degree.

Adult basic education (ABE) programs traditionally have employed public school teachers for teaching adults. These instructors are usually individuals who have skills in a specific subject matter and training in education but no background in working with adults. Noncredit or community education programs which provide courses for special interests, hobbies, or technical skills demand teachers who are knowledgeable in their subject area only; some may never have taught previously. To demand certification of all such teachers would limit the number of qualified instructors, especially in rural areas, where there are few trained individuals and no opportunities for training teachers for adult education programs.

In agencies where adult education is a secondary concern, specialization in the work area of the agency is considered by employers to be of much greater importance than the ability to instruct. Although there is a trend toward obtaining specialized training in working with adults, it seems unlikely that these agencies would agree that certification in adult education is necessary to perform the job competently. Most private organizations would feel that it is more important to have a certified public accountant (CPA) teach accounting or a registered nurse teach nursing techniques than to have a certified adult educator conduct the training.

In response to the demand for professionally trained adult educators, numerous higher education institutions have attempted to identify the knowledge and skills needed to develop effective adult educators. Researchers have only recently begun to develop an empirical footing on which to develop programs.

The identification of general competencies began with the study by Chamberlain (1961) specifying forty-five competencies for practicing adult educators. Aker (1963) sought to establish criteria for evaluating graduate adult education programs by (1) reviewing literature for appropriate evaluation methods, (2) identifying and classifying behavioral objectives related to graduate programs, and (3) surveying students and graduates of adult education programs. Liveright (1964) attempted to arrive at competencies for graduates of adult education programs.

Grigsby (1972) and Veri (1974) continued to refine the process of identifying competencies by updating earlier lists. Grigsby's study was concerned with the development of a competency-based program for community education personnel who are engaged in all types of educational services for adults. Veri initiated a study to develop a "Competencies Assessment" survey for adult educators. His list of competencies was derived from previous investigations which used adult educators as respondents. The multiplicity of these studies indicates that the attempt to identify general adult educator competencies is continuing and that agreement has not yet been reached on a definitive list of required skills.

It is difficult to identify not only general adult educator competencies but also those skills necessary for a more specific situation. What competencies, for example, are needed to teach in an ABE program? Smith (1972) and Fenn (1972) concentrated on competencies needed by ABE teachers. Smith's study attempted to determine competencies needed by ABE teachers as perceived by teachers themselves. Fenn identified a list of types of knowledge, skills, and attitudes needed to achieve effectiveness in an ABE teaching situation and investigated what was needed to certify teachers possessing these abilities. The most comprehensive identification of ABE teacher competencies was conducted by Mocker (1974). This study sought to identify, classify, and rank competencies needed by ABE teachers. In compiling his list, Mocker analyzed all the studies completed until 1974 and condensed them into a list of 293 competencies, which were then separated into competencies of high or low priority.

All these studies illustrate the complexity of identifying the skills that adult educators need for certification. Not only must the entire field of adult education be defined, but so must specific competencies for specialty areas. This problem of identification of the field and the skills needed within it may represent the most complicated hurdle to the issue of certification.

Both the definition of the field and the identification of specific competencies are further complicated by the rapid changes society is experiencing. In Cameron's view, these changes reinforce the need for certification in adult education. Certification, however, will have an adverse effect on the ability of adult education to adapt. Since any plan for certification will have a tendency to become static once it has been committed to paper, the codification of certification would make it very difficult to move as change occurs. Adult education would thus be locked into a secure system that would not promote flexibility but rather would hinder it. The very fact of constant change is, in itself, one reason for rejecting certification.

Level of Competence Required Can Be Established. Even if the competencies needed to function effectively in adult education could be determined, the selection of the degree of competence to be required for certification would still present a major problem. First of all, who is going to set the competence levels? The standards could be established and judged by professors of adult education, other teachers, the teacher being evaluated, students, or a combination of all of these. But there seems to be hesitation on the part of the professionals to judge their peers: "The belief in self-regulation (judgment by peers), which was intended to subject a practitioner to the scrutiny of those best qualified to evaluate performance, has tended to result in a reluctance of peers to throw stones because of the fragility of the glass houses in which they themselves live" (Cameron, Rockhill, and Wright, 1976, p. 3). Individuals do not like to denigrate a colleague, and evaluation can always be influenced by personality conflicts. But if adult educators will not set their own standards, who will do so? Moreover, how high should the standards be? If we wish to certify only highly trained teachers, we shall eliminate many who, though academically less qualified, are excellent teachers. Establishing the precise point at which competence is sufficient will be highly subjective.

Certification Process Can Be Designed. The design of a certification process can be addressed in at least three ways. The first two possibilities work with the systems that now exist; the third would call for the creation of a new method. The first alternative would be to require the attainment of an elementary or a secondary teaching certificate. This approach would undermine the field of adult education by indicating that there is no difference between teaching youth and teaching adults. The second possibility would be to establish an endorsement area for teaching adult basic education, high school equivalency, or adult vocational courses. This is an option that would identify an individual as trained to work with adults, but it would exist within a current, ineffective system. The third option would be the creation of a new process solely for adult education.

This last alternative could be approached in various ways. Jensen (1972) presents three suggestions. The first option is undoubtedly the most traditional—certification based on course work. The second utilizes the demonstration of certain skills to prove professionalism. The third method is based on a written test which would assess general principles of adult education and aspects of good teaching.

In the past, degrees or college credit have served as easy alternatives to certification. Arbitrary standards have been set, indicating that competence is implied by a degree or college credit. But there is no evidence that this type of certification is anything more than a convenient way of determining who is to be certified. Throughout the country, moreover, professional adult education courses are taught primarily on a graduate level—at a limited number of schools. If a degree were to be the basis of certification, as it is in primary and secondary education, most teachers would need a master's degree. But what about areas where teachers have no access to adult education courses? How could the rural teacher get the courses he would need? And, in turn, how could the rural administrator find enough teachers with the necessary graduate degrees?

Demonstration of competence by performance cannot be implemented until agreement has been reached on the knowledge and skill areas required for effective adult education practice. Then it would be necessary to establish how the competencies can be demonstrated and how the quality of performance can be judged. That in itself might prove problematic. For instance, research indicates that the ability to relate to students is one of the most vital teaching skills (Aspy, 1972; Brown, 1977; Gage, 1972). Vescolani (1975, p. 20) asserts that the only attribute of a teacher that makes a difference in pupil performance is a sympathetic, empathetic understanding of the individual. But this is an affective attribute, not a cognitive one, and as such is extremely difficult to measure. A competency-based approach to certification is much easier to discuss than to carry out; it has all the problems associated with any competency-based program (James, 1977).

A written test certainly might be designed, since the medical and legal fields have already established a precedent. However, many people have questioned the effectiveness of the board and bar examinations. These examinations certify doctors and lawyers with respect to knowledge, not bedside manner or the ability to plead a case or file forms. Similarly, given the current state of knowledge in this area, a teacher's classroom effectiveness could not be evaluated through a written examination. It would be difficult to create a valid and reliable instrument. Can a test really discriminate between those who teach poorly and those who do it well?

If certification is to be established, there should be numerous routes to achieving it. In spite of the varying certification requirements that now exist, Aker (1975, p. 15) points out the need for additional variety to meet the diverse needs of adult educators. Certification should be designed for each individual's responsibility and for each different role. All this adds to the complexity of the situation and raises serious questions about the feasibility of instituting such a system.

A complex question in the design of the certification process is: What groups or individuals are to be responsible for overseeing certification? Some of the possibilities are (1) state departments of education; (2) the United States Department of Education; (3) adult education organizations; (4) a certification board composed of representatives of all agencies and all levels of commitment; and (5) the National Council for Accreditation of Teacher Education. Unfortunately, there are problems with each of these options.

State departments of education typically do not represent the wide diversity of individuals associated with adult education and are usually oriented toward literacy or vocational programs. Undoubtedly, the new Department of Education is not interested in adding increased responsibilities to its myriad duties. Education, moreover, is supposed to be a state-level operation. The adult education organizations are currently having problems serving their members. Too many internal problems must be solved before something as major as overseeing certification could be undertaken. The organizations are in such great financial difficulty that they could fold. To support certification as a means of attaining stability is a reverse approach to the problems of both the organizations and the general field of adult education. A board composed of representatives of all agencies would not necessarily provide the depth of training that would be desirable for those passing judgment on the competence of teachers. For example, could representatives of a welfare agency serve adequately as members of a certification jury? Such persons might know a great deal about the welfare system but very little about adult education. The National Council for Accreditation of Teacher Education (NCATE) does not currently accredit any programs that prepare individuals to be educators of adults. Traditionally, NCATE has been associated with the certification of programs for training public school teachers, and most adult education is not associated with the public schools. Many of the people who represent the administration and teams of NCATE are not acquainted with either the goals or the philosophy of adult education and would be at a great disadvantage in evaluating adult programs.

The problems associated with deciding on one approach to certification rather than another, selecting one evaluator over another, and eliminating ambiguities and rigidities are major obstacles to the design of any certification program.

Certification Offers Recognition and Protection. Cameron, Rockhill, and Wright (1976, p. 1) pose the question "If certification provides a means by which the status of adult education might be enhanced and its practice protected from encroachment by persons without similar expertise, can this form of credentialing be anything but good?" The answer to this question can be the opposite of what the authors intended. For, indeed, if the purpose of certification is merely to protect the job market and to increase the status of adult education, it seems a wasted effort. Status can and should be obtained through other means, such as excellent, widely available training programs. As for protection of the job market, does it "protect" the field to have only certified teachers in lightly populated areas to teach cake decorating or basic drawing? Surely the consumer must also be considered. Might it not be better to have an uncertified teacher than none at all? Moreover, though certification may appear to protect the consumer from untrained teachers, it may ultimately remove some effective but uncertified instructors from the teaching market—teachers who, for whatever reasons, cannot or will not submit to the procedures required to receive a teaching credential. Should students be denied, as some proponents of certification would hold, successful experiences with effective teachers simply over an issue of credentialing?

Many individuals in adult education still come from other fields or disciplines, and this tendency will probably continue. Must we protect ourselves from this "encroachment"? It may be that certification merely serves "the self-interest of incumbents in the occupation, enhancing its image and promoting individual and occupational status" (Cameron, Rockhill, and Wright, 1976, p. 3). If adult education is that insecure, perhaps we do need some kind of protection. However, it seems more reasonable to believe that we can learn from and work with individuals trained in other areas who wish to utilize some of the expertise that adult education has to offer.

Certification and Teacher Effectiveness Are Related. One of the assumptions underlying teacher training programs and research on teacher training is that there exists a correlation between the training of a teacher, reflected by a certificate, and the effectiveness of that teacher in the classroom. Research, however, does not substantiate a direct relationship between certification and teacher effectiveness. According to Johnson (1975), McGowan (1975), and Vescolani (1975), there is no relationship between the number of hours spent in professional courses and judged effectiveness in teaching. One study by the Texas Education Agency (1975) indicates that there is no statistically significant correlation between nondegreed (and hence noncertified) and degreed teachers in classroom effectiveness. One of the trends emerging from a study of certification conducted by Jensen (1972) indicated a strong feeling that certification has no relationship to a teacher's competence in adult education. The issue is further complicated by disagreement over what constitutes good teaching and what should be required for certification to ensure such effectiveness, once it is defined.

Alternatives

To require certification of—or even merely to offer it to—all persons engaged in adult education might indeed provide definition for the field and recognition for individuals holding the certificate. But, as I believe I have shown, this arrangement is simply unsatisfactory as a solution to the woes of the field. Yet no one can dispute the need for specialized training in working with adults. What, then, is the answer?

Recognition and respect can be provided relatively simply, through measures such as a listing of trained adult educators or an extensive public relations effort. Another area in which effort would be richly rewarded is that of comprehensive in-service programs. These can be readily adapted to fit the wide variety of adult education situations and should be developed and exploited to the fullest possible degree.

One practical path to recognition might be the design of an endorsement area for those already trained as teachers. For instance, in an effort to ensure that teachers of adults have at least an exposure to working with adults, it might be feasible to have an endorsement area for teaching ABE below the eighth grade, general educational development (GED), or English as a second language (ESL). This would be a compromise between the establishment of a complete certification system and the absence of any way to indicate training in adult education.

Conclusion

Unless a core of knowledge and skills unique to adult education can be identified, unless a level of competence necessary for certification can be agreed on, unless a process and an entity to review and evaluate individuals can be designed, and, above all, unless it can be shown that there is a correlation between certification and teacher effectiveness, certification—whether mandatory or voluntary—will continue to be both unfeasible and unnecessary. Certification alone will not legitimate the field; only striving for excellence within adult education can do that. The practical problems and limitations associated with certification are difficult, though not impossible, to overcome. But to try to institute certification in the face of these difficulties, especially when there are simpler alternatives available, would be an exercise in futility.

Chapter Six

Should Government-Funded Adult Education Programs Meet Established Standards of Performance?

Programs Should Meet Established Standards

Margot Keith Green

The middle 1960s in America were a time of increasing social consciousness, with governmental expansion into social action programs in areas of human service. Many adult education programs benefited from the government largesse, especially in the area of adult basic education through Public Law 91-230, which provided federal funding for local programs. Occupational, vocational, and career education programs, too, have enjoyed considerable federal and local funding, as have other inherently adult education endeavors, such as in-service training of teachers. In addition, state and local agencies have frequently sponsored adult education programs without the participation of the federal government.

With the advent of the 1970s, however, widespread disenchantment with a perceived lack of return on the national investment made itself felt, and a new term, *educational accountability*, became the watchword of the day. The word *accountability* has fiscal connotations, and not surprisingly many writers on accountability stress the economic aspect of education in terms of dollars realized from dollars spent. The word also has a broader meaning, associated with the idea of reporting to an established authority. As Browder (1971, p. 1) defines it, "Accountability is . . . the requirement on the occupant of a role, by those who authorize that role, to answer for the results of work expected from him in the role." One reason for the current emphasis on accountability in education, Browder contends, is that political, social, and economic pressures "are demanding responsiveness to perceived problems" (p. 5) and that education has traditionally been seen as providing ways to deal with such problems. Certainly this view of education is consonant with the tradition of adult education enunciated by Knowles (1960, p. 7), who relates the growth of adult education in America to a belief in and a response to the " 'American Dream'— the notion that everyone who works hard can get ahead."

According to Lessinger (1971), the "publicness" of accountability is its most salient feature, and accountability demands can be
used as a means for achieving responsiveness to demands of the
citizenry: "Outside review tied to a public report probably explains
the popularity of the emerging concept of accountability to the
public at large. Schools in America serve and are accountable to the
citizenry, not the professionals. Since the public served is in reality
many 'publics,' each of whom has legitimate needs for information,
accountability can lead to an opening up of the system to bring in
new energy and new support" (Lessinger, 1971, p. 8).

The need for assessment of adult education programs in
terms of accountability is also making itself felt among adult educators, as evidenced by the two sessions at the Nation's Bicentennial
Adult and Continuing Education Congress devoted to the issue of
"quality control." According to promotional material sent out with
preregistration forms, as funding for many programs diminishes,
demands for accountability and program effectiveness increase.
Roomkin (1972, p. 2) strikes a somewhat similar but somber note:
"The burden falls on adult educators to demonstrate a satisfactory
level of economic performance at minimal costs, compared to
alternative programs and policies. In the jargon of economics,
the benefits and costs of basic education must be identified and
measured."

Many adult educators, however, appear to be somewhat uneasy at the prospect of such evaluation for two reasons: (1) the
emergence of accountability models based on practices arising outside of education and, more important, (2) the requirement intrinsic to accountability that programs be judged by standards
other than programmatic objectives of program developers. The
first of these objections speaks to the means employed for evaluation in accountability terms, while the other speaks directly to the
meaning of accountability.

Objections to Alien Accountability Models

The emphasis on accountability has encouraged educators
to borrow methods from other spheres of endeavor to serve accountability demands. The increasing attention given to quantifi-
cation-oriented accountability measures is an indication of the at-

tractiveness of such techniques, which were developed essentially to monitor the production of goods rather than human service outcomes and which seem alien to many educationists. According to James (1971, p. 40), "Increasingly, state and national lawmakers are asking economists and political scientists for new solutions to old problems in education; and as government makes the study of education both popular and profitable, the number of researchers from these disciplines that are interested in education is increasing. The models they use are . . . adapted from among those long used to describe physical, mathematical, and mechanical relationships. . . . They influence the way we restate the aims of education and the means for achieving those aims."

James (p. 41) describes the four general models in current use as (1) the *investment model*, in which educational expenditures are analyzed as investments (man is the machine, schooling is the input, and the output is a contribution to the gross national product); (2) the *production model*, in which school is the machine, educational expenditure is the input, and the output is "a valuable consumer good"; (3) the *motivation research model*, which leads to a search for "unexpressed needs in a clientele," the development of a "product" to satisfy those needs, and the "engineering" of consensus to arouse a demand for the product; and (4) the *systems model*, in which the management of schools is analyzed in terms of efficiency, through cost-benefit studies, systems analysis, and program planning and budgeting systems.

"Under the rug of technique lies an image of man" (Eisner, 1970, p. 10). Not one of these four models is built on the image of man and of adult education in relation to man—an image traditionally embraced by adult educators. Therefore, adult educators are correct to be concerned that alien accountability models might be used as a framework for evaluation of adult education programs funded at any level of government. Fortunately, within the field of educational evaluation, attention is increasingly being given to models of evaluation based not on the scientific or business-enterprise model of education but on an artistic, humanistic model (Eisner, 1975; Stake, 1967). Attention is also being given to long-term fieldwork of the sort conducted by anthropologists as a methodology for educational evaluation (Clark, 1976; Schwille and Porter, 1976). These new models and methods hold great promise for adult educators who seek to evaluate in a way that will reflect the complexity of programs involving "different understandings by different actors of . . . multiple objectives, processes, and outcomes" (Schwille and Porter, 1976, p. 3) as well as the philosophical assumptions about education on which those programs are based.

Arguments Against Externally Imposed Standards

Even if an appropriate methodology for educational evaluation in the service of accountability could be built on a model consonant with adult education assumptions, many adult educators might reject it because of their antipathy to judging a program according to externally imposed standards of performance. Accountability involves both evaluation and the reporting of the results of the evaluation to appropriate sources outside the program; therefore, outsiders are likely to judge the results according to standards they themselves have set rather than standards that have meaning only within the context of the program itself. This means that accountability demands may not be satisfied by evaluative data indicating to what extent programmatic objectives have been attained. Program objectives themselves may be subject to accountability; they must be shown to be worthy according to some standards. With the massive entry of the government into funding of adult education projects, the climate for accountability raises the issue of whether adult education programs funded at any level of government should meet established standards of performance. Although it is often asserted that adult educators have the responsibility for setting performance standards for their programs, when programmers accept government sponsorship they also incur a responsibility to satisfy the sponsor's requirements.

The literature on adult education program evaluation reveals three major arguments against judgment according to externally imposed standards: (1) Since each adult education program is unique, interprogram comparison is inappropriate. (2) Evaluation should serve only as a means for program improvement. (3) Government may thereby control adult education endeavors.

Uniqueness. According to the claim of uniqueness, each program should be judged only with respect to its own clientele and not in comparison with any other program. The Adult Education

Association's Committee on Evaluation (1952, p. 20) explicitly rejected comparison of one program with another: "Ample experience demonstrates the futility of intercommunity and interprogram comparisons. Such comparisons are usually invalid and may even be dangerous. The sociological conditions, historical development, the leadership structure, cultural backgrounds, and many other factors usually are too dissimilar among communities to permit fair comparisons even if they were useful. . . . Measurement of growth cannot be made against the objectives in some other program. Achievement of one's own objectives is more desirable than striving for objectives of programs in other communities."

From this point of view, each program is essentially idiosyncratic, a law unto itself, as it seeks to meet the unique needs of its clientele in its own unique context. Certainly, no two programs are identical; however, many programs funded by government have the same purposes and are directed toward the same type of clientele. For example, Public Law 91-230 defines its population as adults who (1) do not have a certificate of graduation from a school providing secondary education and who have not achieved an equivalent level of education and (2) are not currently required to be enrolled in schools. Many adults fall into this category, and accordingly many adult basic education programs for this clientele have been mounted. The purpose of these programs, too, has been legislatively defined. The adult programs are designed to help eliminate inability and raise the level of education of such individuals with a view to making them less likely to become dependent on others, to improving their ability to benefit from occupational training and otherwise increasing their opportunities for more productive and profitable employment, and to making them better able to meet their adult responsibilities.

In a sense, all programs funded under Public Law 91-230—being devoted to the same purposes for the same kind of client—are natural competitors, and comparisons among them are inevitable. Moreover, such programs are compared not only with one another but with alternative ways in which monies given them might have been spent. For example, a literacy program for Appalachian adults might be compared with another kind of literacy program—one that employs a different text or class organization or one that uses paraprofessionals instead of certified teachers. Still another kind of comparison might be with noneducational solutions to the same problem. Instead of designing a literacy program for impoverished Appalachian adults, perhaps federal jobs could have been provided.

Some evaluation theorists assert that evaluation is of its essence comparative because evaluation is tied to certain decisions. Scriven (1967, pp. 85–86, 92), for instance, notes that "questions of support, encouragement, adoption, reward, [and] refinement . . . can be given a useful, though in some cases not a complete, answer by the mere discovery of superiority. . . . The conclusion seems obligatory that comparative evaluation . . . is the method of choice for evaluation problems." House (1973, p. 134), too, suggests that comparative evaluation is inevitable in an accountability context, because accountability "involves allocation of resources, which means that some people gain and some people lose."

Each governmentally funded adult education program approaches the individuals who constitute its clientele in its own way. Considered in the aggregate, however, those individuals are members of a class for whom certain kinds of services are being provided with a specific end in view. Therefore, all adult education programs funded under a specific piece of legislation represent alternative means of reaching that end, and it is both necessary and appropriate to compare them one with another as well as with hypothetical alternatives.

Evaluation Solely for Program Improvement. Another argument against externally imposed standards has its basis in a definition of evaluation as a process that serves the purpose of program improvement alone. This interpretation is linked to the curriculum development model developed by Tyler (1950). According to Tyler's view, assessment of the merit of a program should be based on the program's own objectives—a position echoed by the 1952 AEA publication on program evaluation, which defined evaluation as "the process of assessing the degree to which one is achieving his objectives. It is looking at one's present position in regard to one's goal" (Committee on Evaluation, 1952, p. 6). This definition has been embraced in such widely read texts as those by Houle (1972) and Knowles (1970).

Knowles specifically rejects evaluation according to external criteria, as well as comparative evaluation, largely on the basis that the purpose of evaluation is program improvement—the Tyler concept. He appears to reject the idea of evaluation for continued funding as somehow unworthy. However, those who underwrite the cost of governmentally funded programs have a legitimate right to attempt to ascertain the extent to which the programs are accomplishing the purposes for which they were funded—literacy, vocational, and coping skills in the case of adult basic education; improved agricultural practice in the case of cooperative extension; a lessening of recidivism in correctional education.

Programs in agencies not primarily devoted to adult education have always been accountable to elements outside the program. An adult education program conducted under the aegis of a labor union, for example, must involve the participants in activities that will prove of ultimate benefit to the union; and such programs are often called on to account for themselves in precisely those terms. In the same way, a church is not likely to tolerate an adult education program that results in declining church attendance or the serious questioning of ultimate religious precepts; hence, the religious authorities judge adult education efforts in the church by a set of standards external to the objectives of those adult programs. If one considers governmentally funded programs as adult education programs operating in a setting—society—whose main purpose is not adult education but something else, such as maintenance or revitalization, one may argue that it is perfectly legitimate for funders of those programs to demand that the programs account for themselves. Similarly, since most government support for adult education is categorical, that is, given to enable an adult educator to offer a specific program for a particular clientele, it is not unreasonable that such support often entails performance standards.

Perhaps only self-sustaining, specifically adult education enterprises can be considered closed systems where the feedback from any evaluative activity remains within the system and the program's effectiveness is assayed only in terms of criteria the programmers themselves promulgate. All other adult education programs are parts of larger systems and must be accountable at least partially in terms of standards established on behalf of the society which those programs are designed to serve.

Control. Many adult educators apparently fear that judgment of their programs according to standards outside of those programs will lead to control of program content and methodology by outsiders who lack understanding of adult students, of teaching procedures, and of the andragogical assumptions on which adult educators base their programs. This is a legitimate fear. And yet— again considering the fact that government-funded adult education programs are designed to serve society or some segment thereof, and considering the additional fact that the resources of society are not inexhaustible—it seems incumbent on those charged with development and administration of governmentally funded adult education programs to be responsive to the needs those programs were intended to meet. Such responsiveness need not mean the passive surrender of program control to government functionaries. By organizing to collaborate in the evaluative process, by carefully defining the programmatic scope of evaluative efforts, and by setting forth criteria against which the standards themselves shall be judged, adult educators can exert a beneficent influence on the entire evaluative process and in so doing can contribute to the professional growth of their own field.

Questions Concerning Standard Setting

The issue addressed in this chapter is not merely whether adult education programs funded at any level of government should be judged according to established standards of performance. Such judgment is inevitable in view of legislative demands, consonant with the service tradition of the adult education movement, and justified in terms of the needs of a society which is underwriting adult education programs for its own benefit. The issue lies also in the role adult educators assume in the setting of those standards, the scope of applicability of the standards, and the setting of metastandards by which all standards established for the evaluation of governmentally funded adult education programs shall themselves be judged.

Who Sets the Standards? Central to the issue of control is the issue of who should legitimately set the standards of performance for governmentally funded adult education programs. If one agreed that the funding agency ought to set the standards, one might look to the original legislation for criteria by which to judge programs. There are, however, two difficulties with this approach: (1) the goals articulated in legislation are often so broad that they must be interpreted, and (2) the legislative programs themselves, as Weiss (1972, p. 37) has usefully pointed out with regard to federal social action programs, "are the creatures of political decisions. They were proposed, defined, debated, enacted, and funded through political processes and . . . remain subject to pressures both supportive and hostile that arise out of the play of politics." Because of the political considerations, program goals specified in the legislation are often inflated, diffuse, and mutually incompatible. "Again, it is the need to develop coalition support that leaves its mark. Holders of diverse values and different interests have to be won over, and in the process a host of unrealistic goal commitments are made" (Weiss, 1972, p. 39). One cannot look to the legislation and expect to find appropriate standards for the evaluation of adult education programs funded at any level of government.

Another approach, which was suggested in the 1952 AEA publication on program evaluation, is that the standards should be established not by the funders but by program participants and the public at large: "Most of all, particularly in tax-supported programs, we must understand that professional adult educators cannot be the final judges of merit. This role inherently belongs to the public and to the participants" (Committee on Evaluation, 1952, p. 29). If benefit to participants and the public at large is to serve as the basis for evaluation, presumably those groups should generate the criteria according to which effectiveness would be assayed. There are at least two ways of generating such criteria. The first is to base them on ascribed needs of target groups, as derived through analysis of census data and the like. The second way is to base them on felt needs of program participants or target groups as determined by asking them what they want. Stake (1972), for example, appears to endorse this kind of standard setting when he suggests that evaluations be organized according to issues of concern to various audiences associated with an educational program.

Neither of these approaches involves the professional adult educator in a substantive way. Yet to exclude adult educators from such standard setting would indeed be to deny them control of programmatic content and procedures. Ideally, adult educators should be involved in standard setting at four levels: national, state, local, and program.

The optimum for standard setting should be collaboration involving representatives from all the following groups: representatives of funding agencies, of the general public, of proposed program participants, of program staff, and of professional adult educators representing wider constituencies than that of the program. All these representatives have legitimate interests and legitimate points of view which deserve a hearing as standards of performance are derived. The difficulty of incompatible standards alluded to by Weiss (1972, p. 39) can in large measure be lessened by collaborative standard setting which makes explicit the points of view and constraints under which various constituencies operate. A genuine effort should be made to illuminate the points of view and resolve conflicts that might arise. Means such as the Delphi technique (Cyphert and Gant, 1973) or Rippey's (1973) Transactional Evaluation Instrument might be employed. In cases of irreconcilable conflict, differing groups should generate standards and attempt to justify them while considering that these standards reflect divergent points of view.

Griffith (1976) has called on adult educators to unite, possibly through extant organizations such as the Coalition of Adult Education Organizations (CAEO), to influence the shaping of political policy with respect to governmentally funded adult education programs. A part of this broadened role for CAEO might well be activity to coordinate collaborative standard setting by all parties affected by a government-funded adult education program. An organization such as CAEO, representing as it does a variety of adult educators, appears particularly well suited to help funders, local program personnel, participants, and other interested parties to share in collaborative setting of standards according to which programmatic performance would be judged. In this way, CAEO or some similar organization could contribute to the field of adult education, both by fostering professionalism among adult educators and by interpreting the field of adult education to governmental funders of adult education programs. In other words, by participating in collaborative standard setting through an established organization such as CAEO, adult educators could foster both internal identity and external visibility for the profession. In order for this to happen, however, as Griffith (1976) points out, adult educators must organize effectively to lobby for the right to participate in collaborative standard setting.

For What Aspects of Adult Education Programs Should Standards Be Established? Programmatic objectives have traditionally been advocated by adult educators as standards against which programmatic effectiveness is judged. In addition to the weakness of this position with regard to comparative evaluation, a weakness discussed earlier, there are two other objections to employing objectives as the only standards by which adult education programs funded at any level of government should be judged: (1) objectives-based evaluation is too narrow to account for the multiplicity of both anticipated and unanticipated outcomes of an adult education program and (2) objectives-based evaluation tends to focus on programmatic effects to the exclusion of other facets of the program, such as planning, design, and implementation.

As Stake (1972) has noted, objectives inadequately describe programmatic outcomes because (1) countless objectives—some explicit, some implicit—are simultaneously pursued by every teacher; (2) students have more objectives than they can list, and hence any listing of objectives is an oversimplification of what the group wants and a misrepresentation of what any individual wants; (3) there is no language which perfectly represents what a teacher hopes to teach; (4) different objectives have different priorities; (5) objectives change over time; and (6) evaluative judgment of merit and shortcoming does not require an awareness of objectives. Scriven (1967) has struck a similar note in advocating what he calls "goal-free evaluation," in which an attempt is made to determine all the effects of a program without the biasing effect which knowledge of program objectives might have.

Another argument against reliance on objectives as standards for evaluation is that any educational program includes more than outcomes. Adult educators have long stressed the distinction between process and product and have claimed that both are meaningful. Hence, it seems reasonable to include both in evaluation of adult education programs funded at any level of government. Indeed, as Stake (1967) has pointed out, educational programs include antecedents—the formation of objectives and the design of educational programs—in addition to transactions within the programs and outcomes of the programs. Therefore, criteria against which to judge program performance ideally should encompass antecedents, transactions, and outcomes of governmentally funded adult education programs.

It seems apparent that different kinds of standards should be generated for each phase of the program being evaluated. The late Malcolm Provus, for example, articulated five stages of program development, with each stage accompanied by evaluation according to its own set of standards. The CIPP (context, input, process, product) evaluation model developed by Stufflebeam, which has achieved some popularity in cooperative extension evaluation, also employs differential standards by which judgment is rendered according to the stage of program development being considered. Udell (1975) advocates a CIPP approach to assessing the worth of adult education programs, with criteria differing according to programmatic context and sometimes within a context as well. For example, in assessing programmatic results, Udell postulates two types of criteria: criteria of effectiveness, involving the results of the program; and criteria of efficiency, involving the assessing of relationships between program inputs and program outputs. Also within the field of adult education, Bennet (1975) has elaborated a seven-step "staircase for measuring extension's impact," wherein the output of any stage becomes the standard for the next stage.

Another way to conceptualize the programmatic scope of established standards of performance involves the kind of value an educational program might be said to have. In his book on evaluation as an operation in logic, Taylor (1961) describes three kinds of value: exemplified value, instrumental value, and contributory value. Evaluation of an adult education program with regard to exemplified value would entail the assessment of programmatic inputs. It is the model of evaluation employed by accrediting agencies in which educational programs are evaluated on the basis of such factors as teacher qualifications and the ratio of library books to students. Interestingly, the generally critical report of the Comptroller General of the United States (1975) to the Congress faulted adult basic education programs largely with regard to standards of exemplified value: percentage of clientele reached, setting of program goals, recruitment, and coordination with federal anti-poverty and manpower training programs. Evaluation according to standards of instrumental value represents accountability for programmatic results—gains in reading level, in placement of participants in jobs, and the like. Evaluation according to standards representing the third kind of value, contributory value, involves the determination of the extent to which an educational program has contributed to some desirable whole or is seen as a necessary part of a larger good, possibly the good life. While the technical problems associated with evaluating on the basis of standards of contributory value are considerable—and too complex to be treated herein—the contributory value of adult education programs might be seen as their most important attainment—that the programs are not merely instrumental in enabling their participants to obtain some valuable result but that the valuable result is somehow rendered more valuable by participation in an adult education program.

Thus, it seems evident that the scope of established standards of performance for adult education programs should not be limited to programmatic outputs set forth in prespecified objectives but should embrace all facets of an adult education program—from needs assessment and objectives setting through planning and implementation to conclusion—in fact, beyond the conclusion of the program to its contribution to participants' lives.

How Are Standards to Be Judged? According to Taylor (1961), evaluation is by definition a judgment of worth; therefore, when one evaluates an adult education program funded by any level of government, one simultaneously (1) judges the extent to which the program fulfills or fails to fulfill the established standards of performance and (2) claims that it is valid and appropriate to apply those standards in the evaluative process. Hence, there is a need to establish metastandards by which proposed standards of performance can be judged.

Two such metastandards have been suggested previously: (1) that established standards be derived collaboratively to assure that they are responsive to the educational desires of the clientele as well as to the information needs of the funders and (2) that established standards should be comprehensive, encompassing all phases of governmentally funded adult education programs.

Established standards should also represent realistic and attainable performance of an adult education program rather than absolute ideals in comparison with which programs would inevitably be found wanting. Frequently the language of enabling legislation is overly grandiose and might tend to raise expectations of program participants to an unattainable level. Weiss (1972, p. 39) cites an example of the hyperbolic language of legislation, whereby "public housing will not just provide decent living space; it will improve health, enhance marital stability, reduce crime, and lead to improved school performance."

Another metastandard for judging standards developed for evaluation of any governmentally funded adult education program is that the standards should be comprehensible, so that those charged with designing and operating programs will be able to understand what they are to be working toward. Criteria should be clearly written in language which is designed to be understood rather than in jargon or unintelligible statistical formulas.

Closely allied to comprehensibility is the quality of communicability. Established standards of performance should be conveyed to those charged with designing and implementing governmentally funded adult education programs so that they will know what standards will be used in judging their programs. Since standards are to be set collaboratively, at least those program personnel who have participated in establishment of standards will have knowledge of the standards and of their meaning. Those personnel would then communicate the standards and the bases on which they were established to others in the program. Communication, of course, entails not only the transmission of a message but a genuine effort to ensure its reception. Therefore, an important responsibility of those local program personnel who participated in the derivation of the standards would be to institute a series of meetings for the explication and explanation of standards of performance in order to effect the understanding and shared participation upon which enlightened adult education practice is based.

Conclusion

Adult education programs funded by any level of government should be judged according to established standards of performance. Evaluation in terms of accountability is not only a necessity mandated by law; it is also consonant with the service tradition of adult education, and it can be accomplished without turning control of the content of adult programs over to government functionaries. Indeed, to adult educators judgment according to standards derived outside of the program should represent not a threat but a challenge—an opportunity for adult educators to develop a collaborative model for derivation and establishment of standards of performance which will give the field of adult education internal identity and external visibility and which will, even more significantly, result in adult education programs that are responsive to the educational desires of the clientele served by them and to the self-renewal needs of the democratic society that gave those programs birth.

Standards Must Be Agreed to by Adult Learners

Floyd C. Pennington

Adult educators have long valued the notion that fully functioning adults in a democratic society are self-sufficient and self-initiating.

> Goals for adult learning experiences must be self-responsibility, autonomy, individuality, independence of thought, and an ability and willingness to risk choosing. . . . How can adults retain or enhance their own responsibility for learning when we, in the system, insist on, and push for, massive governmentally supported educational programs, which, in fact, continue to institutionalize learning and imply adults learn only when participating in such programs? Are we meeting real needs when, in fact, our programs are basically conducted for repeat customers who have become dependent on us? Are we enhancing independence when adult education programs reinforce this dependency syndrome? . . . Are we encouraging independence of learning when our programs are complex, are lessons in red tape, and consist of prespecified learning? [Forest, 1976, p. 116].

The proposition that citizens have a right to be educated does not appear to be an issue open to debate. Large-scale tax-supported educational programs—for example, right-to-read programs—have been mounted that demonstrate this social posture. Americans assume that being educated is one of the basic rights of citizenship. Underlying this proposition is the notion that someone has the responsibility to provide a service to the holder of such a right, and the limits of the service depend not only on the existence of such a right but on economic and other considerations as well (Duval, 1977, p. 186). The individual, by claiming that being educated is a right, shifts the responsibility for exercising the right from the personal realm to the realm of society.

"More and more the artificer of the possible is society—not the individual; he thereby becomes more dependent on things external and less on his own inner resources" (Knowles, 1977, p. 60). We live in a society where "the idea of individual responsibility" is less salient than the idea of "individual rights, the responsibility of society-at-large, and the steady growth of production and consumption" (Knowles, 1977, p. 60). In that society the distinction between educational need and desire is clouded when need is defined as the minimal requirements for a satisfactory life, and desire is that which adults demand as requirements for what they personally consider an optimal life. This is a difficult distinction for adult educators and the society to deal with. Callahan (1977, p. 28) provides one reason:

> Technological societies are committed to economic growth. Despite the discussions of a "steady-state society," most people still believe that a society which does not continue to grow economically is doomed. The key to continuous growth is the stimulation of production through increasing consumption brought about by the stimulation of desire. People must be induced to want more and more. Hence, to bring matters full circle, "needs" and "desires" become one—the satisfactory life and the optimal life turn out to be one and the same; the satisfactory life is defined as one in which the optimal life can be, and must be, provided. Unless the individual pursues what he desires, and not just what he needs, the economy cannot continue to give him what he needs. Desire becomes king.

A major goal of every individual is a complete state of physical, mental, and social well-being. When this goal is claimed as a right, the educational enterprise and other sectors of society are placed in the untenable position of being required to assure the attainment of an unattainable goal. By even suggesting that adult education can assure these rights, one proposes an impossible and illusory task for it, regardless of the amount of government allocations and explicitly stated standards of performance.

How educated do adults have to be to function sufficiently in this society? How much and what kind of ignorance should be combated? There are enormous variations among individuals and groups in their tolerance for, and perpetuation of, ignorance. Functional illiteracy on one hand and professional obsolescence on the other are at different ends of the continuum, yet both are areas of ignorance and critical concerns for educators of adults.

Should the right to be educated mean that adults are entitled to a standard kind of education stipulated by society or should the right be interpreted to mean being eligible to participate in any education selected by the learner? Are adult educators stressing principles of economic growth to the exclusion of facilitating adults' self-selected educational growth processes? Should adult educators be a part of a system that establishes standards of performance for a passive consumer? Can adult educators believe that their participation in a top-down system will make it any more responsive to the adult as a self-directed learner?

There is no reason, other than lack of political power, for people to curb their desires about what they want the American educational system to deliver to fulfill their notions of the optimal life. The fact is that some will have more ready access to educational opportunities than others, since some groups have more power to shape the directions of education. Adult educators, to keep themselves solvent, will provide the required services and perpetuate an unequal system. As Forest, 1976, p. 116, says: "Are our programs really worth saving if they can't stand on their own merits? Are they worth saving if they don't enhance independent learning? And finally, a most threatening question—can an institutionalized education program even think of enhancing an individual's responsibility, self-sufficiency, and independent learning when it is the antithesis of it?" Traditional principles of adult education are in conflict with the direction in which our society is drifting.

Government Strategy for Funding

The major strategy used by federal and state government agencies to influence educational change has been the paradigm of research, development, and diffusion. The problem is that this basic approach has been relatively ineffective.

In the research, development, and diffusion (R, D, and D) system, the researcher produces the new knowledge and the developers convert the knowledge into marketable products, which are then delivered into the practice setting and adopted by the local consumer. As a result of this effort, education should improve. From the government's perspective, the R, D, and D strategy should result in an integrated system through which the translation of new knowledge to practice settings can occur in an effective and efficient manner.

The R, D, and D strategy is the optimal operational approach for the government to follow. The power of the strategy is not disputable. Those who control the purse strings control the direction of research and programming, and they also influence the outcome. A succession of government programs is guaranteed by bureaucratic career patterns and by constantly changing political coalitions. The government leader finds it expedient to be identified with an innovative program for career advancement: "He must fight for control and resources if he is to be successful, and the longer he does so the less knowledgeable or concerned he becomes about the effect of the program 'in the field'—except as it facilitates fighting his own bureaucratic battles" (House, 1974, p. 206).

Havelock (1971) suggests that the R, D, and D strategies have five characteristics in common. Each assumes a sequence of activities that moves from research to development to packaging before distribution for adoption; a division of labor is required to carry out these activities; massive planning is required to control and coordinate the activities; and a high cost for initial development is required, with an expected payoff in efficiency, quality, and capacity to reach a large audience. Finally, and critical to our deliberation, the strategy used by government agencies for funding projects and programs assumes a passive consumer who, at the end of the entire process, will perform according to the prespecified standards.

The R, D, and D strategy creates a division of labor between those who are doers and those who are done to. "The planning group gets to initiate activities, decide what problems will be addressed, and how resources will be allocated, while the consumers are assigned the difficult and thankless task of implementing. Initiation, control, and rewards reside at the top" (House, 1975, p. 2).

Why should adult educators question the R, D, and D strategy? First, this paradigm treats the adult user as a passive recipient. Each successive recipient in the R, D, and D translation line becomes more inactive and unable to shape the direction of the adult education program or service. Second, for the R, D, and D strategy to operate perfectly, participants all along the translation line must share the same values and desired ends. But self-interests and rewards are not the same for government bureaucrats, adult education researchers, program providers, and adult learners. It is likely that several groups will be working at cross-purposes within the overall process. In a system this complex, no one can force compliance with the overall goals. Further, local administrators know that these funds are short lived and that continuation is not likely beyond that contract period. "The wise local administrator handles federal funds in such a way as to provide maximum help (and perhaps maximum publicity) for his district, while avoiding dependence on a federal program that he knows may soon pass or may have to be funded within a tight local budget" (House, 1974, p. 206). Programs funded by government tend to be operated at a minimum level of output for the dollar. Resources gained through the contract are diverted to the fullest legal extent to support the organization's ongoing activities, which local administrators know will continue beyond the funding period of any government program.

"Perhaps the most significant weakness in the R, D, and D paradigm is the belief that one will be able to define an innovation, the varying contingencies within which it works, and know the generalizable effects it will have from setting to setting" (House, 1975, p. 3). This expectation is not realistic. Interaction effects vary greatly from setting to setting. No matter how many variables are controlled, other factors interfere to upset consistent findings. High-level generalizations are not possible. What the government project officers hope will happen, what they see as the ultimate payoff, often will not happen.

Processes Favoring the Atrophy of Adult Self-Direction

Adult educators are confronted with an impasse where two processes converge. On the one hand, our social structure is making it easier for society to care for major problems by informally proclaiming an increasing number of services as rights. On the other hand, the strategy used by the government to fund programs is generally ineffective. It perpetuates an economy that treats the consumer as a passive recipient who has only the freedom not to buy the end product. When a society insists on service as rights and when a government, by its fiscal power, determines the flow and accessibility of those services, the fundamental choice options of adults are decreased—even though an increase in the choice of brands is offered.

These two phenomena are the antithesis of the historical values which adult educators hold about adults. The fundamental question is not whether programs funded at any level of government should meet established standards of performance. In the context of the current paradigm used by the government, this is an operational question, and the rational response is that adult educators should help set the standards. The fundamental question, given adult educators' historical values about adults and governments' approach to funding, is whether adult educators should accept any government monies for programs, especially funds for programs with preestablished standards of performance. To answer this question, we must move out of the realm of philosophical deliberations and back into the arena of operational realities.

The future of an increasing number of adult education programs is inextricably bound to government funding and perhaps regulation. Without an unacceptable set of central control contingencies, government-funded adult education programs have little chance of significant national impact. Successful adult education programs are dependent on an understanding of how adults should function as responsible individuals and an understanding of how successful adult education programs work internally. This understanding must include a respect for the role of the adult educator and the adult learner. The consumer must not be a passive recipient but rather an active shaper of a system which, over time, will become continuously responsive to the needs of a pluralistic client system. Adult educators must recognize when their decisions are being guided by their own career goals and fights for organizational continuance rather than their role in linking available resources to client needs. Skills in the politics of innovation must be sharpened and applied to contractual interactions with government funding agencies.

New Policies for Government-Funded Programs

House (1974, pp. 244–246) suggests the creation of new policies for government-funded programs. The new policies should avoid a hierarchical division of labor; result in a distribution rather than a concentration of resources; feature the individual as the client rather than the government agency; avoid the indiscriminate pursuit of innovations from other settings; avoid establishing or relying on common measures of payoff; determine the success of government policies by independent, diverse, and honest evaluations of specific projects; and share control of the entire innovation process with those engaged in it and most affected by it.

Implementation of these policies would be a significant step in minimizing the operational problems of the R, D, and D strategy and would create an acceptable collaboration between government funding agencies and adult education programs and services. These shifts in perspectives will not, however, address the unfortunate trends that transpose individual responsibilities to social demands.

When hierarchical divisions of labor are minimized, and when control of innovations resulting from government funded research is shared, more of the ultimate users become involved in the entire process of development and utilization of the innovation. Adults involved throughout the planning process are likely to be strong advocates of the desired outcomes. This will require more than symbolic participation. It requires a dynamic linkage between producers and users in activities of mutual concern.

The adult learner cannot be standardized. A single program cannot serve all persons equally well. Program goals for adult education programs are based on the uniqueness of the local environment. Distributed goals, such as teaching an adult to read, can be achieved only within specific contexts. There should be no ulterior purposes. The adult should be seen as the recipient of educational services that meet his specific learning needs, not outcomes specified by the funding agency or program sponsor. When a government or an agency insists that its standards be met, its programs may become self-serving and may gradually foster values different from those of the adult learner, the ultimate user of the government funds.

Basing educational programs on established standards of performance makes program evaluation manageable. However, education for a diverse group of clients with widely varying reasons for participation cannot be judged adequately by a single measurement of worth. What is suitable for one group of adults may be unsuitable for another group. Programs based on specified standards of performance maximize the values of those who set the standards and provide few opportunities for participants who may prefer to shape the direction of the program to suit their personal learning interests. Ideally, an evaluation of adult education programs uses diverse appraisal mechanisms developed specifically for the context in which the program occurs. To facilitate this broad-aimed evaluation of adult education programs will also require the continuous involvement of the funding agency, the provider, and the client in the design, application, analysis, and utilization of the evaluation data.

The basic assumptions in this approach to funding adult education programs are these:

1. The adult participant—not the government funding agency or the program provider—is the client for government-funded programs.
2. Adult participants can contribute significantly to the development of programs and services. The planners do not hold all social wisdom.
3. Educational needs for adult learners cannot be equivocally defined.
4. Program providers may not be able to achieve consensus on goals among adult participants.

5. More adults will be served if government funds are used to facilitate innovation in a wide variety of settings.
6. Government funds should be restricted to supporting new programs reaching new audiences rather than being made available to administrators to cover the costs of operating existing programs.
7. The quality of an adult education program is more likely to be dependent on the level of caring and involvement than on the achievement of standards selected by others for the learners.
8. What works in one location may not work in another location.

New Mechanisms for Democratic Program Planning

To establish a more democratic process for funding projects will require a major shift in government's attitude toward the process of translation of information and services. Persons to be affected by the program will have to bargain with persons controlling sources of support throughout the entire program and raise a variety of questions. How far should the program go? What are mentors, learners, and innovators to get out of it? What resources are available to implement the program? Whose definition of needs is being met? Payoffs for the program will be distributed by a dialectical bargaining process among the concerned parties. Various mechanisms, including vouchers and workers' sabbaticals, have been suggested for an equitable distribution of monies for adult education program funds.

One intriguing suggestion is negotiated innovation (House, 1975, p. 8). In this approach, the advocacy group bargains with authorities over resources to be allocated to the specific local program or project. Each local group argues for elements it deems most important. Differing goals are mediated through negotiation, so that the resulting program will take on a different form in each program environment. A single set of preestablished program standards is not appropriate in this system. "Democratic innovation . . . calls for a strong government presence but one in which local authorities, particularly those who must do the actual work, have equal power in key decisions. In fact, government should be concerned with stimulating innovation generally but not with determining what the content of innovation shall be. In the long run, government policies should promote equality rather than deny it, but individuals should be left to determine for themselves what is good" (House, 1975, p. 10).

The challenge is to make the adult learner the real client. At the same time, adult educators must make certain that program resources are used for programs that will have real impact and not for more of the same. If the negotiated innovation approach is used, an equitable way to support innovative practice must be developed. House suggests an innovation credit. The major stipulation of an innovation credit is that the funds be spent on good practice. The government cannot define what good practice is. The program sponsor may spend innovation credits in supporting new programs to reach new audiences to achieve new purposes. The credits may not be used to support any existing programs.

Flexibility without responsibility is not what is being suggested. A monitoring system would still be required. Some adult educators would still cheat. The monitoring system could be regional. State authorities could monitor programs in their state with overseeing audits by federal authorities. This arrangement allows government agencies to do what they do best—distribute money, audit, monitor, regulate—but takes away the necessity for them to pass judgments on new ideas or the quality of practice, something they do not do well.

Mechanisms like the innovation credit, negotiated innovation, workers' sabbaticals, or vouchers return to the people the responsibility for educational direction. They force the adult educator into broad educative roles. They do not allow the government to treat the adult learner as a powerless and passive consumer. They provide an alternative to current practices that perpetuate an ineffective system of schooling. The power is at the local or regional level, where the quality of the efforts will be judged. Power is not in government bureaucracies, where local citizens are consumers to placate every two to four years.

Conclusion

Should government-funded programs meet established standards of performance? Only if the standards are negotiated at the local or regional level and agreed to by the clients—the adult learners. Adults must have their independence of thought and participatory rights restored. The government must change its strategy for funding programs and projects. Otherwise, we need not spend time deliberating the issue raised in this chapter. The issue then becomes: Are adult educators willing to change their basic values about how adults learn and what adulthood means in order to function in a government-subsidized adult education system that relegates adults to passive acquiescence?

Chapter Seven

Should Adult Education Be Competency Based?

Programs Should Be Tied to Behavioral Objectives and Achievement of Competence

Noreen M. Clark

As a result of careful reading of this chapter, you, the reader, will be able to recognize my views on behavioral objectives and achievement of competence as a basis for program planning and organization. Specifically, you will be able to:

1. List three factors that have influenced development of competency-based education.
2. Specify whether I disagree or agree that
   a. Competence formats describe a process.
   b. Educational hardware is critical to competency-based education.
   c. The test of a behavioral objective is whether or not it facilitates learning.
3. Determine whether I agree or disagree that
   a. Explaining values is appropriate in competence formats.
   b. The content of an affect must be specified in advance in competency-based education.
4. Describe two characteristics of competence, list three sources of data for defining competence, and identify the most important source for adult educators.
5. Indicate whether or not I believe that competency-based education can fit with humanist philosophy.
6. Specify the extent to which you agree with me and analyze why you feel as you do.

The criterion of mastery will be correct completion of all tasks in the five checkpoints appearing at the end of each section.

Even as the concept of competency-based education increases in popularity, some critics contend that the approach is incompatible with humanistic adult education practice. This criticism, to a great extent, grows out of misunderstandings surrounding the application of competence formats among a surprising number of educators in general and adult educators in particular. These misconceptions give the approach an undeserved bad name in some quarters and discourage otherwise enlightened adult educators from utilizing the approach in their professional practice. To support the position that program planning and organization should follow a format tied to behavioral objectives and achievement of competence, it is important to examine these several points of contention one by one.

Accountability, Personalization, and Application

Point One: Concern for competence did not arrive, without invitation, in a Skinner box. Three factors have generated interest in and shaped the development of competency-based education: accountability, personalization, and application of learning.

The welcome or unwelcome presence of competency-based programming is reflected in words filling the literature and vocabulary, not to mention administrative directives, of the educational community: behavioral objective, performance level, criterion-referenced instruction, mastery learning, and so on. Essentially, this language jungle reveals an old problem for everyone engaged in education; that is, getting clear on what the processes entail and are intended to accomplish. The conceptual sources for competency-based education have been identified and discussed at length: behavioral psychology (Glaser, 1962), learning theory related to modeling (Bandura and Walters, 1962), and systems analysis (Gagné, 1962b). The research findings and models emanating from these areas of investigation in the social and behavioral sciences have provided the theoretical framework for competence formats. Why, one might ask, the great and seemingly sudden interest of educators in something called competence?

Houston (1974, p. 5) has discussed two relatively new forces in society which have influenced the development of competency-based approaches to education: demands for accountability and personalization. The demand for greater accountability from providers of service in all fields of endeavor (medical, social, educational, commercial) reflects the belief that the buyer must get full value for the dollar, regardless of who ultimately foots the bill. This expectation also implies that quality and accountability are intertwined. Accountability is an aspect of the idea that service is rendered on the basis that one is able to do something needed by another. For example, Henry is able to assist Mary to learn to bake a cake, and she contracts with him to do so. Henry therefore becomes accountable to Mary. Whether or not Mary learns is observable in the quality and quantity of her cakes after Henry's instruction. The point at which Mary begins her baking sequence should correspond to the level of her readiness and should be diagnosed by Henry as part of the exchange. In other words, there must be reasonable assurances that Mary can count on Henry and that he delivers effectively the instruction she needs, regardless of whether it is purchased through payment of fees, through taxes, through barter, or by another means.

The burgeoning of mass education and the wide range of functions, interests, and concerns of an incredibly heterogeneous population have resulted in another expectation on the part of American consumers. Along with accountability has come the demand for more personal and individualized service. If Mary is interested in chocolate cake baking, is able to study only in the evenings after work, and lacks confidence in her ability to cook, she wants an instructor who can respond to her particular needs; that is, one who will personalize the service of education so that Mary's goals can indeed be met.

Interest in competency-based adult education is being fostered, as well, by a more subtle force. This influence is the importance placed by adult educators on educational philosophies that value observable application of learning. Obviously, the behaviorists view learner performance as the critical factor. However, it appears that they are not alone. A quick review of some major nonbehavioral philosophies shaping adult education thinking will illustrate the emergence of this value. We might begin with the Thomists, who claimed that knowledge is a value and an end in itself, that there is no other foundation for the educational task than the eternal saying "It is the truth that sets men free" (Maritain,

1955). Enter Adler (1955) and his conviction that the ultimate ends of education are the same for all men at all times and everywhere—they are absolute and universal principles. Dewey (1920) believed that education must be reconceived, not as merely a preparation for maturity but as a continuous growth of the mind and continuous illumination of life. He felt that the school can give us only the instrumentalities of mental growth and that the rest depends on an absorption and interpretation of experience. Lindeman (1956) argued that learning which is combined with action provides a peculiar and solid enrichment and that all successful adult education groups sooner or later become social action groups. In Freire's (1970) view, education leads to social and political acts. His goal is to debunk the concept of education that ends in conformity. Rather, he exhorts, education must liberate, acknowledge individual experience, and lead us to freedom and control over our own destiny. It must be problem posing; it strives for the emergence of consciousness; it attempts to achieve a critical intervention in reality; it employs the method of dialogue; and it ends not in talk but in action. Although it may be difficult to reconcile the assumptions of Freire with those of competency-based education, the concepts of personalization and observable change through application of learning are common to both.

The idea of action, or application of knowledge, as it has emerged in important educational philosophies apart from the behaviorist, has influenced interest in competency-based education. We have come to believe that the truth sets people free if it is translated into action. In addition, a measure of our success as educators increasingly is seen in the extent to which the adults with whom we work are able to perform independently as a result of educational intervention. That is, we are to be accountable as educators. Learners must be able to demonstrate in behavior what they have recognized or acquired. Finally, we have become aware that the route to freedom must be personalized, since it may not unfold the same for thee as for me, and you may travel by jet while I go on foot. One result of these influences has been the development of educational approaches concerned primarily with demonstrating learner outcomes; and these three factors, in a sense, can be considered descriptors of competency-based education.

Checkpoint:

Check yourself here by filling in the blank
spaces below. If you feel you are not ready
to complete the statement, reread
to this point. Correct answers immediately
follow this checkpoint and are italicized.

Development of competency-based adult
education has been influenced by an
increased interest in _____ ,
_____ , and _____ .

Competence formats, then, incorporate *accountability*, *personaliza-*
tion, and *application* of learning. These factors, without doubt, constitute a solid basis for program planning and organization for the
education of adults.

Demonstrated Outcomes and Selective Use of Hardware

Point Two: Competency-based education is not an evil plot
devised by behavioral objective fanatics and teaching-machine sales
representatives. It is a process for learning that centers on demonstrated outcomes and sometimes employs educational hardware.

In the flurry of activities surrounding the arrival of competence formats, a great deal of attention has been paid by program
planners to teaching machines, videotapes, recorders, programmed
texts, and the like. Various versions of these tools have been thrust
at teachers by some planners who are fervent in their conviction
that the use of such machinery and devices will enable adults to
learn like magic. Concurrently, some program planners require
teachers to specify in the smallest of units the behavioral objectives
related to each step of skill development. A primary focus of
competency-based education is on the application of systematic approaches to achieving observable outcomes. Given, however, a
parade of teaching-machine sales representatives and seemingly
infinite possibilities for documenting the most minute of behavioral
objectives, the words *competence format* often engender horrible visions of hardware and endless reams of paper in the heads of some

adult educators. Fixation on these artifacts blocks understanding and acceptance of the primary characteristics of competence formats. The ideas that underlie the use of the educational tools associated with competency-based education are the focus of disagreement. McDonald (1974, p. 25) suggests that there are three characteristics of almost all competency-based programs: organization of what is to be learned into interdependent components, precise specification of what is to be learned, and provision of feedback. Similarly, he identifies three tasks for the program planner: deciding on the critical features of the process of acquiring skills, determining whether the components of the skill are discrete and independent or interdependent, and selecting a training model that fits. Nagel and Richman (1972, p. 49) outline the competency-based instructional system as one in which (1) instructional objectives are given to the student, (2) readiness for the piece of instruction is diagnosed, (3) evaluation procedures are designed which adequately reflect the objectives, (4) some arrangement is made for giving each student the amount of time needed to learn, and (5) students work at their own rate.

Given these definitions and tasks for the programmer, we are again reminded that competency-based education describes not what one learns but how. It is a process in which a variety of tools and techniques may be used. The content or substance of learning fitted into this process can range widely from nursing care to nursery rhymes. The hardware which may be used is to enhance the process. It is not mandatory and is in no way by itself synonymous with competency-based education.

Another major concern of those who avoid competence formats is that setting objectives is an imperfect process because of the breadth of behavioral outcomes it is possible to identify for a learning event. Objectives currently in use vary greatly in quality and precision, from general (such as "The learner will be able to lead a meaningful discussion") to narrow ("The learner will be able to select and activate the correct knob to adjust focus on an opaque projector") (Broudy, 1974, p. 61). Much of the opposition to stating outcomes in behavioral terms has originated with those critical of the minute levels of specificity used in many systems models, where tasks to be learned are analyzed and subsequently broken into the smallest of discrete units; for example, "Wrapper Stemming for Pipe Tobacco: (a) select leaf; (b) grasp with thumb and first and second fingers of right hand; (c) grasp selected point with thumb and first finger of left hand; (d) release hold on leaf with right hand; (e) regrasp stem; (f) remove stem, holding at right angle to body" and so on (Seymour, 1966). The major criterion for determining the level of specificity for learning objectives, however, is not the relative size of the item of performance but, rather, whether or not the objective enables a learner to acquire a skill or apply a concept. Houle (1972) observes that an important test of an objective is achievability. Several characteristics are related. Objectives must be rational and practical. Objectives require judgment and flexibility in their use. They must be hierarchical and discriminative.

Objectives are constructed for purposes of clarity, on the basis of independent components of a skill or concept, and to enable sequencing. "Will lead a meaningful discussion" is not a reasonable and clear objective unless *meaningful* is defined and characteristics of discussion leading are specified and sequenced. Dissecting psychomotor aspects of a skill, so that following a procedure may actually interfere with learning to perform, similarly may be unworkable. The extent to which an objective serves to articulate and facilitate learning from the learner's perspective is the measure of its appropriateness. How well an objective works is determined in several ways. Learning procedures and events themselves always must be subject to formative and summative evaluation. Banathy (1968, p. 31) states that the assessment has two major purposes: evaluation of learner's performance and monitoring of the instructional system's effectiveness and economy. This continuing assessment considers how well the specific learning experiences are producing the desired changes in skills and the intended increase in the capacity to utilize the concepts covered in the instruction. This determination is reached through trial and error, through learner and teacher assessment of means and ends, through observation, through exercise of judgment, and so on. Rejecting competency-based education as accommodating objectives that may be too general or too specific is begging the question. Critics using this argument well may be the same people who respond to the query "How long should my term paper be?" with "long enough to handle the subject adequately."

Checkpoint:

Check yourself here by circling the word
which reflects whether I
disagree or agree with statements
listed below. If you are unsure of the
responses, reread the preceding section
before continuing. Correct answers
immediately follow this checkpoint.

Competency-based education is a process.

Disagree   Agree

Educational hardware is necessary in an
effective competence format.

Disagree   Agree

The test of a behavioral objective is
achievability.

Disagree   Agree

Allow me to reiterate: I *agree* that one can only define competency-based education as a process, and I *disagree* that hardware is critical to the process. Achievement of competence in a sense is guided by behavioral objectives, and I *agree* that the test of an objective is achievability, not level of specificity.

Cognitive and Affective Objectives

Point Three: Competence formats are not cold, heartless, and imposing (although sometimes teachers are). They incorporate affective as well as cognitive learning objectives.

Competence has most frequently been discussed in relation to the cognitive domain of learning. Competence formats do, however, incorporate learnings related to values, feelings, and beliefs, in which specific content outcomes cannot be predetermined. Again it is necessary to say that the approach describes how one learns, not what one learns. Expressive concerns are as critical to the process as are instructional ones. Many enthusiasts who urge "help stamp out nonbehavioral objectives" (Kurtz, 1965, p. 31) have expounded on learning outcomes related to technical or clinical skill development and have not paid the same degree of attention to the equally important affective domain—probably because content is more manageable than the slippery arena of affect. The pioneers of competence concepts, however, did not avoid this territory (Krathwohl, Bloom, and Masia, 1964). The issue is not that the teacher who advocates competency-based education imposes his belief any more or less than another teacher does. A competence format does not specify what values, feelings, or beliefs a person will have as a result of a learning event but rather what the learner is able to do related to them; that is, articulate values, express feelings, explain beliefs.

Learning activities focused on expressive objectives, like those focused on instructional objectives, utilize a variety of tools and techniques to reach measurable outcomes. For example, if an instructional objective is that learners will define perception and list influences on the perceptual process, a lecture or programmed text may be an appropriate technique for achieving the outcome (Bullmer, 1975). In contrast, if an expressive objective is that learners will draw conclusions about how they perceive members of a group and analyze their perceptions, an entirely different mode of learning—such as dialogue, discussion, structured group experience, or exercise—may be necessary (Pfeiffer and Jones, 1974). The nature of the learning activity is determined by what is to be learned. The behavioral objectives specified are to enable learners to clarify affective concerns. The objectives do not dictate the content of the affect. Behavioral objectives provide an essential basis for evaluating achievement. Sharing the objectives with the learners may also be motivational, for as Mezirow, Darkenwald, and Knox (1975) have reported, adults in basic education programs perform better when they have a clear idea of what is expected of them than they do if the desired outcomes are unclear.

Checkpoint:

Check yourself here by circling the word
that describes my view
on the statements below. If you
feel that you are not ready to respond, reread
the preceding section. Correct answers
immediately follow this checkpoint.

Being able to explain what one values
as a result of a learning experience
is an appropriate outcome in competence formats.

Disagree   Agree

To use a competence format effectively,
one must specify in advance of a
learning event *what* feelings and *which*
beliefs a learner will have afterward.

Disagree   Agree

The ability to reach expressive outcomes is integral to competence formats. I *agree* that explaining values is an appropriate
objective. I *disagree* that what one is to feel or believe is imposed
before the fact.

Learner's Role in Defining Competence

Point Four: Competence is not unilaterally determined
by experts. Definitions of competence abideth in at least three:
official mandates, research, the learner. The greatest of these is the
learner.

Describing what a person should be able to do after a learning experience, in order to demonstrate his competence, logically
precedes educational program development. If one is learning to
drive a car, for example, one's performance in obeying signs and
signals and executing turns in accordance with official criteria for

public safety is a measure of achievement. If one is studying nursing, one's ability to carry out a series of skills and to apply certain concepts will be evaluated against nursing profession requirements and legal standards for patient care. If one is learning to operate a widget machine, minimal competence is judged in relation to standards for widget production, safety measures, efficiency, and so on. In order to qualify as a licensed driver or as a certified public accountant an individual readily accepts the fact that he must satisfy fixed standards of performance. Developing a definition of basic competence, however, is not a function solely of some monolithic group of experts, nor is it easy, even for driving teachers, nursing directors, and widget makers.

The process of defining is made difficult by at least two factors. One is that standards for competence change over time. A case, for illustration, is the definition of *literate*, which until recently constituted the end-point objective in adult basic education (ABE). Initially, ABE programs were concerned with making literate adults who, for one reason or another, had not learned to read or write at the sixth-grade level. Harman (1970, p. 226) and others have noted that, currently, the total number of "illiterates" in the United States is startling "if literacy is defined to include the ability to complete necessary everyday functions in addition to basic reading and writing." It seems that the definition of literate adult has changed and now includes functional literacy; that is, minimal competence in carrying out daily tasks which have become routine in our technological society. Another factor making competence difficult to define is that it is relative. Two people, for example, may meet minimal standards and each acquire a driver's license. One, however, may go on to win the Indianapolis 500 race while the other piles up traffic violations. Each has personal goals related to how good a driver he wants to be or can be.

The dynamic nature of competence, that it changes and is relative, requires that we utilize several sources of data for working definitions. One has been mentioned previously; that is, official and professional and legal mandates regarding minimal standards of achievement. Another source is research. Research in all areas is conducted to develop the knowledge base. Each new discovery, improved technique, and refined idea contributes to our collective and individual ability and expands our concept of competence. As an illustration, we can again refer to the ABE definition of literacy. A survey conducted by the staff of the Adult Performance Level Project at the University of Texas (*Adult Performance Level Study,* 1973), somewhat in response to the criticisms by Harman and others, attempted to assist in redefining literacy and to catalog the minimal tasks and functions adults currently need to be able to perform. Findings of research in the social, behavioral, and physical sciences are pervasive and continually shape our definitions of acceptable performance in virtually every learning arena.

Another source of data, and the most important, is the learner himself. The individual learner may make determinations that coincide with or go beyond legal and professional and official mandates or research findings. For example, a father enrolls in an adult education course because he wants to learn about parenting. The program may incorporate objectives which draw on several sources of data for defining competence as a parent. A legal standard of minimal parental competence is that one feeds and clothes and refrains from abusing a child. Research findings suggest that a desired behavior for a parent is to provide direction and positive reinforcement, so that a child will develop self-confidence. The father himself may want to learn to negotiate with his child to reduce conflict and stress at home. Learner-defined competence is the most important single data source for adult educators and is consistent with guidelines of adult education program planning and organization. Adult educators speak of identification of learner priorities—that process by which the substance of learning is formulated from the concerns of program participants—as critical to needs assessment. The skilled adult educator uses a variety of approaches to help learners articulate problems and identify priorities. Essentially, learners provide the data on what will help them reach their educational goals and improve their performance in selected areas.

It is difficult to accept the claim of some "experts" that learners are incapable of defining competence. Hall (1975, p. 27) outlines several points that are likely to be part of a set of guidelines found in any adult education text: (1) Programs should be based on adult needs. (2) Adults, unlike children, are able to articulate their learning needs. (3) Adults often work out quite complex learning strategies to achieve desired goals. An effective adult education program depends on effective needs assessment. Effective needs assessment yields learner-determined objectives. Some who reject competency-based education do so because they fear elitist definitions of competence. Competence is the what of learning, and it is to be generated primarily from the people. Precepts of adult education specify identification of participants' objectives and priorities, and these lead to learner definitions of competence.

Checkpoint:

Check yourself here. If you are unsure
of responses, reread the preceding section.
Answers follow this checkpoint.

Competence precludes unilateral
definition because of its _____
and _____ nature.

There are several sources of data
for defining competence. Three are
_____ , _____ , and _____ .

The primary source of data for defining competence for adult education
program planning is _____ .

Risking redundance, I submit that the *relative* and *changing* nature of competence requires that many sources—including *official mandates*, *research*, and *the learner*—be tapped continuously for working definitions. The tenets of adult education make clear that the *learner* is the primary source.

Competence Approaches and Learner Autonomy

Point Five: Competency-based education is not antithetical to humanistic philosophy. Competence formats can foster autonomy, growth, and participation.

The humanist philosophy—with its stress on fulfilling one's potential, self-determination, and the use of the learner's personally defined goals for education—is essentially concerned with the autonomy of the learner. For the humanist, learning is active participation. In competency-based education, content derives from a philosophy of education; that is, what one should be educated for. Critics who argue that competence formats are manipulative and antihumanist fail to note that the approach essentially uses organized and systematized procedures to achieve growth, autonomy, and participation. To paraphrase McDonald (1974, p. 28), autonomous growth processes are stimulated in a competency-based format in two ways: first, by stimulating the learner's information-gathering and -interpreting processes; second, by teaching procedures that provide for feedback to him. The rationale and substance of competence programs are rooted in the nature of what is to be learned. A behavioral description of outcome performance is necessary because program design and models of teaching and learning are eclectic.

Performance can be enhanced through a variety of learning situations. Hefferman-Cabrera (1974, p. 47) suggests that competency-based education, in fact, can be an organizer for humanists. She states that programs are congruent with humanist philosophy because of the principles on which they are built. First, "a competency-based curriculum is a transparent curriculum; that is, terminal objectives are made public and the learner knows exactly what he will be doing and the criterion by which he will be evaluated. In addition to transparency in the curriculum, the learner assumes management of his own destiny. He participates in the decision-making process by designing instructional activities to achieve successful completion of enabling objectives or making choices if optional instructional activities are given." Critics of competence formats, one suspects, feel safer in unspecified teaching situations, where the educator, in fact, retains control through concealing his objectives and the criteria by which students will be evaluated.

There is little reason for the learner to be inactive in any phase of competency-based education. The learner's role most logically includes participation in defining competence, setting behavioral objectives, selecting instructional activities, determining criteria for assessing performance, and so on. In fact, learner involvement is necessary for the viability of the competence format itself. As discussed previously, competence is a complex construct. However, with the involvement of learners in definitions of competence (which in no way precludes building and refining with other sources of data), its relative and changing nature becomes less of a problem. When behavioral objectives are made public, the baseline of a learning activity or program—that is, what it intends to achieve at a given time—is made clear and explicit. Objectives can be revised, adjusted, and refined to meet inevitable changes, in part, through reality testing by the very individuals who are using the learning experience as a vehicle for developing competence. It is the learner who confronts transference of principles.

When one uses competence formats, as in all adult education approaches, one does not ask whether learners should be involved but, rather, how they can participate most effectively. Some educators currently write contracts with learners, who collaborate in setting performance objectives and determine methods to assess their own competence. Other educators negotiate with their students at the beginning of the course so that there is agreement between teacher and students regarding both the instructional objectives and the criteria to be used in evaluation. Instructional strategies are similarly negotiated, some of which are designed for groups, some of which are individualized. It is also possible to involve learners at the program level, and the mechanics of doing so clearly have implications for the organization of most adult education programs. Client participation in the goal setting of a formal organization necessitates creation of special mechanisms. Arrangements such as client policy boards, councils, and planning committees are possibilities and long have been employed by many adult educators.

When one considers that clients can be involved in defining intended program outcomes in terms of the kinds of behavior, skills, and attitudes required of the learner at the end of the course, one envisions a richer and more relevant form of participation than is usual. Dolinsky (1974, p. 351) describes in detail her effort to involve learners in decisions regarding competence outcomes for a teacher education program. The process has a high potential for frustrations for both planners and clients, in part because many administrators and teachers fear losing control, and some learners demand that the experts supply all the answers. Nonetheless, by involving learners in setting objectives and assessing performance outcomes, a competency-based educational format—more than any other—can assure accountability, personalization, and emphasis on application of learning.

Checkpoint:

Check yourself here by circling the word
that best expresses my view on
the following statements. If you do not
feel ready to respond, reread the preceding section.
Correct answers follow this
checkpoint.

It is possible to use a systematic
approach to achieve growth, autonomy,
and participation.

Disagree   Agree

Competency-based education, more than any
other approach, can ensure accountability,
personalization, and application of
learning.

Disagree   Agree

To summarize, I *agree* that autonomy, growth, and participation can be fostered through the systematic procedures of competency-based education. And I *agree* that the process—because it is transparent, involves learners, and is based on reality testing—is accountable, personal, and centered on application of learning.

Conclusion

Now that some major points of contention surrounding competency-based education have been discussed, you no doubt have formulated your own position on the issue. Make your view explicit by circling the number that best describes the extent to which you agree or disagree with my views as summarized above.

Disagree				Agree
1	2	3	4	5

Jot down on a piece of paper some key words or phrases which describe why you feel as you do. Review the checkpoints in this chapter to help stimulate your thinking. Develop these statements into a paragraph or two synthesizing your views. Once you are satisfied with your paragraphs and have sufficiently clarified your position for yourself, move to the next paper and see how your ideas fit with those of an author who is opposed to competency-based education.

Competency-Based Adult Education Does Not Ensure Accountability

Herschel N. Hadley

The issue implicit in the title of Noreen Clark's paper is that program planning and organization should follow a format tied to behavioral objectives and achievement of competence. At the end of that paper is the statement "A competency-based educational format—more than any other—can assure accountability, personalization, and emphasis on application of learning." Linking these two statements, we come up with "Program planning and organization should follow a format tied to behavioral objectives and achievement of competence because this format, more than any other, assures accountability, personalization, and application of learning."

To the last statement, I responded (on the five-point scale) with a 3—it depends. That was my position when I started reading the article.

Looking back, I find five points discussed in the article. (1) Pressures for accountability, personalization, and application of learning motivate development of competency-based education (CBE). (2) CBE is a process for learning focused on achievable and demonstrable outcomes, and educational hardware can be used to facilitate the process. (3) CBE formats can incorporate affective as well as cognitive learning objectives. (4) Definitions of competence (learning objectives) can come from at least three sources—official mandates, research, and learners—and such definitions are always changing and relative to specific conditions at a given time. (5) Competence formats can foster the autonomy, growth, and participation which humanist philosophy endorses. With these points, as presented, I generally agree (on a five-point scale a 4 or even a 5). However, I can still say, "It depends," to the main issue stated. What is missing?

Questions of Practice

Decision on the stated issue calls for experiential (empirical) data. Which CBE formats worked? Which did not? Under what conditions? What were the significant variables in each case? What were operational definitions of these variables—including "success" and "failure"? In other words, evidence is needed before I can judge whether CBE formats are effective. And before we can decide what evidence is needed to make decisions, we must consider questions of practice.

Learner's Role in Defining Competence. A learner is the primary source of definitions of competence. In Clark's article this assumption is accurately identified as a tenet of adult education. A tenet is a statement of principle, belief, or doctrine. How we rationalize the distance between our tenets and our practice has been and is a fertile area for research in many fields, not only adult education. Before this specific tenet can become a guide to practice, my experience indicates that major transformations are necessary in educator, in learner, and in methods. These transformations are necessary, whether CBE or any other format is used, if we are to achieve the full learning potential of adult education.

A major barrier to learners' becoming primary sources of definitions of competence is that over a long period the rites of education have frozen and continue to reinforce two dichotomous roles—teacher and student. Worthwhile information flows only one way—from teacher to student. A student receives information. To say that a student achieves learning is not a significant difference in the rite as long as the student depends on the teacher for direction (the objective) and recognition that learning has been achieved (the test). As long as a person depends on another for direction and achievement of learning, the dependent person is not adult, nor is the process adult education. Only when a person assumes responsibility for direction and achievement of his own learning can adult education be fully realized. Corollary: Adult education can be realized only when the relationship between teacher and student is interdependent and collaborative. Does CBE aid or hinder such a transformation? Experience so far indicates that CBE could have potential either way. My observations indicate that CBE as practiced (like other formats) is more often a hindrance than an aid. The underlying problem is the attitude or orientation of an educator to the learning process and production.

In every bureaucracy and for members of a bureaucracy, rational planning and production control lead to standardized approaches that try to achieve a consistent product. Hypothesis: Teachers and students usually perform their roles in a manner suitable to the bureaucratic production context. In such a context, CBE is likely to be used to reinforce traditional teacher-student roles with no fundamental changes. It can be argued, in fact, that CBE requires more advance planning and prior product development and therefore is more likely to block using the learner (raw material) as a primary source for defining competence objectives. CBE may encourage freezing programs before the fact in order to make them impervious to tampering by learners. CBE or other educational formats do not have to freeze teacher and student into traditional roles. But if CBE or other formats are to develop other relationships for teacher and student, fundamental changes in attitudes and practices for individuals as well as educational organizations must be accomplished.

Students are conditioned to their dependent roles through many years of educational ritual. Faced with the demands of a self-directing and self-achieving learning role, persons (both teachers and students) react with a complex range of defensive behaviors, which is a measure of the depth of transformations required. Nor have the humanists been outstandingly successful in helping individuals cope with this transformational role crisis. Too often it has been a matter of sink or swim. Much more examination of this role transformation process is required to develop practical aids to help learners and educators cope with it.

Desire for Closure. There is another dimension of adult education where practice seems to reinforce attitude and attitude reinforce practice, with the result of limiting learners' achievement.

The Zeigarnik (1927) effect denotes a work group's need for closure with respect to a particular task. There seems to be a desire for closure in education. First, the institution of education has established points of educational closure by denoting kindergarten, elementary, secondary, postsecondary, graduate, and adult education. Within these points of closure are smaller closures in the form of grade levels—freshman through senior, for example—and even smaller units of closure, the courses. Thus, the goal of learning can be displaced and become education, meaning a progression through a series of closed experiences.

The structure of closed experiences can work against growth and learning. From one point of view, the effect is positive. A course or year completed (whatever that indicates) does answer a person's need for completeness (closure) and is a mechanism for recognizing achievement. However, the closed structure can lead an individual to interpret life and learning as separable, unrelated fragments, or to see life as a series of closed events rather than as a continuous pattern of growth and learning. We are then left with such abominations as terminal learning experiences which result in terminal degrees—something like cancer.

The impact of CBE on this aspect of learning and growth is not clear. On the one hand, CBE seems to reinforce packaged learning in ever more neat, separable, and closed packages. On the other hand, if CBE can be used to help the learner become aware of ever more complex and different but related learnings, CBE can encourage growth.

Time. A competency-based format requires arrangements that contribute toward giving each student the time needed to learn or, in the case of criterion-referenced instruction, to permit students to work at their own rate. How much flexibility of time for individual learning can or will a specific institution—educational, manufacturing, or business—permit in a competency-based format? How does this constraint affect the format? How essential is the time dimension? Or, stated another way, are time constraints so rigid that competency-based formats become hurdles, as in other formats that select out those who underachieve because too little time can be allotted their needs for learning? If the time dimension is critical for learning, it would seem that, given the same constraints, the value of CBE formats reduces to whether more raw material can be processed to a certain level of expertise in a given time, with comparable amounts of resources, than can be achieved by other formats.

Accountability, Personalization, and Application

Accountability. In her discussion of accountability, Clark describes the accountability of an educator to a learner. This is the appropriate model for adult education (omitting accountability to an establishment which provides place and accreditation for learning). In her example, Henry, the instructor, is accountable to Mary, the learner. Henry, it appears, is accountable for two items: (1) assessing whether Mary is competent and ready to profit from Henry's instruction and (2) delivering effectively the instruction Mary needs. In practical situations, the measurement of Henry's assessments and his instructional performance are very difficult.

If in CBE readiness to learn is interpreted as the demonstration of a prerequisite competence, this assessment is relatively easy to conduct. Of course, it requires as much effort, at least, to specify prerequisite competencies as to specify learning objectives. Assuming we are operating without time constraints, assessment is not a difficult problem. However, Mary's readiness for instruction in another competence may not be demonstrated by demonstrating prior achievement. It is not just Mary's readiness for instruction toward a new objective that must be assessed but also her readiness to accept Henry as an instructor in learning the new objective, and her willingness to utilize other resources that are part of the instructional process.

The second area of accountability is the converse of the first. Is Henry effective in delivering the instruction Mary needs? Mary's acceptance of Henry as her instructor is shown by her willingness to follow his directions at the beginning of the instructional program. If she fails to learn what she had sought to learn, then one could question whether Henry was effective as her instructor. But her objectives may have changed during the course of instruction and so an instructor who achieved the original but not the new objective would be regarded as less than effective—at least from

Mary's perspective. It could be that Mary is simply a human being with many motivations affecting her behavior and the assessment was unable, before the fact, to predict her changing needs.

A problem, then, in practice, is the extent and character of assessment required—continuously, not just prior to a course—to deliver effectively the instruction a learner needs. But this continuous assessment of needs is an operation in which both Henry and Mary are accountable to each other, not just Henry to Mary. Continuing assessment can be thought of as an interdependent accountability in which all involved possess assessment competencies and share relevant data. To become competent in self-directing learning, one develops the competencies of a self-educator, including competencies in assessment of oneself and of other resources.

Personalization. Practice is the art of making do. For example, there is the goal of personalization. This could mean how to match an instructor's finite range of competencies with a much wider range of behaviors necessary to meet the needs of each individual learner. If the CBE format is constructed before the fact, such matching requires a range of possible formats which would be much too large for realistic budgets. If it is unstructured before the fact, a good deal of time and effort is required during the course to develop different structures that meet learners' needs. The unstructured approach too often short-changes the students by making do with whatever is available. In practice, personalization—given the usual limitations of money, time, and effort—provides a choice of two or three approaches. Fortunately, or unfortunately, everyone who has gone through any formal schooling has received approximately the same conditioning, including the competence of making do, and is prepared to settle for one out of a few standard choices. In practice, a CBE format may be packaged as self-paced instruction, which usually precludes group-learning activities. The only so-called personalization is the use of additional resources and no time restriction.

Application. Despite the Thomists cited by Clark, it is questionable whether the emphasis on application of learning is a distinctive feature of CBE. Learning has always been valued for its usefulness. But that is not quite the meaning of application as used in her article. Apparently the message of application is that CBE formats emphasize demonstrable change in behavior as a result of a learning experience. The learner must perform in a specifically different way as a result of the learning process. The distinction between CBE and other formats is that CBE requires that both the behavioral objectives and the criteria for evaluation of learning are explicit and specific whereas these are frequently vague or not revealed in other kinds of instructional systems.

Conclusion

The change to CBE, as described here, appears to consist in trying to do more precisely and understandably what educators have attempted to do all along. The asserted gains in precision and public understanding of objectives may have a revolutionary effect on educators' viewpoints and impacts on their practices. The effort to increase precision and agreement on learning direction may have enormous impact on students' learning also. But, by itself, the change does not seem a change of kind. The form of delivery—especially packaging—may be different, but the relationships and roles may be unchanged.

A general option might go far to make CBE an effective adult education system. First, learning hierarchies of competencies (objectives) are determined and defined by experts working in the field—experts meaning persons who practice these competencies. Educators then construct a variety of potential learning activities, which should lead to achieving the skills necessary for each competence. Objectives and learning activities are then presented to potential learners, who, with the help of educators and other resources, select competencies they decide they should learn. To fit the wishes of the learner, objectives may be altered and learning activities altered. This collaborative redefining and reshaping of basic material by educator and learner continues during the learning process. Ultimately, the learner performs an objective that he and the educator consider to be of value.

This CBE format uses the learner as the primary source of objectives and learning activities. It personalizes learning. Accountability is shared between learner and educator. Competent performance is the criterion. The claim that program planning and organization should follow a format tied to behavioral objectives and achievement of competence because it assures accountability, personalization, and application of learning cannot be supported or refuted on the basis of existing empirical data. Rigorous research is required to test the validity of this claim.

Chapter Eight

Should Colleges Grant Credit for Life Experiences?

Educationally Relevant Life Experiences Should Be Credited

John C. Snider

A self-made storekeeper had little patience with formal education. When a young man applied for work in his store, the owner said: "Sure, I'll give you a job. Sweep up the store."

"But I'm a college graduate," protested the young man.

"Okay, I'll show you how."

The implication of this story is reflected in the proverb "Experience without learning is better than learning without experience." A counterthought equalizing the concern might read: "Experience combined with learning is the best of both worlds." This is especially true for the adult population in American society today.

The simple truth is that American adults are looking at alternatives for advancing their educational achievement. The middle-aged adult, for example, works full time and also is rearing a family, managing the home, taking on civic responsibility, and adjusting to aging parents. Should this middle-aged adult stop the pursuance of full-time work, rearing of family in an accustomed life style, and management of home in order to attain a degree or certificate (which is needed to continue and improve that pursuance of full-time work, rearing of family, and management of home)? To many the answer is yes. And to them goes the utmost encouragement and understanding. They will likely need both. Many other adults, although they desire additional education, are unwilling or unable to give up job and other responsibilities to do so. These people need an alternative. The traditional time and space concepts of education do not fit. What, then, are the alternatives? On paper they are numerous and quite varied. They range from weekend colleges to correspondence schools. There are independent-study television programs and a host of outreach courses sponsored by nearly every postsecondary and higher education institution in the country. However, although genuine exceptions exist, there seems to be something missing in most alternative programs. An ingredient has been left out. The ingredient: credit for important life experiences. Such credit is being largely disregarded by American higher education institutions. Hence, the thesis of this chapter: Credit should be granted to adults for important life experiences when those experiences allow the adult student to demonstrate attainment of the desired competencies identified by the educational institution.

The Conditions

The storekeeper indeed wants to hire a person who can sweep the floor properly. The office manager wants a secretary who can type 50 words per minute accurately. The high school principal wants an English literature teacher who can communicate the messages of Shakespeare. If, then, a 35-year-old homemaker enters a local community college in pursuance of a secretarial science degree and can type 65 words per minute, should she be required to enter the beginning typing class along with those students who have just finished high school and who know little about typing? In many schools the answer to this question is a rather hard yes. If a veteran of twenty years of military service returns to the campus to certify as a public school English literature teacher and has previously become a self-taught Shakespearean scholar, should he be required to enroll in "Introduction to Shakespeare" (English 201 and 202)? Again, the answer often comes rather hard. Most institutions, even in their nontraditional approaches, are not readily prepared to handle the credit for experience. It is the missing ingredient. It is missing for four rather salient reasons: (1) granting credit for life experience is complex, (2) it is sensitive, (3) it is threatening, and (4) it is ambitious. More specifically, the resistance to real acceptance is delineated as follows:

1. Granting credit for past accomplishments is a complex undertaking because each individual adult possesses many unique life experiences. New technology and major career changes coupled with longer life spans and shorter work periods dictate life-long learning. Concurrent with this notion is the thought that each new learning period need not start from zero. New learning can be facilitated if important past experiences are recognized and utilized in new learning, both for instructional and credentialing

purposes. The trick of the whole matter, and the major complexity, is that of identifying those past experiences which are in fact critical to the conditions for attaining new knowledge. This responsibility rests squarely with the institution providing the program. If it can be ascertained that an adult student has mastered certain competencies through experiences, then one of two routes can be followed: the factor of time for completing the program can be shortened, or new and enriching competencies can be added to the overall program. For example, the 35-year-old homemaker entering a community college in preparation for a secretarial science degree might be advised that, because of her already developed typing skills, the school will make available its "Listening Communications" course or its "Motivating People" course instead. Consequently, the student earns the desired credential and enjoys an enriched program of studies. Or, in recognizing the adult's typing experience, the school could exempt participation in that portion of the total program and grant the credential in a shortened time period (nontraditional time period). Whichever the case, it should be a decision made between the student and the institution. The real challenge belongs to the institution because the task of eliciting, sorting, and assessing direct relationships between experiences and the competencies required by the institution for a particular degree or certificate is monumental.

2. Sensitivity is the second factor that deters the granting of credit for life experiences. The reasoning: Educators and other professionals are concerned about the public image that could be created by an educational alternative that allows credit for life experience. They feel that, if misconstrued by their consumer populations, such a program would be negatively characterized as an easy shortcut, a prostitution of education, or a complete breakdown of all that is good and proper. This type of sensitivity is normal and can be handled only if all parties involved are given sound justification and realistic evidence of need.

3. To state that granting credit for life experiences is threatening provides much academic food for thought. Though not meant in a negative sense, the statement implies a normal, healthy reaction to any radical innovation submitted to the institution of higher education for consideration. "Granting credit for

past experiences?" "Allowing students to exempt English 201, Math 184, Horticulture 106, Physical Education 310?" "What about the loss of student credit hours?" "What about the faculty?" "What about the state legislature?" "Will this affect the budget?" "What about academic respectability?" These are all very real questions. Unless they are answered with sincerity and resolve, the threat will not be removed. Answers should include assurances that this alternative is designed only for mature adults who have gained some rich experiences during their lifetimes—experiences that allow students to demonstrate that they have attained the desired competencies identified by the educational institution itself. Answers should assure the faculty that only minimum numbers of adults relative to the total enrollment will be eligible for exemption from particular classes, hence freeing faculty to work more closely with other aspects of their academic endeavors. In addition, it should be noted that faculty will be needed to assist in assessing life experiences and that perhaps credit production hours as well as academic fees might be generated through such activity. Answers should emphasize that alternative programs cost money the same as traditional programs and that adult students will be required to provide tuition and fees to the institution. Answers should point out that the total academic program will likely be strengthened as a result of the faculty's identifying the competencies that adult students must possess in order to secure credit for life experiences. Finally, it should be remembered that adult students are the voters, the taxpayers, the producers, and the consumers of the state; hence, their successes in higher education can lend support to the total institutional program.

4. Designing a sound alternative program that grants credit to adult students is an extremely ambitious undertaking. The prospect of identifying competencies for the various programs of study within an educational institution is just short of overwhelming. Competency-based education is a system quite applicable in today's world. It is a system that allows for individual attainment of pre- specified levels of task-appropriate skills, attitudes, and knowledge. *outcomes The development of such a system would require extensive effort on the part of the faculty, not to mention genuine cooperation. Such effort and cooperation could be obtained only for an admit-

tedly marginal alternative program under the best of conditions. Hence, only the ambitious, sincere, and extremely dedicated adult educator would undertake such a challenge.

A Strategy

Implementation of a plan for developing credit for life experiences within an institution of higher education involves a process which can be viewed in a three-step sequence based on the conditions previously described. The process involves a series of actions conducive to a desirable outcome; namely, a program that is acceptable to the faculty, respectable from the standpoint of the community, and realistically attainable by the adult student.

Step 1 of the process involves the systematic education of faculty by providing evidence of need and corresponding academic rationale. Evidence of need can be gained today from a myriad of sources, including the reports of the Carnegie Commission on Non-traditional Study and the many published statements of the National University Extension Association. In addition to the use of national and regional evidence of needs, it is likewise critical that local evidence be included in this educative effort. In order to secure local evidence, some type of survey would have to be completed. The exact type of survey would be dictated by the nature and setting of the community itself. Whatever the type of survey, the results must reflect a good representation of the adult population in terms of age, sex, and socioeconomic status. The demonstration of educational needs to a faculty can do much to whet curiosity and provide initial thought on the subject of granting credit for life experience. However, initial thoughts need nourishment, and at this point an academic rationale that is down to earth and to the point can sustain and encourage the thought processes. Developing a down-to-earth academic rationale means simply that both the advantages and the disadvantages are openly discussed, with as many of the disadvantages shown to be of minor consequence in the discussion as possible. Only through this open and honest look at the needs and the rationale can the alternative of credit for important life experiences get off to a proper start.

Step 2 of the process deals with the establishment of a customized competency-based system for granting credit. Nationally as well as regionally, there are standardized examination programs for granting credits to adults. The College-Level Examination Program (CLEP) is an outstanding example. It enjoys wide recognition and has furnished that much-needed first step in providing credits for experience to adults around the country. Most colleges and universities in the United States accept the CLEP in varying ways. In addition, comparable programs are being developed in several regions of the country. All such programs have numerous merits. The point is that each institution must further legitimize the whole notion of credit for experience by customizing a credit-granting system that is unique to the philosophy and goals of the individual institution. By customizing the program, the institution ensures faculty involvement, which is necessary to the long-run success of the program. Even more important, the customized program for credit granting will allow the faculty to sort out the knowledge, skills, and attitudes that are critical to the goals of the institution and the students.

This knowledge and these skills and attitudes are defined as competencies. A competency-based system is as important to the college that grants academic credit for experience as accounting is important to the business world in communicating financial information. Such a system, however, is not easy to operationalize in an institution that has for decades engaged in a traditional mode of academic operation. A competency-based system forces faculty to look hard at courses and programs within the curriculum and ask themselves "What are the skills, attitudes, and knowledge that students should attain as a result of these typing, literature, history, engineering, and other courses?" Concise answers to such questions often prove difficult and frustrating to develop. Only the persistent and cooperative faculty will succeed. And the success will beget success. Not only will the credit-granting program take shape, but also the traditional curriculum will be strengthened in the process.

A hypothetical profile of an adult student who has entered a college or university program which has operationalized a competency-based system allowing for the granting of credits for critical life experiences is presented as a typical case.

Fred Brown is currently employed by one of the large furniture-manufacturing plants located five miles from the community where he resides. He has been an assistant sales manager with the firm for over twelve years. It is likely that he will be in a position to move up in the organization within the next three years because of normal retirements within the hierarchy. However, all positions above the one that he now holds require specialized preparation in business management, and the firm will consider only those candidates who possess the credential which symbolizes that specialized background (B.S. in Business).

Before his education was interrupted because of military service, Mr. Brown had completed 72 semester hours toward a B.S. in Business at the state college fifteen miles away in the next town. It has been several years since he last attended the college. During the service years, he married and became the father of one son. Upon discharge from the military, he and his family returned to their home town, where he accepted the position with the furniture manufacturer. The addition of two daughters and the financial burden of an invalid mother have prevented him from completing his college work.

He now has two goals: (1) to complete his college education and (2) to earn a promotion and upgrade the standard of living for his family. He needs a new option for attaining his goals. He is good at his profession but needs the official credential to advance. However, he cannot afford to leave the job and return full time to college. He cannot secure sabbatical leave for college work. If a leave of absence were financially possible, loss of seniority would probably occur. Some type of nontraditional academic program is apparently the only viable option.

Mr. Brown enrolls in a business management program offered by the state college. It is characterized as a nontraditional or alternative degree program for adults who need new options for study. It is a competency-based system which among other things grants credits for important life experiences.

His faculty adviser, a member of the academic department

in which he has enrolled, identifies with him those critical life experiences that he gained during his three years in the military, his twelve years as an assistant sales manager in furniture manufacturing, as the son of an aging, invalid parent, and his fourteen years as a husband and father. His faculty adviser then equates these experiences to the degree program competencies that the college and the department have previously delineated. Through this careful and concise assessment procedure, Mr. Brown is granted 21 academic credits toward the degree. Subsequently, evening classes, independent-study programs, and some traditional daytime classes are planned for him. He earns his B.S. in Business within two years and maintains his full-time employment as assistant sales manager of the firm. He is graduated with the same competencies that those young adults possessed who completed the traditional degree program in business. Quality was explicit primarily because the faculty had agreed to identify those skills, attitudes, and knowledge that graduates would possess upon leaving the campus. Hence, credits for experience presented no threat.

N.B.

Step 3 involves a continued monitoring procedure, which has a twofold purpose: (1) that adult student life experiences are being adequately equated to academic credits based on pre-specified competencies and (2) that the total competency-based system is constantly upgraded to reflect the needs of society in keeping with the college's philosophy and goals. Although this step is the easiest of the three, it is no less important. An innovative program soon becomes a stale program without constant internal monitoring. For best results, this evaluation looks at both process and product.

Process evaluation involves looking at procedures beginning with what happens from the time when that adult student takes the initial, anxious step and comes to the campus to seek information and assistance. Process evaluation then includes all that transpires while the adult student matriculates and completes the program and resumes his growth as employee, manager of the home, family member, and citizen. The whole process as it relates to the institution and the student must be monitored.

Product evaluation delves into the outcomes and results. It

answers questions about how many adult students finished, what their grade point averages meant, and how financially acceptable the program was overall. Product evaluation is certainly important, but it is just one of the ways to view the total program.

Conclusion

Lifelong learning is coming of age. Adult and continuing education is growing at a rate not equaled by any other area of education. Concurrent with that growth is the emergence of the expressed need for alternatives for attaining educational degrees and credentials. The adult student has demonstrated that he will accept, appreciate, and utilize viable options. However, the options are found in only a few institutions. The credit for life experience is in its infancy. It has to be developed and nurtured in the coming years. Advanced technology, creative use of media, and rapid career changes will all dictate lifelong learning—lifelong learning that has no time to start from zero but makes optimal use of life experiences. The future of education promises excellent opportunity for the adult student—a heretofore sometimes neglected species.

Crediting Life Experiences Can Lead to Fraud

Leo McGee

The concept of granting credit for life experiences has much support, and the number of advocates may well continue to increase. Miller (1975) believes that to expand the learning opportunities of all citizens, due consideration should be given to the granting of credit for life experiences. He maintains that while learning for the sake of learning is a noble and worthy proposition, most students are interested in tangible awards. Miller's position is supported by Meyer (1975, p. vii): "Like it or not, we are a credentialing society." Cross and her associates (1974) argue that granting credit for nontraditional experiences represents the greatest challenge to higher education. Hesburgh, Miller, and Wharton (1973) advocate that universities ought to lead the way in granting credit for meaningful experiences. However, there is reason to believe that caution should be exercised in the promotion of the idea of granting individuals college credit simply for living.

No matter what terminology is used by institutions to classify life experiences being evaluated, in the final analysis it boils down to awarding individuals credit for living. The fact that hundreds of institutions of higher education are awarding credit for nontraditional experiences is not reason enough for all institutions to endorse the concept. Conversely, a number of educators seem to believe that it is sufficient reason to exercise caution or even to express opposition.

Trying to determine the worth of certain life experiences is almost an impossibility. Cross and her associates (1974) suggest that this is one of the most difficult problems facing proponents of the concept. It is difficult enough trying to give credit for traditional college experiences, let alone trying to evaluate, justify, and give credit for the varied life experiences.

Progressive adult educators ought to take the lead in avoiding the perpetuation of societal demands for credentials. Moreover, adults should be encouraged to live wholesome, well-rounded lives without being concerned about whether some institution will consider a specific experience deserving of academic credit.

Credentialing and Economic Success

The American society has generally accepted the proposition that there is a direct relationship between having credentials and enjoying economic success. The literature is replete with evidence that employers prefer workers with superior credentials. Jencks and his colleagues (1972) suggest that the primary purpose of this arbitrary rationing system for jobs is to reach a balance between those trying to enter the high-status occupations and the number of places available; that, with respect to employment, credentials represent no more than a rigorous screening device for job applicants; and that economic success is not primarily determined by the amount of credits an individual has but by luck, on-the-job competence, and any number of unmeasured differences in personality.

In many jobs, credentials have little to do with work performance (Little, 1968). In fact, employers seldom complain of an employee's academic competence; they are much more concerned about his inability to relate to his supervisor or to other employees, tardiness, failure to follow orders, failure to call when absent, and absence from work.

The myth of the positive relationship of economic success and credentials is adamantly refuted by Vermilye (1974, p. 15): "In some cases higher credentials and job performance appear to be inversely related." Possession of college-level credentials is no guarantee of fortune or fame. In fact, Keats (1965) reports that from a socioeconomic point of view it is difficult to distinguish individuals with college credentials from those with no degrees. Often college degree recipients are unable to show a relationship between what they studied and their job responsibilities. The only logical reason why any adult thinks that he needs credentials is his belief that everybody else thinks so.

The Adult Learning Society

Increased societal pressures are being brought to bear on all citizens to obtain academic credit. Because the pressures are never ending, Ohliger (1974b) points out that some adults will feel inadequate all their lives. According to Taylor (1954), education is to assist individuals in the enjoyment of their own lives and the enrichment of the lives of others. An excessive concern with academic credit and credentials will impede progress toward this ideal.

Despite the fact that our lives are becoming more regimented in this technological age, the purpose of education should be to show concern for the whole man, not just those skills he needs as a wage earner. As Hutchins (1971) observed, this country has been far too concerned with the form rather than the substance of learning. Consequently, America will never have a learning society until it gets over its infatuation with the forms rather than substance of learning.

Adult education should facilitate the development of a learning society—not be totally preoccupied with awarding credits, diplomas, degrees, and certificates. It should serve to improve the intellectual skills and raise the level of critical consciousness of all adults. Taylor (1971, p. 91) says, "There is something absurd in the whole concept of academic credit"—a position supported by Rogers (1969, p. 19) and Bird (1975). Essentially, educational institutions should provide for learners to discuss topics of concern to them with teachers who have a high level of competence in the area under discussion. They should become centers of independent thought and criticism, intertwining the great intellectual disciplines and confronting the important issues facing modern man.

Conclusion

Presently, the American educational enterprise is far too concerned with the awarding of credits, credentials, and grades. Many educators believe that the perpetuation of such an irrational reward system is counterproductive in the development of a learning society and that adults should not be urged to seek credit for living a well-rounded life. Rather, they should be guided toward becoming lifelong self-initiating learners.

Whether we like it or not, pressure from all angles is being brought to bear on adult learners to accumulate credits. In turn, they are pressuring institutions of higher education to credit their life experiences. The overreaction by institutions to this demand raises some serious concerns with regard to these institutions' ability to maintain academic integrity. While the education profession has received more than its share of criticisms from the general public, the initiation of programs to give adults credit for living has a potentially debilitating effect on the entire system of higher education. Perhaps the most critical factor is that the process of crediting life experiences may lead to further dishonesty, chicanery, fraud, and corruption in students' attempts to receive credit for what they may or may not truthfully consider to be worthwhile experiences. It is next to impossible to accurately assess the numerous and varied experiences of the inordinate number of individuals who are currently demanding such.

Finally, if we expect to have a free and open adult learning society, adult educators can ill afford to allow the present-day demand for academic credit for life experiences to set the pattern for higher adult education.

Chapter Nine

Should Adult Education Require Self-Support from Learner Fees?

Fees Should Support Adult Education

Howard A. Sulkin

Hyman Kaplan, the fictional character in Rosten's (1937) book *The Education of H*Y*M*A*N K*A*P*L*A*N*, understood the meaning of adult education. Kaplan knew very well why he was attending the American Night Preparatory School for Adults. He needed to learn English and Citizenship. He wanted to become part of the "melting pot," and he needed the language as a tool for survival in a world alien to his background. There was relevance in the subjects he demanded to be taught. In order to learn to speak English properly, Kaplan had to learn how to conjugate verbs correctly, and he was willing to pay for the knowledge. ("Die, dead, funeral," he learned, is not an acceptable conjugation of the verb "die.")

Today, of course, the process of adult education is much more complex.

In the next article, Harold Beder, who believes that adult education should not require self-support through learner fees, admits to difficulty in defining adult education. According to the *Encyclopaedia Britannica* (1953), the term originally meant the "education of adults who have not been properly educated as children. As the educational system improved, the need for such education diminished, but as democratic government developed, it brought with it the need, felt by everyone, for education in citizenship." In the United States, the term "is used to denote an educational movement for men and women, young and old, who no longer are in contact with formalized education and whose primary interest lies in a vocation but who possess a secondary interest in their own educational improvement as a sustained and continuing process"— in other words, continuing education. The term *adult education* is used here in the most generic sense. As long as there are adults, as individuals or in groups, in a learning situation, for any purpose whatsoever, what is taking place is adult education. It can be a work-oriented issue, a survival-oriented issue, or a leisure-oriented issue. It can be for credit or noncredit, for degree or nondegree.

Those are irrelevant concepts. All learning of adults is within the scope of adult education. This does not mean only a university or adult high school experience. It can be setting up a private independent study at a library, workers' education through a labor union, or executive education through an employers' institute of management.

We must set up a system that encourages pluralism of learning and of methodologies, so that a diversity of learning styles can be made available. It is difficult to accept the premise that a learning activity can be economically viable only if the learner is willing to pay a fee and if learners exist in sufficient numbers to cover the cost of instruction. The issue should not be one of financing only but, rather, a pluralistic approach to the importance of getting people to think in terms of lifelong learning. Economics must not be the sole criterion of whether a course should be given. No matter who pays for the course, government or foundation or student, certain classes should be held whether they are economical or not. But my own experience is that when public money subsidizes all classes, which Beder advocates, many more of the uneconomical classes are given than should be. In many instances, if the institution were forced to think through the economics of the course, if it had to justify the economics more, then fewer of the uneconomical classes would be held. An alternative model for adult education for small groups—a model that is more creative and more economical—would be much more desirable. Instead, the traditional model of a class with a teacher is used simply because the funding is available.

In certain circumstances, some subsidy is certainly appropriate; but when education is totally subsidized, as in many instances today, the tendency is to develop a grandiose monolithic concept with the danger of institutional conformity.

Hansen (1974, p. 14) has noted the extremes for educational finance: at one end, the "let them pay" approach; at the other, the "free ride" model. It is here where arguments by the protagonists for full and complete support by the taxpayer break down. It is incorrect to debate the question "Should Adult Education Require Self-Support by Means of Learner Fees?" as an either-or proposition. There can be no simple "yes" or "no." The policy must be looked at pluralistically. One must consider the socioeconomic levels of the students, as well as alternative sources of funding—for instance, the companies for which students are working.

As Kurland (1975, p. 4) points out, "No one can ever consider his learning needs fully satisfied." Adult education, like the entire American society, has changed in the past twenty years and continues to change, and these changes will include the way in which adult education is financed. People will live longer and have more leisure time, and it will be necessary to have activities available which can enrich and enhance those hours and years.

Are financial contributions likely to create motivation? Will existing motivation be sustained if adult students pay fees and sacrifice income? According to Edding (1974, p. 245), the answer to the first question is "probably no"; to the second, the response is that "people normally value goods they have paid for, and as a rule consumers associate high prices with high quality." That is, charging participants "would presumably motivate only those already motivated and would not create new learning motivation."

At the same time, it must be noted that "family income (or individual income) alone is not the only important variable in determining an individual's decision to seek postsecondary education. Parental education and occupation may be even more important" (National Commission on the Financing of Postsecondary Education, 1973, p. 348).

Arguments favoring support of adult education through learner fees or public funds are similar to those proposed in the traditional debate between public versus private educational institutions. It is argued that, because universities contribute to the social good, society should pay for the student's education. Proponents of private financing argue that education benefits the individual and so the individual should pay the bill.

But there is a subargument which is just as important: that public funding for adult education was designed to help social equalization. There is a growing belief, however, that those who seek higher education, and hence accrue the benefits of available funding, tend to be in the middle and higher socioeconomic groups. Thus, the socioeconomic spread gets wider as more public money goes to upper-income students. The result is an emphasis on serving one group at the expense of the other.

So the question remains: How should adult education be paid for?

Kurland (1975, p. 2) proposes that every adult American over 25 should receive what he calls an "annual Education Entitlement (EE)," which should "put emphasis clearly on education beyond the college years." The unused portion of EE would remain available throughout the individual's life, supporting Kurland's suggestion that "no one can ever consider his learning needs fully satisfied." The voucher system as proposed by Kurland is a viable alternative and one to which educators and government should seriously address themselves. It must be emphasized, however, that the voucher would be assigned to the student and not to the institution. In this way, the student can enroll in any institution that accepts him.

The primary goal is to give each adult who wants higher learning a multiplicity of choices, since in a pluralistic society it is desirable for each individual to have the maximum number of options from which to make decisions. This conforms to the ideology of the basic free-market economy. The student makes the choice based not only on wants, needs, and interest in the class but also on the effectiveness of the teacher. With vouchers acceptable at all schools, the student will always gravitate to the one he considers the best.

"After two decades of unprecedented growth, postsecondary education in the United States," according to a report of the National Commission on the Financing of Postsecondary Education (1973, p. 67), "has become, in round numbers, a $30 billion enterprise." In 1971–72 about "$5.9 billion was provided by students (after deducting student aid) in payment of tuition and other educational fees, $9.3 billion was provided by state and local government, $8.1 billion was provided by the federal government, $2.7 billion came from gifts and endowment income, and $3.5 billion came from auxiliary enterprises and other institutional earnings. Tuition and fees generated the largest income, an estimated $10.3 billion in total. Of this total, a little more than half,

$5.9 billion, came from students and their families. State, local, and federal governments and private sources supplied the remaining $4.4 billion in the way of financial aid to students. Although these figures are not measures of all adult education, they do reflect the pattern of all kinds of postsecondary institutions.

Despite those impressive figures, the central issue of adult education is more than a financial problem. It is to get people to think in lifelong-learning terms. We must maintain a pluralistic society, with each individual having the maximum number of options from which to make decisions. Only in this way can the highest quality of education be maintained.

When the learner has to pay for his education, he will look for relevance and the institution will be forced to come up with cost-effective alternate methods instead of subsidy requests for public funding. In the long run, this approach would be more beneficial to the lifelong-learning concept than a totally free system.

Adult Education Should Not Require Self-Support from Learner Fees

Harold W. Beder

As a principle of public policy, adult education should not require self-support through learner fees. To begin, let us define and clarify the issue. The first phrase that requires more elaboration is "as a principle of public policy." Public policy refers to high-level, overall plans embracing the general goals and acceptable procedures of governmental bodies. The purpose of public policy is to guide governmental decision making at the local, state, and national levels; and, functionally speaking, public policy guides what a governmental agency will do and how it will do it.

Though a cursory glance at a dictionary will yield a definition of public policy, strangely enough the term *adult education* gives us much more difficulty. No consensus has yet been reached on the definition of adult education, and if the outcome of debates in introductory graduate courses in adult education is any indication, we will have to wait a long time for that definitive definition to emerge. In the absence of the definition, let us propose an operational definition. As used here, the term *adult education* will refer to those educational activities that are purposely organized and conducted for adults. Although this definition is still quite broad, it does rule out most adult learning that is purely experiential in nature.

The last phrase to be dealt with is "require self-support through learner fees." Here we are talking about how adult education is financed.

As Clark (1958) and others have pointed out, adult education agencies tend to experience considerable financial insecurity. For elementary and secondary education, which are legally mandated, having basic operating funds is rarely an issue. Yet in the field of adult education, decreases in public funding have decimated entire programs. In the 1950s, for example, public school adult education in California was nearly strangled by severe cutbacks in state support, and adult education programs in New York City were severely harmed by the withdrawal of municipal support in 1976. The specter of financial disaster is always with us.

Meeting the Needs of Adults

The manner in which a program is funded tends to affect the kind of education delivered. For example, Lawson (1975) and others have noted that adult education seems to have a distinct service orientation, which in turn produces a highly student-centered approach to instruction. When adult education programs are voluntary, and when they are funded purely from student fees, it becomes incumbent on adult educators to provide the educational service that learners want, or they will not participate. If learners do not participate, the program suffers a loss in fee income, which threatens its existence. Hence, only those activities that meet learner needs will survive in the free market. There is little doubt that financing through learner fees does promote educational relevance in any adult education program regardless of funding source.

Some problems inherent in fee-supported programs, however, limit their ability to meet certain needs. One problem is that, in order to make a learning activity economically viable, there must be a sufficient number of learners to pay the cost of instruction. Let us assume, for example, that we wish to offer a course in braille to adults in a medium-sized community. After all, few would argue that blind persons do not need braille. But let us also assume that only five blind adults in our community have not learned braille.

Now, the cost of instruction for our braille course will be quite high considering the need for expert instructors, braille-producing machines, and braille materials—in all likelihood so high that to require self-support through learner fees would require us to charge our five students prohibitively high fees. The point is that at least two factors govern the amount of fee we must charge: the cost of instruction and the number of students among whom the cost must be divided. If the cost of instruction is too high or the number of interested students too low, the fee to be charged will price the learning activity out of the market, regardless of how much learners need it.

Moreover, the logistics of fee financing can have a direct effect on the organization of instruction and an indirect effect on the ability of a fee-supported program to meet needs. First of all, if a fee is to be charged, there must be some way of restricting the education solely to those who have paid. As a result, it is nearly impossible to finance programs through fees if the programs rely on radio, television, or community development, for in these cases the education is delivered to a general audience rather than to specific, identifiable learners who can be charged. Second, fee-supported programs must develop a rationale for the fees they charge. They must be able to tell learners that they must pay x fee for y program. In short, the learner must know what he is receiving for the fee dollars spent. This means that fee-financed programs must typically have a precise beginning point as well as a fixed termination point, and they must generally specify the number of sequences or meetings the course of study will entail. It is probably no accident that most fee-supported programs depend on classroom instruction or correspondence study, since these instructional modes are particularly compatible with the logistics of fee financing. Unfortunately, many learners have needs that cannot be met effectively through the kinds of instruction generally associated with a student fee approach. Though the rural isolate or the housebound elderly could be reached by radio or television, for example, it is generally difficult for either to partake in formal classroom instruction.

One might respond, "I know of student fee-supported programs that offer braille and similar courses, and I even know of a fee-supported program that delivers part of its instruction over radio." Well, programs supported through student fees occasionally earn a surplus on some courses, and this surplus is then used to subsidize other courses that do not attract enough students to be self-supporting. There are two problems with this approach. First, the ability to continue to offer learning activities which consistently lose money is rather limited, for if money is lost on too many activities, the result is economic collapse. Obviously, then, requiring funding through student fees constrains adult educators from offering socially desirable learning activities with high price tags. Second, when the surplus from courses that make money is used to subsidize courses that lose money, the learners in heavily enrolled learning activities are, in effect, subsidizing the learners in other activities. If we are going to subsidize some activities in adult education, why do so with a hidden educational tax on learners in more economically viable learning activities? Why not spread that subsidy throughout society by promoting public funding from a progressive state or national tax?

External and Personal Benefits from Education

In looking at who benefits from education, economists distinguish between personal benefits and external benefits. Personal benefits are those that accrue only to the individual—for instance, increased personal income or prestige—while external benefits accrue to society in general. An example of an external benefit might be the reduction in welfare costs that could result from educating the unemployable to the extent that they could gain employment. Economists argue that if the benefits from education are primarily personal, the learner should pay, since he alone will reap the rewards from the investment. If, however, the benefits are primarily external, society should subsidize the education through tax receipts, since society in general will profit from the investment. It might be argued that the benefits of adult education accrue primarily to individuals or to sponsoring organizations. Hence, there should be no subsidy. Although I disagree, let us assume—for the sake of argument—that adult education provides primarily personal benefits.

Becker (1964, pp. 77–78) estimates that the personal rate of return to an investment in higher education is about 14.5 percent. Hansen (1963) estimates that the individual rate of return through the eighth grade is about 29 percent, that a high school diploma may yield a 15–20 percent return, and that a bachelor's degree will net about 12–15 percent. How much does an investment in adult education net the learner? The question is extremely difficult to study, and we cannot supply a figure. Yet even if the benefits to adult education were primarily personal, should we fail to subsidize it by requiring funding through learner fees? First of all, it is clear that the government does subsidize activities that yield primarily personal rather than external benefits. Take, for example, the substantial subsidies allocated to the arts or to recreational facilities such as state and federal parks.

There is still a stronger argument, however. From the point of view of the taxpayer, one might consider the payment of taxes an individual investment which is expected to return personal benefits. If, for example, citizens did not benefit directly from the tax dollars they paid, it would be almost impossible to levy taxes in a democratic society. I am willing to pay taxes because I benefit directly in having police protection, safe roads, fire protection, and so forth. What does an American taxpayer receive for his tax dollars allocated to education? Increased opportunity for the taxpayer's children might be an answer, but many taxpayers, especially the elderly, do not have children in school. A subsidized higher education might be another answer, but most Americans still do not complete college. Almost by definition, taxpayers are adults. Does it not make sense that those who pay taxes for education should receive direct educational benefit from the taxes paid? If it does make sense, then the obvious conclusion is that public tax dollars should be used to subsidize adult education to at least some degree. The point we are trying to make is simply this: Even if the benefits to adult education were primarily personal benefits, that would be no reason not to subsidize adult education, because the taxpayer has a right to expect a direct personal return for the tax dollar he pays. Second, since federal and state governments already fund some activities that are primarily personal in their benefit, why should adult education be excluded?

At this point, let us change perspectives and agree with the economists who claim that public subsidy should be allocated only to educational activities that provide external benefits. We will argue that adult education does provide external benefits.

Bolton (1969, p. 34) explains the concept of external benefits as follows: "The external benefits [of higher education] are the ones which increase the satisfaction of other members of society, but for which, as a practical matter, the educated person cannot be compensated. His education increases the welfare of all society, but his own income does not reflect this." What are the external benefits to adult education, and how great are they? The first part of the question is much easier to answer than the second, since external benefits are difficult to measure. Let us discuss a few of the external benefits that apply to adult education.

Weisbrod (1964, p. 28) categorizes external benefits into residence-related benefits, employment-related benefits, and benefits to society in general. Residence-related benefits accrue to the learner's family and neighbors. For example, certain kinds of adult education may increase family income, and adult education which promotes self-actualization contributes to a fuller family life. Parent education contributes to better child care; in addition, children whose parents are well educated seem to achieve better in the public schools and are more likely to engage in postsecondary education than children of parents with less education. Weisbrod (1964, p. 30) argues that education also affects the learner's neighbors. For example, the farmer who has learned new farming methods from cooperative extension serves as a positive example to other farmers and thus functions as a conduit for new and more productive farming methods. The adult who has learned home repair at the local public school contributes to a more attractive neighborhood with increased property values for everyone. Taxpayers in general also benefit, as Weisbrod (1964, p. 31) states: "Related to the effects of education on neighbors are the effects on those who pay (directly or indirectly) for the consequences of lack of education. For example, insofar as lack of education leads to employment difficulties and crime, law enforcement costs will tend to be high. Thus may education provide social benefits by reducing the need for incurring these 'avoidance costs' to the advantage of taxpayers." Employment-related benefits accrue to the learner's employers and fellow employees. Assume, for example, that a medium-sized business has been performing all its accounting, billing, and inventory functions manually. Assume also that the company has found it increasingly difficult to compete with similar companies which have modernized their business functions through computerization. To solve the problem, several employees of the company are sent to continuing education courses where they learn how to operate and maintain a computerized system. The new knowledge gained by these persons results in computerization; a better competitive position for our hypothetical company; and increased profits, which are allocated to other workers in the form of higher salaries and personnel benefits. Thus, the new knowledge gained by one or several workers eventually benefits all workers in the form of increased remuneration.

Finally, there are benefits that accrue to society in general. The fabric of our society is stitched together by an intricate web of communications without which no subsystem could function. Unless people can read, newspapers, books, and other written forms of communication are irrelevant. Our whole technological order cannot function without the symbolic language of mathematics, and there can be no meaningful communication unless we have a common language. Hence, the external benefits from forms of adult education that improve communication are enormous. Moreover, our system of government requires an electorate that can make informed, reasonable choices, and adult education has traditionally played a role in this regard. External benefits also accrue to the extent that adult education assists the unemployed to gain employment and the welfare recipient to withdraw from public assistance, for in these cases we have a healthier society and a concomitant reduction in the rate of increase of taxes used to fund such social services.

Equalization of Opportunity

In recent years it has become clear that opportunities provided for individuals in our society are unequal and that, in all probability, we cannot long endure the tensions produced by that inequality. Thus, the promotion of equality has become a major governmental responsibility. There are two ways in which inequality may be corrected by public bodies. First is the redistribution of wealth, where in effect money is transferred from the rich to the poor. This is the objective behind progressive income and inheritance taxes. The second method is to remove the barriers to socioeconomic mobility through governmental intervention. Affirmative action regulations are an example of this approach. Adult education promotes equality and, therefore, should be subsidized under the equalization-of-opportunity principle.

First of all, when tax revenues are used to support the education of poor and disadvantaged adults, income is redistributed to the extent that these students no longer must pay tuition to support their own education. In most cases, however, this redistribution of income represents a minimal transfer payment. The major effect of public support to the education of disadvantaged adults is in helping to remove the barriers that promote inequality. Clearly, basic communication and computational skills are prerequisites to social mobility in the United States, and courses in adult basic education and English as a second language help to remove these formidable barriers. Adult vocational education provides occupational skill training to those who have been denied jobs for lack of skills, and cooperative extension has been successful in upgrading the agricultural practices of many marginal farmers. Economic inequality is addressed by consumer education, and inequality in health care delivery is partially remedied by prenatal programs and continuing education programs in preventive health care. These programs are examples of adult education programs designed to remove barriers to equality. In general, the educationally disadvantaged sector of our society tends also to be the economically disadvantaged section. These people deserve subsidized education as a matter of public justice; moreover, they must receive subsidy if they are to participate in adult education, for they cannot afford to pay.

Problems of Coordination

The coordination principle of public funding argues that the government should subsidize programs which are impossible to coordinate effectively on a local basis. Part of the reason for co-operative extension's success has been the ability to coordinate the activities of the local extension agent with the activities of land-grant universities and their agricultural experiment stations. Imagine the waste and chaos if each county were required to maintain its own experiment station. Large-scale coordination is also crucial to disseminating extension's advances from one state to others. Thus, because of governmental coordination and communication, new agricultural advances developed in Iowa quickly find their way to Kansas, Missouri, and other states. Large-scale coordination is likewise crucial to adult education in the armed forces. Needs for the entire military must be translated into specific learning activities that will enable a trainee at Fort Dix, New Jersey, to apply his skills anywhere in coordination with soldiers trained at other posts. What chaos if soldiers at Fort Knox, Kentucky, were taught infantry tactics that substantially differed from those taught at Fort Sill, Oklahoma. The point is that, if it is to work, large-scale coordination must be the responsibility of agencies that transcend localities. This coordination generally entails governmental involvement and subsidy.

Extreme Local Need: High Cost

It is generally accepted that public monies should be allocated to activities which meet extreme local needs and are also too expensive for individual financing. This is the theory behind federal disaster relief, for example. The need for adult education is not randomly distributed in our society. It is clear that the problems addressed by adult education can create situations approaching emergency. In Kentucky, for example, the median family income in 1969 was $7,439, as compared to $11,808 for Connecticut, the second-highest state, and $9,586 nationally (United States Bureau of Census, 1975, p. 387). In 1970 the median number of school years completed for persons aged 25 and over in Kentucky was 9.9, as compared to 12.2 for Connecticut and 12.1 nationally (United States Department of Health, Education and Welfare, 1974, p. 15). Although differences in population distribution and cost of living within states can render comparisons between groups somewhat misleading, individuals living in the Appalachians have had considerably less formal education and are more economically deprived than the norm. How do we solve the problem? One answer might be the infusion of industry into the Appalachian area to stimulate the economy and create more jobs, but where is the skilled labor to come from? Where will we find the managers? Clearly, the problem goes beyond geographical logistics. A solution must include the upgrading of human capital. Yet, because of its rural mountain nature, people living in Appalachia are costly to reach for the purpose of providing basic and vocational education. Self-support through learner fees is probably out of the question given the income level of potential participants. The answer then becomes public subsidy for basic and vocational adult education.

The Ability to Pay

It has been argued that public funds should be used to subsidize only those important activities for which the intended participants cannot pay. Children cannot pay for their elementary and secondary education, and there would be too great a burden on the parents of large families if elementary and secondary education were financed through learner fees. Similarly, 18- to 24-year-old college students do not have the means to pay for their education, and the burden would be so great for low-income families that only the well-to-do could attend college if either the parents or the students themselves had to pay the full cost of instruction. What about adults then? The argument is that adults are wage earners and therefore are able to pay for adult education. That argument is so weak that we will discuss it but briefly. The unemployed, the underemployed, the handicapped, immigrants, and the elderly do not have available capital to spend on education, and these populations are among those that could benefit most from adult education. In 1974, 24.3 million Americans had incomes below the federal low-income level, and 5.1 million were unemployed (United States Bureau of the Census, 1975, p. xvii). In 1972, 25.9 million Americans had chronic conditions which impaired their activity (p. 85); and in 1970, 9.6 million Americans were foreign born (p. 34), and 9.8 percent of the population was aged 65 and over (p. 31).

It is also argued that those who do have the ability to pay should pay. This argument may be valid for some areas of adult education, especially those areas that are primarily avocational, but what about the field of adult education in general? One reason why public monies are used to subsidize education is to reduce the cost to the learner to the extent that he will consider participation an investment that is expected to yield a profit. If adult education does indeed appear to be a profitable investment, participation will be stimulated. This was the theory behind forgiving a percentage of National Direct Student Loans for teachers and for granting National Science Foundation fellowships to incipient scientists. The same principle should apply in many areas of adult education even though the potential participants have the economic means to pay. Take, for example, those areas of adult education which are primarily vocational in focus. Though unemployment has been a constant problem in our economy, the cause is not necessarily a lack of sufficient jobs. Frequently there is a surplus of jobs in one technical field but a deficit of jobs in others. Those employees who are displaced in the deficit areas and become unemployed must be retrained if they are to gain employment in areas where jobs exist. At the same time, entering a new occupation is an unpleasant situation for many people; for, among other reasons, their self-concept is frequently related to occupation. Hence, if these people are to be motivated to seek retraining in new or underemployed occupational areas, the training often must be subsidized.

Conclusion

What would be the implications if, as a principle of public policy, adult education were not required to support itself through learner fees? The sanction of such a policy by the taxpaying public would amount to de facto recognition that the benefits of adult education are important enough to the general welfare of the United States to warrant public funding above and beyond current levels. Such a statement implies that we would expect more public funds to be allocated to adult education. Just how much more funding is impossible to predict, but that will not deter us from speculating. In 1972 the average per pupil expenditure for elementary and secondary education in the United States was $1,147

(United States Bureau of the Census, 1975, p. 121). In the same year, there were approximately 140 million Americans aged 18 or over (p. xiii). If we arbitrarily computed the public commitment to adult education at a modest one tenth of the public commitment to elementary and secondary education, the net result in 1972 would have exceeded $16 billion. Figures are not available to show the state and local governmental allocation to adult education, but it is useful to note that the federal government reported a total expenditure for cooperative extension, veterans' education, correctional education, vocational and technical education, and general continuing education in 1972 of about $3.7 billion (United States Bureau of the Census, 1975, p. 143). Even if the combined state and local contributions to adult education equaled the federal allocation in 1972, the total public contribution to adult education would not have exceeded $7.4 billion. Thus, an allocation of $16 billion to $20 billion for adult education would in all likelihood represent a great increase. Moreover, $16 billion to $20 billion for adult education is certainly paltry compared to what is expended on elementary, secondary, and higher education each year. In 1972, $53.9 billion was expended on elementary and secondary education, and $29.2 billion was expended on higher education (United States Department of Health, Education and Welfare, 1974, p. xiv).

It is important to note that public financing of elementary, secondary, and higher education does not prevent the institutions providing such programs from charging fees, and there is no reason to suspect that the same principle would not apply to adult education. Though fee income for adult education would likely decrease as free programs became more numerous, increased public expenditures would not completely supplant fee income.

An increase in funds to adult education, so that there was no longer a need to rely on fee income, would have an enormous impact. We would expect less reliance on part-time staffing as funds became available to pay full-time staff. Subsequently, more educators would make adult education their career, and we would see an increase in the degree of professionalism. The benefits of adult education would be extended to many who previously could not pay or were reluctant to do so for economic reasons. Increased funds would also permit greater experimentation with and use of approaches to adult education which are difficult to finance through fees.

Increased public funding carries with it several dangers, which must be guarded against. We must resist a movement to a high degree of institutionalization, which can stifle creativity and flexibility. We must also protect the autonomy that enables local programmers to address the needs of adult learners. Nevertheless, increased public financing for adult education is worth the risks.

Chapter Ten

Should Adult Education Program Goals Be Established at the Local Level?

Goals Should Be Set Locally

Laverne B. Forest

Who should set adult education program goals?

Before trying to answer that question, consider one of Charlie Brown's experiences.

His little sister asks, "How come you won't help me with my homework?"

Charles replies, "You don't really want help. What you really want is someone else to do the work for you!"

She retorts, "THAT'S EDUCATION, ISN'T IT?"

Is it? That's the question! Is adult education what someone does for a learner or what learners experience themselves? The answer to this question is the basis for dealing with the issue of who should set adult education program goals.

Regardless of one's philosophy, goal setting is a planning and decision-making process, not simply an instantaneous choice. It involves several subprocesses: deciding to offer a program, identifying alternatives, identifying selection criteria, choosing, and reflecting on the choice. In adult education goal setting, a person or group or institution decides that one goal (desired outcome) is more important now than other goals.

Regardless of who makes them, goal-setting decisions must be good ones. The dilemma is that all goal alternatives usually have some merit and the criteria for deciding the best alternative will probably lack clarity and consensus. Maier (1963) presents a way of dealing with this dilemma. Since the worthiness of goals depends on their context, Maier argues, the merit of a decision depends on its subsequent outcomes. The consequences of the choice are the bases for knowing whether the choice was good.

What are the subsequent events in adult education? Regardless of type or agency, "good" goal-setting decisions are those which lead to valuable programs. Valuable programs are effective, relevant, and efficient. Effectiveness means that they achieve positive results, whether initially intended or not. These results are new knowledge, attitudes, skills, ways of doing things, and benefits from applying the learning. Relevant programs provide learning opportunities related to participants' lives, problems, and concerns. The learning is appropriate and useful for the participants' own current situations and future concerns. When efficient, the program has a high ratio of effectiveness compared with the amount of resources and time expended.

Are such programs more likely to result when local people are setting the goals than when they are not? I believe that local involvement in deciding program goals is more likely to effect program success than nonlocal input. This belief is based on five reasons supported by philosophy, research, and experiences of adult educators: (1) democratic ideals, (2) more inclusive identification of needs and decision alternatives, (3) program acceptance and support, (4) learning benefits, and (5) nature of reality.

Democratic Ideals

The ideal that people can and should decide their own destiny has been the basis for action throughout our history. The freeing of slaves, the resistance to totalitarian governments like the Third Reich, legislation on civil rights and equal opportunity, and the alarmed reaction of many to Watergate and the Vietnam War are all examples of thoughts and efforts based on the original premise. More specific to education, Thomas Jefferson believed that the population can and should learn so as to be more competent in the democratic ideal of self-governance. Accordingly, local school districts, most of them governed by locally elected school boards, have established educational policies.

The interdependence of the educational system and government has been apparent from the early years of the country. The government needed intelligent people if such an ideal were to succeed, and local educational systems, with local support, accepted responsibility to help people learn. Local self-governance depended on interested people and participation in the educational system, and many adult education programs developed accordingly. Chautauquas and Lyceums preceded cooperative extension work, established in 1914. From its earliest efforts, extension practiced the "grass roots" approach to program development. Municipal libraries, public forums, town meetings, and adult evening classes are other historical examples of adults participating in their own locally determined programs.

Recent decades have brought changes. The movement away from local goal setting is typified by the proliferation of federal programs such as Title I of the Higher Education Act of 1965; increases in state monies to local school districts (up to and beyond 50 percent of local budgets); and more area and regional educational programs, such as vocational and technical institutes. Control and power originate with sources of funds. Local units are losing control of goal setting as the proportion of their funds from higher levels of government has increased.

However, these trends do not negate the original democratic or participatory ideal on which the United States was founded and has developed. Though at times inefficient, inequitable, and ineffective, this basic principle has been the impetus for this country's growth and improvement.

Are citizens currently involved? Many studies, particularly since 1970, describe people's feelings of alienation from the decision-making processes affecting their lives. In a study of local extension leaders in a rural Wisconsin community, Forest and Marshall (1977) found that 45 percent of leaders believe local people do make decisions. And the many who do not so believe have had "little" or "no" contact with local extension planning committees—only 17 percent of those who had had little or no contact felt that local people do make decisions on programs. Moreover, leaders' perceptions of educational benefits went up if they had been involved with local extension agents in committees. These results suggest that increased committee contact with local extension agents probably increases the committee's feeling of being involved in decisions and in advancing education. But, for reasons of democratic ideals, should more local levels be involved in goal setting? In the same study, local leaders said "yes." Of leaders involved "a great deal" with local extension agents in committees, 71 percent felt that they had enough opportunity to influence. Of those who had no such contact, only 27 percent felt that they had enough opportunity. A Chi-square test of significance showed this relationship to be significant at the .005 level of probability.

These data illustrate current feelings about participation in goal setting in one community. Those leaders who think that they have not had enough opportunity to influence program decisions are saying, in effect, that the democratic ideal is not practiced enough.

More Adequate Needs Identification

Boshier (1971), Forest (1973), Houle (1961), Sheffield (1964), and others have found that the needs and motivations of potential learners are crucial to deciding program goals. If learners have a right to make input to decisions, and if high-quality decisions are more likely when all alternative needs are identified (Maier, 1963), does involving local people in needs identification enhance the process? Whale (1966) has shown that needs identification in the decision-making process is enhanced by local involvement. In four replications, he found that important needs identified by local citizens significantly differed from those identified by professionals and agents. Of fifty-four important needs identified by both groups, only nine (17 percent) overlapped. Local citizens identified twenty-two (41 percent) unique needs, and professionals identified twenty-three (42 percent). Local citizens do add to the quality of the goal-setting process because they identify additional unique alternatives not identified by others. In a sense, they can validate the needs identified by professionals.

Two crucial outcomes can be drawn from motivation theory. First, learners know their specific wants and orientation better than external professionals. Second, the voluntary nature of adult education necessitates that adults perceive the program as meeting their own needs. Under these conditions, they will be more motivated to participate and learn. These two outcomes are more likely when goals are set locally. The closer the goal-setting process is to the local level, the more likely will goals be specific to the local participants and unique to their values and needs. The higher the process goes in the hierarchy, or the farther it is removed from the local level, the more general and abstract the goals have to become to ensure that specific learners' goals will be included. If one sets specific goals at higher levels, more risk is involved to arrive at goals seen as credible and acceptable to specific local individuals.

Gaining Program Acceptance and Support

That involvement in goal setting enhances a potential participant's acceptance of an adult education program is suggested by the findings of various theorists and researchers.

Experiential Philosophy. According to Dewey (1939), the value of a goal to a person depends on its having evolved from that person's own experiences. A learner attaches more significance to a goal such as "to learn how to do electric arc welding" if he has attempted to join metal in other ways, such as riveting, has experienced some setbacks, has been unsuccessful when trying to weld, and has suddenly discovered how to become a better welder. The goal is his at that point. It is psychologically real, meaningful, and acceptable.

Goal Commitment and Participation. Since adult education participation is voluntary, adults will only participate if they accept the goals of a program. Successful extension planning involves representatives of the learners in setting program objectives. The resulting programs then are promoted in part by giving recognition to the community members who participated in the planning. Subsequently, both the planners and those on whose behalf they planned are much more likely to participate than would have been the case had the program been planned entirely by the professional staff. Local program planning committees are utilized as a way of institutionalizing this process of involvement.

Research on Resistance to Change. The goals of adult education programs, regardless of who sets them, imply change—movement toward different levels of understanding or behavior. Coch and French (1948) have shown that resistance to change can be overcome by involvement of a group in the decision-making process. It seems that resistance will be reduced if administrators, teachers, board members, and community leaders feel that the project is their own, not one devised and operated by outsiders; if the project accords with values and ideals which have long been acknowledged by participants; if participants feel that their autonomy and their security are not threatened; and if participants have joined in diagnostic efforts leading them to agree on what the basic problem is and to feel its importance.

Adoption and Diffusion Theory. Katz (1961), Lionberger (1960), Rogers (1962), Wilkening (1958), and others have developed an extensive body of research and theory on social diffusion, that is, the ways in which ideas move through and are accepted by the various segments of any social system. The evidence is overwhelming that the social system within which adults live strongly influences whether new ideas are accepted, how they are accepted, and the speed with which they are accepted. The general conclusion of this research is that educational strategies must consider the values, knowledge levels, power bases, resources, and past experiences of the social systems within which potential participants live and perceive their needs. Again, the closer the goal setting is to the participants, the more likely the success, because they themselves determine whether the new ideas will fit the social environment.

Participation Effects on Acceptance of Goals. In a small community social system, Forest (1973) found 68 local leaders' overt commitments and involvements directly related to their acceptance of intended goals. Faced with sharp increases in tourism and changes due to outside forces, leaders' commitments toward two nonlocal goals which they could not control (state highway and coast guard relocations) were significantly lower than their commitments toward four local goals (park improvement, mobile home location, sign control, and residential replatting). These findings support the notion that local involvement greatly influences the level of local acceptance.

If programs conducted over time are thought to reflect goals of the institution, then judgments about the programs and institutions also indicate level of acceptance of goals. Forest and Marshall (1977) determined how local community leaders judged University of Wisconsin extension programs. Leaders generally perceived extension to be effective, important, and worth tax dollars. However, these perceptions related directly to the leaders' amount of contact with extension agents through local committees set up by extension for planning. Forty percent of leaders having a "great deal of committee contact" rated extension's effectiveness as excellent, whereas only 10 percent of "no-contact" leaders gave such a rating. Also, the percentage of leaders saying that extension "does important things" dropped off sharply as leaders had less committee contact. Finally, leaders' judgments of extension's worth increased as they had more local committee contact. For instance, 38 percent of leaders with a "great deal of contact" judged extension excellent or "worth the dollars." Only 6 percent of the no contact leaders gave that judgment. Conversely, only 11 percent of the "great-deal-of-contact" leaders rated extension as fair to poor on such a factor, and 56 percent of the "little" and "no-contact" groups also made such judgments.

Learning and Other Benefits

Local goal-setting experiences can benefit participants in several ways. Local citizens can achieve new ideas, attitudes, values, and skills by it. They can apply ideas gained from the experience, and their learning and application of ideas can result in better living, more income, cleaner environment, and healthier lives. Specifically, the process of setting goals allows local people to learn more about their situation, practice and experience need analysis, value and choose, set realistic goals, compare current behavior, and design further learning experiences.

Lewin (1952), in a classic study, showed that greater involvement, freedom of decision, and resulting public commitment in an educational program increased housewives' use of objectionable foods during a time of food shortage. With increased participation and discussion, 32 percent of the women tried the foods; in contrast, 3 percent of the women tried the foods after hearing only a lecture. The results, persistent after four weeks, illustrated that learners accept suggested learning when given a chance to set their own goals.

Herzberg and associates (Herzberg, 1966; Herzberg, Mausner, and Snyderman, 1959) and Clegg (1963) have shown that people are motivated by such factors as felt achievement of a goal, recognition for achieving goals, responsibility, opportunities for growth, advancement, and work itself. These factors are more likely to be found when an individual learner is personally involved in a goal-setting experience than if he participates in an established program. If an individual is responsible for setting goals, that responsibility triggers motivation toward reaching the goal. This act of setting goals stimulates individuals to work toward accomplishing them.

Forest and Marshall (1977) found that the more local leaders were involved in local committees planning extension programs, the more likely they were to perceive educational benefits from extension to themselves and their communities. Fifty-eight percent of the leaders who had had a "great deal" of local committee contact said that extension benefited individuals, groups, and communities in educational ways. Only 41 percent of the "no-contact" leaders felt that way.

In summary, theory on adult learning and evaluations of adult education programs strongly support the concept that people learn and benefit by being involved in setting goals. If we want program participants to benefit, the more successful and valuable programs will be those in which they have learned and benefited during the goal-setting process at their local level.

The Reality of Goal Setting

According to Dewey (1939), any goal predetermined by nonlocal levels is not a "set" goal but is vulnerable to being made more specific and meaningful by the adults who eventually participate in that program. Pirsig (1974), in a recent but parallel philosophical argument, implies that reality is determined by individuals on the scene. Reality is not and cannot be determined and imposed by others. People determine for themselves the appearance and importance of a program goal to their lives, and they must understand the underlying reasons for the goal if it is to be their reality.

Sigfried (1975), Bahm (1971), Freire (1970), and others representing different fields of inquiry argue likewise. Technology, science, and rationality are sterile without interpretation and judgments of those to be affected.

Pirsig and Dewey and Freire say that it is philosophically impossible for individuals at nonlocal levels to make the choice if learners are assumed to be active. Learners and participants at local levels establish the goals prior to and during learning transactions. Research on classroom learning supports these positions. Much of the curriculum is determined in a classroom (Jackson, 1968), even when specific goals and lesson plans are predetermined. Adult education programs and learning experiences are even more dynamic than elementary and secondary classrooms.

Conclusion

We hear it said that people are apathetic toward participation and involvement in decision making. That is a myth. People are interested in things that affect them. They are not interested in matters they consider abstract or irrelevant. Nonlocal goal setting, as is occurring in many federal programs, is an excellent example of what alienates many people. As the use of such a process increases, local people will increasingly become apathetic because they see less and less opportunity for input and for making an impact on decisions.

In a 1975 *Issues Facing Kentucky* report, for example, a representative group of citizens named "government-citizen relations" as the primary problem in the state. Many representatives said that citizens do not bother to become involved in decision making because officials do what they want anyway. Yes, apathy exists, but not because citizens are naturally apathetic. Apathy is due to their increasing experiences and perceptions that it does not do any good to be involved because others at higher levels are actually setting the goals. Since local goal setting has several plusses and is currently underused, several things must be done.

First, adult educators should realize that educational goal setting occurs at various levels, from local to national, but the origin of those goals and the persons who finally "set" them are local. Local levels must initiate and clarify. Though some national goals for education currently exist and guide local programs, they have been accepted by local people who have psychologically experienced them as related to their own lives. Unaccepted national goals are ones they have not psychologically experienced. How local should the decision making be if it is to have meaningful consequences? Just as local as possible.

Second, adult educators should realize that setting goals is a decision-making process. What is known about decision theory must be utilized. Local leaders and potential participants must be involved in the entire process: (1) identifying and clarifying the basic problem situation, (2) identifying alternative goals, (3) identifying selection criteria, and (4) making the choice(s).

As problems are delineated, alternative goals identified, and choices made, these experiences will give rise to further goals at local levels and will affect goal setting at higher levels of bureaucracies. The higher-level goals will be indirectly grounded in the specific experiences of local goal-setting experiences. Philosophically, it makes sense and in practice it works.

Have faith, Charlie Brown. Not all educators believe that education is doing the work for learners. The optimistic position taken here is that many adult educators espouse ideas like individual growth, self-direction, and self-responsibility among our adult population—ideas which are more likely to be advanced through local goal setting. These arguments and strategies are simple. If people are inherently responsible and wish to retain that responsibility, they must be involved in decisions that affect them. Adult educators who use this idea will increase the probability of program success as defined by both professionals and participants, an ideal to which we all aspire but often fail to reach.

Nonlocal Units Should Be Involved in Goal Setting

J. David Deshler

The increased influence of state, national, and international organizational units is a welcome change for the field of adult education. The involvement of these nonlocal organizations, with their accompanying perspectives and resources, promises to strengthen the role of adult education in society. In the past, the adult education movement has been blessed with all the autonomy that localism can provide, but it has also had a host of accompanying difficulties and limitations. Some of the more self-defeating characteristics of localism have included (1) excessive cost and wasted effort from "reinventing the wheel"; (2) provincial inertia in resisting innovation; (3) unequal educational opportunity as a result of catering primarily to those who could pay; (4) undemocratic practice through excluding many minorities in local planning; (5) practitioners' tending to identify with their parent institutions rather than with their practitioner peers in the movement as a whole; and (6) low professional standards due to ignorance about any national norms for excellence.

These characteristics are being modified through the influence of (1) national affiliates of local adult education agencies and institutions; (2) state and national voluntary associations, agencies, and organizations which conduct adult education as part of their mission; (3) professional associations such as the Adult Education Association of the U.S.A. and its counterparts in other parts of the world; (4) units of national and state government which fund adult education and in some cases operate program efforts; (5) international organizations such as the International Council for Adult Education and the Adult Education Section, Division of Structures and Content of Lifelong Education, UNESCO; and (6) nonlocal private foundations which engage in funding adult education efforts in the United States and abroad.

Those who have labored to establish viable national and international structures for adult education are happy that these organizations now have some influence in the setting of program goals. Those who have struggled with local budgets welcome the increased intervention of federal and state governments in providing tax dollars (National Advisory Council on Adult Education, 1976b, p. 19).

What is not at issue here is the responsibility and right of individual learners to be involved in setting their own learning goals or to be engaged in organizing a program effort for themselves or possibly others. Neither are the alternative purposes for setting goals at issue. Goals may serve as stimulants to action; as guides to operational decisions; as bases for bargaining, building coalitions, or co-opting others (Thompson and McEwen, 1961); as reflections of what has already been achieved and found valuable (March, 1972); and as criteria or standards by which evaluative judgments can be made (Stake, 1970). What is at issue is the significance of the benefits resulting from active involvement of larger-level organizations in goal setting for institutionally organized learning activities in adult education and, more specifically, whether these benefits outweigh or supplement those accrued from uninhibited local-level goal setting.

Benefits from Higher-Level Goal Setting

Degrees of tension will always exist between institutional goals at the local level and institutional goals at larger levels. This tension is profound and long standing. Organizational theorists have described it as the tension between centralization and decentralization. The tension among levels is clearly manifest in discussions regarding alternative forms of federal funding—between categorical grant-in-aid programs and revenue sharing. Educators and politicians have discussed this tension as it has related to federal aid to education. The pendulum tends to swing. The development and strengthening of larger-level organizations attest to the impetus to respond to forces that cannot be adequately addressed at the local level. The emphasis on strengthening local-level decision making in organizations from time to time attests to the need to bring about a balance of power through new definitions of the separation of powers. This tension pervades our society, public and private. It was recognized as a basic tension by our founding fathers as they struggled to create a constitution that would balance national interests with state interests. They recognized that complete local autonomy could mean anarchy, while complete centralized authority could mean dictatorship or a mass society.

Without denying the benefits to learners that come from their involvement in local-level program goal setting, I believe that participation by representatives of nonlocal levels is essential to the field of adult education. Nonlocal participation strengthens the program development process because it brings with it increased capacity to analyze need more comprehensively, to design and appraise programs more adequately, and to stimulate increased experimentation and research. The programs that result from nonlocal participation in program goal setting are more likely to address large-scale problems, to focus a critical mass of attention on problems, to protect the public interest, and to equalize educational opportunity than are programs designed entirely at the local level.

More Comprehensive Analysis of Need. On the surface it sounds reasonable that local people know best how to assess local needs. On closer examination, however, it becomes evident that the local perspective is also quite narrow. Bradshaw (1974, p. 185) has provided a helpful differentiation among four dimensions of need: (1) felt need, which can be defined as what people or organizations say that they need; (2) expressed need, a felt need that has taken the form of a demand—for instance, when someone signs up for or uses a service; (3) comparative need, a need based on the inequality between the services available in one area and those in another; and (4) normative need, a condition that does not meet the standards set by acknowledged experts or authorities. Local leaders often tend to be more responsive to the expressed need of politically articulate segments of the local population. Felt needs of minorities or less articulate persons may be less likely to be addressed if there is a bias against these types of persons. Local leaders also may be less aware of need that is defined either as comparative or normative. Perception of need can be more comprehensive when local-level need analysis includes larger perspectives.

More Adequate Design and Appraisal of Programs. State and national officials usually bring to their program design and appraisal task comparative and normative judgments about the adequacy of programmatic responses. Macro program evaluation also is likely to be undertaken (Steele, 1977). Larger-level evaluations tend to reflect the normative standards of practice acceptable to the field as a whole. This standard-setting impact through evaluation on the part of state and federal levels has been extensive in fields other than education (Graves, 1964). It has operated to some extent in adult education. For instance, Knox and his associates (1974) designed a national evaluation guide for adult basic education programs. This guide reflects criteria derived from evaluative research conducted by the authors in a number of local programs across the United States. Without federal intervention, this technical assistance probably would not have been provided.

Increased Experimentation. The stimulation of experimentation, the demonstration of new approaches, and the sponsorship and dissemination of research findings are major goals of many organizations which conduct programs on a state, national, or international level. Large-scale research efforts ordinarily require large investments with accompanying risks that go with experimentation. Local administrators are understandably conservative about making such investments. "It is the federal support of educational research and development that places the United States in the leadership in the application of resources to research and development for education" (Organization for Economic Cooperation and Development, 1971, pp. ix–x). The Organization for Economic Cooperation and Development has as one of its functions the exploration of educational policies of individual nations, especially the policies that relate to the role of research and development for education. Although investments in educational research and development have not produced as much change in local practices as those sponsoring them had hoped, very little activity in this area would have occurred without the involvement of state and national organizations such as the Adult Education Association of the U.S.A. and its affiliates.

Increased Attention to Large-Scale Problems. Reagan (1972), in discussing the new federalism, has suggested that more and more problems are national in scope and that these problems are indivisible across the nation. Our society has become thoroughly interdependent in its economic, transportation, and communication patterns (Reagan, 1972; Sufrin, 1962). It is becoming clearer that educational deficiencies in one part of the country have negative impacts on the country as a whole. The population has become mobile, and there is an interdependent relationship between human resource development and economic development. For instance, the development of adult minimal competency levels of our population can no longer be viewed exclusively as a local responsibility. The adult basic education task is now recognized as national in scope. To mount separate campaigns in one thousand towns or in fifty states independently requires much more energy than to address the problem at the national level through multilevel decision making. On the international level, the problems of environmental conservation, energy supply, overpopulation, and human rights call for community learning on the part of millions of citizens around the world simultaneously. At the second International Conference on Adult Education at Montreal (UNESCO, 1960), it was declared that mankind's survival requires that the citizens of the world learn to live together. This learning requirement is not likely to be fulfilled if we are dependent only on local initiative. The content of that learning should be suggested by the experience of persons from all over the world. Problems of such magnitude cannot be addressed adequately if program goals are set at the local level.

Focusing of Attention on Problems. Program goal setting at the larger level is essential to focus a critical mass of attention in a given area of need which otherwise would be ignored or neglected. If we have learned anything from the struggle for desegregation, it is that a goal is likely to be ignored without such attention at the national, state, and local levels (Orfield, 1969). Several examples from the history of adult education in the United States show that the focusing of attention on a specific problem at the national, state, and local levels has produced results that otherwise would not have occurred as rapidly if the problem had been left entirely to local initiative. The first major federal intervention in education, the Cooperative Extension Service in 1914, brought about a number of quite significant changes in the quality of life of rural America. The Adult Education Act of 1965 brought aid to an important target population. The National Advisory Council on Adult Education, which was brought into being through that legislation, has subsequently focused national attention on adult functional competencies (Barron and Kelso, 1975). Lowe (1970, 1975), Ward (1974), and the International Bureau of Education, Geneva, have reported that anything short of a nationally focused adult education effort for most of the developing nations has been considered less than adequate to make the rapid changes desired in their nation building. Without state, national, and sometimes international attention, a massive effort cannot be mustered.

Protection of the Public Interest. Walter Lippmann (1955, p. 44) described the public interest as "what men would choose if they saw clearly, thought rationally, acted disinterestedly and benevolently." One of the tasks of government and other organizations beyond the local level has been to assure the common good through mediating conflict among interests and between local interests and the interests of the general public. Ensuring that the public interest is adequately protected is a delicate role for a state or national unit to play (Berdahl, 1971). However, the federal government has increasingly been called on to articulate policies that attempt to embody ideal definitions of the public good (Derthick, 1972, p. 94). The notion that the public interest will more likely be protected by persons who act in organizations beyond the local level is based on the belief that officials at the state and federal level—because of their distance from the pressures of local conflict—are "free, much freer than local officials, to stand publicly for progress and high principle" (Derthick, 1970, p. 94). Persons filled with local idealism sometimes assume that demonic tendencies in human nature are more likely to appear at the state or national levels. There is evidence, however, that corruption, prejudice, ineptitude, closed-mindedness, recalcitrance, rigidity, and protective self-interest have become visible in American society at all levels. Probably the public interest is best protected when there is a balance of power among levels. This tension among levels can help to preserve conflicting values, so that domination and harm to the public interest are less likely to occur (Litwak and Rothman, 1970).

Equalization of Educational Opportunity. Local independence is not compatible with the value of equality (Derthick, 1970). As long as the vestiges of independence and local autonomy remain, either in principle or in fact, the goal of equal educational opportunity is in jeopardy. To provide equal educational opportunity across the nation, local governments must be willing to give up control of some of their resources, so that they can be equitably redistributed to other localities through a mechanism beyond the local level. The inclination to provide equality of opportunity and the mechanisms for the redistribution of resources have been relatively weak in the field of adult education due to the reliance for the most part on voluntary donations and contributions, fees from learners, foundation grants, and local tax revenues. As a result, opportunities for adult learners have varied widely. This unevenness of opportunities has been modified to some extent as federal and state governments have increasingly assumed the function of raising revenues and redistributing them, often under the concept of equal opportunity or on the basis of a broad conceptualization of need. Certainly, the raising of revenue is increasingly and overwhelmingly a function of the national government (Reagan, 1972, p. 51). The basis of redistribution—not only in the area of education but also in health, welfare, transportation, and other service functions—has been at issue for years. The tension over forms of distribution has been primarily between those who favor categorical grants-in-aid and those who favor formula grants such as revenue sharing. Graves (1964), Reagan (1972), Stolz (1974), and many others have reported on the continuing struggle between the proponents of these opposing views over the years. The move toward balancing grants-in-aid with revenue sharing began in the 1960s and has continued with strong support from local levels. The categorical grant-in-aid mechanism has been regarded as a better means for obtaining a distribution that benefits the disadvantaged and the poor, since skepticism still remains about the ability of these persons to compete locally for their share of the revenue-sharing dollars (Reagan, 1972). In any case, program goal setting at the federal, state, and local levels is required to determine not only the priorities but also the means of distribution. Equality of educational opportunity as a goal is affected by the means of redistribution of resources as well as by the nature of formulas used. It is unlikely to occur without the participation of larger-level goal setting because of resistance on the part of some local publics.

Strategies for Integrative Planning and Goal Setting

The complexity of intergovernmental relations has been recognized by social scientists—perhaps most graphically in Grodzins' (1966) rejection of the "layer cake" view in favor of the "marble cake" image. Hahn (1972, p. 4) has suggested that the emerging picture of intergovernmental relations is one in which "the various levels of government are 'equal partners'—in which policies may be enacted at a particular level but in which participation and influence in shaping the policies, and shaping their implementation, is widely shared among actors from all levels of government (and the private sector as well)." The conditions for conflict as well as cooperation usually exist simultaneously over the array of national, regional, state, and local resources and interests. The focus of interests from the local level and from larger regions takes place in what has been termed integrative planning, a process whereby program goals affecting action at various levels are developed collaboratively.

Even though integrated planning within the field of adult education in most instances is quite new and its practice quite diverse due to the multiplicity of programs and organizational units involved, the following strategies are being proposed as having promise for facilitating the program goal-setting process.

Use of External Scanning. Drucker (1969, p. 109) and Farmer, Deshler, and Williams (1974, p. 46) have found that administrators generally tend to scan internally and downward within their own organizations and often fail to scan upward to the next level (state or national) or outward to the larger environment in order to identify critical issues that could profitably be addressed through mutual problem solving or goal setting among levels. Etzioni (1968, p. 284) has described a process of scanning that calls for rapidly and broadly viewing internal and external environments to identify potential danger or strategic opportunity spots, which are subsequently analyzed and scrutinized in detail for purposes of making both all-encompassing decisions (goals) and incremental decisions (objectives). This mixed-scanning approach to planning can help to overcome the tendency of administrators to scan downward—a tendency which has exaggerated negative consequences when multiplied by the distance between the local and the state and national levels of decision making. Failure of persons at each level of planning to scan externally may result in costly mistakes and missed opportunities.

Avoidance of Rigid Goal Stipulation. National, regional, and state organizations sometimes stipulate rigid program goals, objectives, guidelines, and performance characteristics. This practice has been found to be antithetical to successful program implementation, especially when programs are undertaken as development efforts in turbulent or uncertain environments. When such organizations insist that programs be run by the book or prescriptively, local implementers may ignore significant uncommon obstacles or fail to take advantage of unique resources that may be unknown at the outset of an effort. Hirschman (1967, p. 77), upon examination of World Bank development projects, suggests that funders and implementers should periodically redefine their goals and expectations in order to take advantage of emergent knowledge, resources, and programmatic possibilities. This process can prevent the waste that may occur when unproductive efforts are continued without modification. Farmer and colleagues (Deshler, Farmer, and Sheats, 1975; Farmer and Knox, 1977; Farmer, Sheats, and Deshler, 1972), in evaluation projects in California, Colorado, Connecticut, Georgia, Minnesota, Oklahoma, and Tennessee, have concluded that the flexibility permitted by national and state organizations contributed to the productivity and positive outcomes of these efforts. Because federal agencies often interpret their guidelines rigidly, those individuals who seek to overcome the limits they impose have endorsed revenue sharing as a means of restoring discretionary authority to state and local levels. Such local discretionary authority is essential if innovative programming is to be encouraged.

Provision for Incentives. Another strategy conducive to an integrative planning process is the provision for incentives, penalties, and rewards. According to Schultze (1969, pp. 201–225), "objectives, plans, and budgets are not synonymous with actions and results. Promises are not performance." He suggests that attention be given to the use of incentives for "inciting" and "inducing" individuals, public employees, and private decision makers to undertake the actions necessary to produce desired results. Incentives in addition to money should be considered from the perspective of those who have the greatest power to make the efforts successful.

Increase in Public Participation. Program goals reflect the values and perspectives of those who set them. Integrative planning is unlikely to work unless provisions are made for increased participation and greater representation among various publics at both local and larger levels. It is through interaction among these publics that the public interest can be protected (Thompson, 1970). Although some people believe that the local level is more likely to provide for widely representative participation, the federal level has been called on time and time again to intervene in order to guarantee the rights of participation of local citizens who have been denied these rights by local self-serving leadership. It has been at the federal level that leaders have expressed their concern for mandates to increase "maximum feasible participation" at all levels and have written public participation requirements into numerous pieces of federal legislation (Federal Regional Council, 1976) governing commerce, health, education, law enforcement, labor, transportation, environmental protection, and energy. If integrative planning is to be viable, public participation must be increased.

Improvement in Interlevel Communication. Two-way communication between levels is essential for an integrative planning process to occur. National, regional, and state goals will be unrealistic, and local appreciation of them will be unlikely unless settings and processes are created to allow for the free exchange of information among all levels which facilitates the continuing improvement of operating procedures. According to Kaufman and Couzens (1973, p. 79), when shortcomings in the feedback process occur, the cumulative impact of faulty communication results in nonresponsiveness at all levels or actions which are faulty because they are based on incomplete or incorrect impressions of the situations at other levels of the system.

Another communication problem that must be overcome is the sheer volume of information that must be communicated when planning occurs at state, regional, and national levels. One possible strategy is to emphasize holistic communication. Holistic communication has been described by Rhyne (1972, p. 93) as "a brief communication which provides a map of the whole for complex issues." It is an increasingly important form of communication between levels of an organization and between organizations. Persons engaged in macroplanning do not have the time to read lengthy detailed proposals, including reports on situations of need and programmatic responses. A holistic communication process known as Chartering, suggested by Lopez (1970) and tested with revisions by Farmer, Deshler, and Williams (1974), has been found to aid communication between levels of the vocational education system.

Conclusion

The benefits from involving state, regional, and national thinking in local program goal setting are considerable. Integrative planning in the field of adult education is increasing and is here to stay. Strategies exist to facilitate this process. The field of adult education as a whole may now need to engage in larger-level goal setting as an occasion for facilitating learning. No one location has a corner on innovation or on useful information. Nonlocal representatives can facilitate learning about adult education practice—not only through dissemination of information through publications and through clearinghouses such as the Clearinghouse on Adult Education and Lifelong Learning (ADELL) and the Educational Resources Information Centers but also through interaction among interested publics, official publics, and the general public in what has been described as community learning.

Chapter Eleven

Should the Federal Government Assume a Major Leadership Role in Adult Education?

The Federal Government Must Assume a Leadership Role

Allen B. Moore

Adult education is not the sole responsibility of any one agency, organization, or institution. Public high schools, community junior colleges, proprietary schools, libraries, museums, military organizations, college and university extension programs, labor unions, business and industry, religious organizations, centers for older persons, and other agencies offer continuing education activities for adults throughout the nation. According to Christoffel (1976), more than 275 different adult education programs are administered by as many as fifteen different departments in the federal government. Given the multitude of activities under the broad umbrella of continuing education, is there a single unifying source or agency that assumes leadership for organizing, facilitating, coordinating, or evaluating these educational programs? The answer is no. Should there be a single agency leading the development of adult education? The answer depends on who is asked the question. In my opinion, the federal government should assume a major role if not become the key leadership agency in adult education.

Critical Functions Essential to National Leadership

At least six functions are essential to a national leadership role in adult education: (1) establishing national policies and future directions, (2) adapting to change, (3) encouraging citizen participation in adult program development, (4) achieving governance and program flexibility, (5) stimulating and supporting research and development, and (6) developing consumer awareness. Expressed in another way, the federal government should (1) establish national policies and future direction; (2) assimilate changes into existing and new program efforts; (3) involve professional and volunteer adult educators as well as the public in policy and program development; (4) set guidelines for achieving goals that are flexible enough for a broad range of participant interests; (5) promote and support research and development efforts to generate knowledge, programs, and technology; (6) establish and maintain a national, state, and local communication system for dissemination of information, materials, technology, and research findings.

Policy and Future Directions. The federal government can assume a major leadership role in adult education by (1) coordinating the efforts of the various departments that sponsor programs for adults, thereby eliminating overlapping and duplication of programs; (2) establishing a comprehensive but flexible policy for adult education programs at the state and local level; (3) supporting continuous improvement of legislation for adult education (see National Advisory Council on Adult Education, 1976a); and (4) supporting the identification and study of barriers to educational opportunities for adults (see Broschart, 1976).

Change. Two situations illustrate the need to assimilate change into adult education programs. First is the ability to serve Vietnamese and other persons who are refugees from their native lands. Educational programs for immigrants into the United States have been in existence for decades; however, the need to update and change these programs was accelerated by large numbers of Vietnamese coming into the United States since the end of the Vietnam War. As a result, more basic literacy and cultural awareness programs for the Vietnamese are now offered. The second example is the energy crisis, which has created a new life style for Americans. Adult education cannot solve the energy crisis, but programs for adults can be designed to help them better understand the energy problem.

These two examples illustrate the need for adult education organizations to respond to change. Some changes can be identified and dealt with in a short period of time by existing policies and legislation. Other changes suggest new policies, new legislation, and new programs.

Citizen Participation. Recent legislation (Public Law 95-561) requires citizen advisory committees to be involved in the design, development, implementation, and evaluation of adult education programs for low literates. Mandatory review by citizens is one way to stimulate participation in policy and program development. The federal government, to be a viable leader in adult education, must develop other ways of stimulating citizen participation in educational programs and other activities (see Langdon, 1978).

Governance. Although the federal government must exercise initiative and leadership in stimulating activities at the local level, it must not usurp the legitimate rights of the citizens to participate in shaping and governing local adult education programs. Policies, legislation, and guidelines must be flexible enough to provide discretionary authority for state and local leaders to direct adult education programs. States need the authority and flexibility to develop programs that serve the specific needs of local citizens. A program in South Carolina may be similar to that of Georgia but not to those found in Wyoming or Montana. Coping skills, literacy education, and vocational training for adults may be needed nationwide (Northcutt, 1975), but the program could require a different delivery system in certain regions or states because of economics and the labor market.

Research and Development. The federal government should support research and development efforts in the area of adult education as one of its leadership roles. Short- and long-term research efforts are needed to identify and solve current and future problems. Data regarding contributions of past research to adult education (Kreitlow, 1968, 1975) have indicated the need for studies about learners, adult learning, participation in adult education, program planning, and evaluation. Reports identifying current problems and research needs can assist the development of adult education. Studies documenting the need for research and research agendas (College Entrance Examination Board, 1978) stimulate educators and others to meet the continuing education needs of adults. The federal government should lead in making the needed research possible.

Much of the funding to support adult education research is limited to short-term research projects, with sponsors requiring fiscal reports after a single year's work. The federal government is in a good position to take the long view and to provide support for long-range research. Long-term, long-range research attempts to answer policy questions that have an enduring effect on individual learners, whereas short-range research, while important, can answer only a few important questions.

Consumer Awareness. Another essential element of adult education leadership is the development and support of a national, state, and local communication and dissemination network. For the most part, the federal government has taken a leadership role in this area. At the national level, federal legislation has supported a Clearinghouse on Adult Education and Lifelong Learning (ADELL), and one of the clearinghouses in the Educational Resources Information Centers (ERIC) system has adult education as part of its scope. However, the 1980s will be the "age of information sharing." The consumer (adult learner) is and will continue to be bombarded by media and messages from a variety of sources. The federal government can demonstrate leadership in this area by establishing local linkage to state and national information-sharing centers. By its ability to respond accurately and quickly to consumer needs, it will build a "track record" of trust and competence that is the basis of leadership.

Examples of Activities

The federal government should engage in some of the following activities to carry out its leadership role in adult education in the United States.

Policy Studies. The federal government can commission policy studies via contracts and grants or encourage other agencies (such as the Brookings Institution, the Rand Corporation, and the National Advisory Council on Adult Education) to conduct such studies. A policy study should include an overview of international issues and problems in adult education. The linkage between international problems and United States policy on adult education should be described. Equally important areas are the problems within the United States that are related to work, employment, inflation, energy, transportation, and housing, and the need for adult education to solve these problems.

Policy studies sponsored by the federal government should clearly identify issues, possible outcomes, and roles of public institutions, private agencies, and organizations in adult education. A summary of research related to adult education should be part of the policy study. The policy study should address such questions as: What research is needed? What research has been done? What questions have already been answered? What are the priority research areas for the next five to ten years? What should be researched now?

The leadership role of the federal government in policy studies would be to initiate the study; identify the issues; develop priorities of short-range, intermediate-range, and long-range benefits; and coordinate the efforts of individuals and agencies toward solving these problems.

National Planning Commission for Continuing Education. In the adult education field, there are a number of leaders who could work together for planning purposes. These leaders could form a national planning commission, with subgroups studying the following and other issues related to adult education: (1) mid-career change (Dubin, 1974; Leider, 1976); (2) continuing professional education (Houle, 1980; Knox, 1972); (3) preparation for retirement (Otte, 1971); (4) career planning (Hill, 1976); (5) basic survival skills (Northcutt, 1975); (6) education and work relationships (Hodgkinson, 1976; Wirtz, 1975); (7) movement back to rural areas (Beale, 1975); (8) on-the-job learning (O'Toole, 1976); (9) futures for adult education (Mandel, 1975); and (10) life-style changes as a result of current energy problems (O'Toole, 1978).

Planning at the national level requires cooperation and commitment to action. In the planning phase, the leadership role of the federal government should be to facilitate the commission's formation for a specific task and to assist in carrying out the commission's plans and recommendations for action. The members of the commission ought to devise its own mechanisms for implementing its own recommendations rather than having the federal government create yet another structure just to enact recommendations of the commission. This panel or commission, similar to the Carnegie Commission, would help the federal government make an extended study of continuing education, its problems, its future, and possible alternative solutions.

Future Assemblies. A nation of 240 million or more people obviously cannot hold a single meeting or conference on adult and continuing education. However, each village, ward, neighborhood, and district could hold discussions on the need for adult and continuing education. Future assemblies could be planned and conducted in such a fashion that citizens living in local neighborhoods and communities can express their ideas, interests, and needs for continuing education. Data from these assemblies would be compiled at the county and state levels for local action. The federal government leadership role in the operation of future assemblies would be to establish the national priority and provide support via funding or cooperative ventures to meet continuing education needs.

Telecommunication Links for National Discussions. To establish communication between citizens and leaders about continuing education issues and problems will require an electronic mechanism. In some instances it is not convenient to travel to a convention or meeting for these discussions. The technology exists today for a national linkage of universities, agencies, and organizations to hold conference telephone meetings, open-line seminars, and two-way audio/video communications. A periodic series of seminars or discussions on continuing education priorities could be conducted to focus the best national thinking on critical problems. Educational TV and cable TV facilities could be used to encourage local discussion and input into these national seminars. The federal government leadership role would be to identify and encourage agencies now operating facilities to participate in the national program. Regionally located institutions, such as universities and community colleges, could be responsible for coordinating parts of the program and any resulting reports. Summarization of reports and national dissemination could be conducted under contract with the federal government.

Conclusion

Is the federal government the *only* agency that can assume a leadership role regarding the six functions discussed here? I believe that it is. The authority for performing these functions is found in federal legislation passed by the Congress of the United States. No other agency or organization has such support for adult education.

214 of the Federal Government

Private institutions, foundations, trust funds, and humanitarian organizations can and often do assume major leadership roles in adult education. However, the long-term leadership role appears to be prescribed by the legislative authority of the federal government. Having the authority to do something is not the same as being a leader of continuing education programs for the nation. The real issues about federal government leadership are:

1. How do program participants, local citizens, program directors, and professional educators make sure that the people working in federal government agencies are leaders?
2. Will cabinet-level appointees, department administrators, mid-level managers, and program specialists actually be leaders?
3. Will adult education program personnel, throughout the nation, cooperate and work with the federal government leadership?

There is a critical need for individuals within the federal government to exert leadership in the six areas noted above. Taking action to establish policies that allow for change and promote citizen participation is a leadership function. Long-term financial support is needed for research and development, local governance of programs, and a national communication system.

The National Leadership Role Belongs to Professional Adult Educators

Robert A. Fellenz

A unique form of adult education is going on in the little town of Mountain View, Arkansas, where the culture and homemaking skills of the people of the Ozarks are being preserved and taught to future generations. Young men and women apprentice themselves to furniture makers, wood carvers, and weavers. They learn, for example, how to select the right tree, split it, and devise designs for objects to be carved. Their crafts are demonstrated to the general public in the Ozark Folk Center established for this purpose as a state park. In a paper mill in Wisconsin, an experienced trainer is striving to make the company's educational program one that will develop not only human resources for increased production but also human beings for more productive and enjoyable living. At times this trainer is on loan to other companies to help them develop complete educational programs of their own. In a church in Florida, a young man combines music and theology to inspire people and to teach them of the Spirit of God. And so throughout the nation men and women are developing successful continuing education programs—some similar to those mentioned but each unique in being directed to needs of the local community.

Some of this uniqueness is due to the fact that a major portion of the programming is conducted through agencies not primarily educational in nature. Johnstone and Rivera (1965), in their famous study of participation, found that agencies such as churches, businesses, and service groups were conducting more than half of the programs for adults. Schroeder (1970, p. 33) summed it up this way: "As we have seen, adult education in the United States developed somewhat chaotically in response to a great variety of special interests and needs rather than systematically in response to some overall plan and purpose." The question now before us is: Should the federal government be given major leadership over this unique movement? Allen B. Moore thinks so and argues this position strongly in the preceding article. However, I contend that giving the federal government the major leadership role in adult and continuing education would not only be ineffective but would likely be detrimental to the continuing education of adults in America.

It seems to me that Moore's arguments and assumptions run basically like this. There is no single unified leadership in adult and continuing education. But leadership is a good. Therefore, a single unified leadership role should be given to someone. Further, the federal government can fulfill leadership functions such as the establishment of policy, the stimulation of citizen involvement, and the promotion of research and development. Therefore, the federal government should be the one given major leadership rights and responsibilities in the education of adults. I contend that two of these basic presumptions are false and dangerous. Leadership is not necessarily an unmitigated blessing; it can be a destructive force. Installing the wrong agency in the major leadership role could be detrimental to adult education. Second, the federal government is not well equipped to carry out leadership functions in the broad field of continuing education. Other agencies and groups are providing better leadership to the field. A simple review of the history of adult education in the United States demonstrates the weakness of Moore's argument and at the same time keeps this discussion rooted in reality. First, however, we need to be clear about the topic under consideration. A brief examination of the nature of leadership will provide the perspective needed to review this complex issue.

Leadership in Continuing Education: A Review

One difficulty in the examination of leadership lies in the various connotations and innuendoes attached to the concept. For some the very mention of the word brings forth visions of noble heroes such as Jefferson and Franklin; but others hear it and cringe before the remembered atrocities of a Hitler or an Idi Amin. In the last decade, theorists of educational leadership, such as Lane, Corwin, and Monahan (1966), played down the effectiveness of the charismatic individual as leader and gave more importance to a system or management approach to leadership. Although this is not the place for an involved examination of the theory of leadership, several points should be borne in mind. For example, because of the historical "lack of leadership" in continuing education, it is tempting to think in terms of some national structure. Positing such a structure and automatically presuming its effectiveness is an oversimple approach. Perhaps no such structure has arisen because no such structure would be effective. Moreover, conceptualization of leadership in terms of structure tends to stress control; yet control is so foreign to much of adult education that the very mention of mandatory continuing education raises eyebrows and voices around the nation. Certainly it is more profitable to discuss leadership in terms of essential functions, as Moore attempts to do, rather than to focus on structures.

Congruent with this view is the concern that leadership cannot be separated from a consideration of those who are to follow that leadership. In this instance we might properly ask: What would move educators of adults to follow some national standard bearer? What would be the source of power or authority that would make such leadership effective? How, indeed, would any unified national leadership role be maintained and how would it interact with those cast in the role of followers? These are not irrelevant concerns but issues essential to the nature of leadership in continuing education.

Because of the uniqueness and complexity of the field of continuing education and because of the high potential benefit or danger to the movement of endorsing any single agency or group as the "major" leader, it seems advisable to anchor our further examination of the issue in a review of leadership as it has been and is presently being exercised in the field. Rather than use any complex definition of leadership or exhaustive listing of its functions, we will identify it simply by its results. Where there was noticeable advancement in the field, leadership will be presumed to have been exerted.

A historical review of adult education was presented by Grattan (1955) in his classic *In Quest of Knowledge*. The eleven eras he used to examine the growth of adult education from the settling of our country to the 1950s provide a fitting outline for our review of leadership. The early history of our country and of its adult education was largely a tale of strong individual leaders, such as Franklin and Jefferson, together with an underlying national stance that advocated and promoted broad diffusion of knowledge. Ben Franklin and his famous Junto, or discussion club, are of particular interest, for Franklin utilized this educational methodology not only for continued self-education but also as a vehicle for promotion of social and cultural enterprises. This dual purpose, self-improvement plus some pragmatic accomplishment, became characteristic of many adult education efforts in America. While others of this period have not gained the public recognition of Franklin, hundreds of individuals organized learning activities such as discussion clubs, subscription reading rooms, and lecture associations —so much so that various historians marked these efforts as characteristic of our democratic society. Moreover, such individual initiative also marked the next two major events noted by Grattan. Josiah Holbrook promoted the Lyceum with a visionary's zeal, for he anticipated that such learning activities would lead to social harmony as well as continued education. Although his dreams were never fully realized, Holbrook provided us with an adult education methodology that remained effective well into the twentieth century. However, more impressive in its long-range impact on American adult education was the Chautauqua. Begun as a training program for Sunday school teachers, it soon began to promote broad educational improvement, utilizing residential short courses, traveling, lectures, and correspondence study. Although the

Chautauqua was originally developed by the Methodist Episcopal Church, major credit for the movement is usually given to two individuals, Reverend John Vincent, a Methodist leader, and Lewis Miller, a prominent businessman.

Another major development noted by Grattan—the extension of the resources of the university to the general public—was an outgrowth of movements such as Jacksonian democracy, the example of British programs, and the lectures of numerous American professors. Grattan gave special credit to a number of university presidents, such as Daniel Coit Gilman, C. R. Van Hise, George Vincent, and William Rainey Harper. He also acknowledged the special efforts of the American Society for the Extension of University Teaching, which "originated in Philadelphia, drew its leadership from the citizens of that city, and conducted most of the classes in the city, eastern Pennsylvania, and in New Jersey across the Delaware River, though it had offshoots farther afield" (Grattan, 1955, p. 186).

To these cooperative efforts of local citizens and universities was soon added a third force, that of the federal government. The Smith-Lever Act of 1914 became the milestone marking the birth of the Cooperative Extension Service, which many still recognize as the largest organized adult education enterprise in the world. Credit for its inauguration must, of course, be given to Senator Hoke Smith and Representative Asbury Lever but also in a special way to Seaman A. Knapp. As early as 1882, this former teacher and superintendent advocated vocational education for adults and was influential in the adoption of the Hatch Act of 1887. But today he is especially credited for the promotion of demonstration methodologies favored by the extension service.

Grattan next noted the service that public schools have provided for adults—service so extensive that by 1951, in his estimation, four million adults were participating in public school programs. Leadership in this movement apparently arose from a number of different sources: from Henry Leipziger, the inspiration behind the New York Free Lecture System; from the Americanization movement, which promoted citizenship education through the local schools; and from the National Education Association and its Department of Adult Education, organized in 1924, and its offshoot, the National Association of Public School Adult Educators, founded in 1952.

For the purposes of this review, the next three developmental movements noted by Grattan—educational programs for adults sponsored by libraries, labor unions, and complexes of civic and social groups—can be considered together. Each of these movements undoubtedly has had an educational impact on many citizens in numerous and diverse areas of learning. However, the development of programs in each of these areas is episodic rather than continuous—never reaching the heights envisioned by proponents in each field. Moreover, it is very difficult to identify either individual leaders or specific methodologies through which such growth did occur. The impact of individuals was usually restricted to certain libraries, unions, clubs, or agencies. Complete analysis would call for hundreds of individual studies of such groups as the libraries of New York, the International Ladies Garment Workers Union, the YMCA, and the Great Books movement.

The final development noted by Grattan should be of particular interest to us here, for it concerns "Organizing the Adult Educators." The first effort to unite educators of adults throughout the country resulted in the formation of the American Association for Adult Education in 1926. Although a number of educators were involved in calling for or helping to organize this association, Fredrick P. Keppel is recognized as its principal instigator. As president of the Carnegie Corporation, he used that foundation's resources to promote the American Association for Adult Education (AAAE) during a fifteen-year period, from 1926 to 1941. In Keppel's mind, the AAAE was not organized to provide direct service to individual members but rather to assist other agencies involved in adult education. Its major efforts seemed directed toward increasing communication among adult educators; it also promoted research and a positive public image for adult education. In 1945 the association reached a turning point. Left without the financial support of the Carnegie Corporation and anxious to move forward from complete absorption in a world war, the association first had to turn its efforts to the individual communities to help them determine needs, develop programs, promote leadership, and unite in establishing learning opportunities for adults. In 1951 a new effort was made at organizing the adult educators when the members of the AAAE and the Department of Adult Education of the National Education Association joined together to form the Adult Education Association of the U.S.A. The National Association of Public School Adult Educators (NAPSAE) soon split off from the AEA—a division that has lasted to this day despite efforts by members of both groups to design a single organization to serve the purposes of both.

Even this brief historical review makes it clear that the federal government has played a minor leadership role in the development of adult education in the United States. Instead, the major role was played by insightful individuals. Each individual whom Grattan recognized as a leader in the development of American adult education had two special characteristics. First, each recognized some distinct need in the people he proposed to serve; second, each concomitantly recognized some appropriate strength unique to the environment or organization with which he was associated—a strength that could be used as an instrument to meet the needs of his clientele. Vincent and Miller, for example, recognized the yearning of people for intellectual and spiritual stimulation and tied this need to the power of the organized church and its desire for trained Sunday school leaders. Seaman Knapp used the far-reaching voices of the university and the federal government but harnessed them to the demonstration methodology, which was meaningful to rural Americans and essential to their adoption of innovative practices. Repeatedly throughout this saga of the involvement of diverse sponsors and clients, we see this dual tendency repeated—the strength of an organization is manipulated to serve the needs or yearnings of a special group of adult learners. When the educator was not able to use his institution—to twist it to serve the needs of the people—the adult education program failed to coalesce. It became "discontinuous."

This individual exercising his leadership on the local, state, or national level may be further characterized by several attributes. First, he showed leadership, in the sense of causing events to happen and not simply announcing direction or policy. Second, whether directly intended or not, each of the above movements seemed to inspire a spirited and energetic following, which guaranteed promotion of this concept apart from the efforts of the instigator. This is reminiscent of the insistence of modern theorists (see Sergiovanni and Carver, 1974) that leadership includes group sensitization and maintenance functions as well as organizational abilities. Or, as Knowles (1960, p. 26) implies, adult education programs have survived by developing their own spirit rather than through dependence on an institution. In each instance, leadership was a liberating rather than a limiting or controlling force. Perhaps it is easier to conceptualize this leadership as noncentralizing, leading to diversity of programming rather than to tidiness of organization.

In *The Adult Education Movement in the United States,* Knowles (1962) posited several genetic principles exhibited in the development of adult education in the United States. In so doing, he reinforced the notion that successful adult education programs result from efforts to alleviate specific human needs rather than as an overall design for the continuing education of adults and that the growth of continuing education has occurred in spurts rather than consistent patterns. His sixth principle, "the institutional segments of the adult educational field tend to crystallize into organized structures without reference to any conception of a general adult educational movement" (1962, p. 260), seems particularly relevant to this discussion. It provides further testimony to the fact that adult education in the United States is not a simple movement of allied forces but a diverse field of scattered efforts, often oblivious to efforts of cohorts in the field. Yet growth has been dramatic, even though no single agency or organization has assumed the central leadership role.

This may seem a simplistic explanation, perhaps good enough for the first three centuries of American adult education, but what of the dynamic decades of the 1950s, the 1960s, and the 1970s? Certainly there were societal trends that had a great impact on the demand for continuing education. The growth in production spurred on by World War II consequently produced a demand for more and more skill training. The growth of the economy, and the consequent "rise of the minorities," the explosion of technology and the resultant increase of time and resources for leisure activities, the changes in the proportion of adults of different ages, the energy scares and bewilderment about alternative futures are but a few examples of societal changes that have spurred the development of educational activities for adults. As a result, we read frequently of the "greying of our campuses," the increased use of neighborhood schools for "community education," and the second chance or "last gamble on education" for many through adult basic education. These last three decades have witnessed a phenomenal expansion of learning opportunities for adults in community college systems, in business and industry, in extension and nontraditional programs of universities, and in professional continuing education in such fields as the military and health services. What we have witnessed is not the result of efforts of a single leader. Instead, the leadership in the field has been diverse and creative.

Effectiveness of Federal Involvement in Adult Education

A brief look at the history of federal involvement in continuing education is sufficient to call into question the effectiveness of federal leadership in such activities. Although it is feasible to expect unified programs to flow from federal initiative, the director of governmental relations for the National Association of State Universities and Land-Grant Colleges points out that the expectation has not been realized: "The success of continuing education in the past has been scattered. The federal government has been funding extension and continuing education for a long time, but there is no one program of federal funding of extension and continuing education. A study in September 1976 by the Institute for Educational Leadership at George Washington University identified 275 federal programs of support to some form of lifelong learning" (Roschwalb, 1976a, p. 6). These words are reminiscent of the consternation expressed by the National Advisory Council on Adult Education (1972, p. 7) in its report to the President: "Congress funds educational assistance programs for adults through a large number of agencies. This proliferation makes the task of cooperation extremely difficult, often resulting in duplication of effort, program gaps, wasted funds, and unnecessary competition by agencies for participants. Without agency cooperation and co-ordination, successful new methods for working with adults, developed and tested in one program, are rarely disseminated to other programs. The problem is major, the amount of money expended in the federal adult education effort is large, the need is great, and the confusion is often overwhelming." Is this not what can be expected from a political entity? Loyalties are scattered; many different groups must be satisfied. Unity in programming is simply not a primary goal. In itself, this would not be completely disastrous, but it also is inadequate for each of the specific educational programs. The federal government's own analysis by the Comptroller General of the United States (1975) indicates that there has been inadequate funding for adult basic education. The report concludes that the program has had little impact on reducing illiteracy among adults and that the biggest obstacle to effective adult basic education programming has been the inadequate funding. Hunter and Harman (1979) report the same inadequacies.

It is not only funding unity that is inadequate in federal programming in continuing education. Frequently the conceptualization and spirit of such programming appear parochial. Rivera (1976, p. 288) has summarized some of the discontent with such leadership: "The ABE (adult basic education) program as presently conceived . . . is stymied with a one-purpose mandate—raise formal educational levels." In his view, the lack of leadership is exemplified in the inability to develop an independent Adult Education Act separate from the Elementary and Secondary Education Act. The change in control of funds from the Adult Education Act for staff development and demonstration projects might also indicate where leadership should reside. Originally these funds were dispensed by the Division of Adult Education in the U.S. Office of Education. For a three-year period in the early 1970s, they were administered on a regional basis. Since then, the funds have been given directly to the individual states, which determine how the funds are to be used. Even though state and local leaders later elected to allow minimal discretionary funding to be returned to the control of federal officials, no funds were appropriated for this purpose in the 1979 or 1980 fiscal years.

In her capacity as guest editor of the special bicentennial issue of *Adult Education*, Rockhill (1976, p. 204) pessimistically concluded that "adult education's most important role has been as a finishing school for entry into the middle class." This may be true of most institutionally directed programs where structure was valued above people. In the same issue, Stubblefield's (1976, p. 266) comments on education of adults for citizenry, especially during the 1920s and 1930s, seem more optimistic: "This period, rich in its diversity, produced no final answer or program for promoting an intelligent citizenry. The issues of the relation of adult education to social action and what knowledge, values, attitudes, and skills intelligent citizens should possess were not resolved. But the diversity was good; many approaches were needed. Perhaps the most significant legacy of this period lay in the conception of adult education that emerged: the idea of adult education as a process of helping adults to use their experience and knowledge in understanding and handling situations in their lives."

Appropriate Leadership Roles for the Federal Government

The federal government has a leadership role in adult education, but it is not *the* major leadership role. The fifty states are united because this unity promotes the common good and guarantees the rights of each individual. Thus, the federal government can gather revenue to fund broadly based programs that address national needs. But even here programs must be adjusted to local needs.

Paul Delker is an adult educator who has been in a leadership position in the federal government for more than a decade, and his long tenure gives weight to his analysis of the appropriate role of the federal government in continuing education. His conclusions are based on two principles that he believes should regulate governmental roles in our society. "The first of these is that government should have no role in providing social services . . . if these can be achieved with reasonable effectiveness by nongovernmental units. The second is consistent with this; namely, that nothing should be carried out by a higher, more centralized unit of government that can be effectively achieved by a lesser unit of government" (Delker, 1974, p. 28). Delker goes on to point out appropriate roles both of a regulatory and educative nature. In core education, for example, he sees the federal role limited to identification of national priorities and the targeting of resources in a manner supportive of state and local leadership. In the promotion of multiple learning activities for adults, he believes that all governmental units can play supportive roles through incentives offered to sponsoring agencies or through regulations promoting educational services. The federal government might exercise a major role, however, in guaranteeing equitable access to education and promoting learning opportunities on behalf of all citizens. Throughout his analysis, Delker holds true to his original contention that the federal government should not usurp the leadership role in providing services that can be effectively supplied on a less centralized level, and he maintains that the greatest promise lies in placing the decision for determining what shall be learned, when, where, and how in the hands of the learner. The government's role is to support this right and responsibility of the individual.

In the preceding article, Moore suggests six functions essential to national leadership in continuing education and maintains that the federal government is in a position to carry out these services. The history of adult education, along with strong traditional conceptions of the role of the federal government in our society, challenges the appropriateness of some of these roles. For other roles it may be more appropriate for the federal government to provide continuing support rather than assume the leader's position.

"To establish national policies and future directions," the first function suggested by Moore, is certainly an appropriate one, for the federal government is concerned with issues vital to the welfare of the nation as a whole or essential to the protection of the rights of individuals or groups. However, I would maintain that in a field as complex as adult education, and especially where success is based on meeting the needs of the individual, the major portion of policy and decision making must occur on an operational level much closer to the learner than that of the federal government. Much the same can be said of Moore's second role suggestion, "to assimilate changes into existing and new program efforts." Federal regulations and appropriations, together with the judicial system, are powerful inducements to change. However, they are a bit cumbersome and have only a secondary impact on educational programs in agencies such as churches and businesses. Two additional functions suggested by Moore, promotion of research and support of communication systems, seem appropriate federal efforts provided local and state leaders are involved in such exercises. As Kreitlow (1975) points out, administrative and governmental priorities need to be balanced with the needs for research as seen by the professional.

Two of the leadership functions that Moore suggested seem most inappropriate. The first, "to set guidelines for achieving goals that are flexible enough for a broad range of participant interests," violates the traditional role given the federal government in our society; the second, to involve citizens "in policy and program development," is more practically performed at a local or regional level.

Moore has pointed to some legitimate roles of the federal government in adult education; however, they are supportive rather than major leadership roles. Suggestions for federal governance, control, or dominance are inappropriate; for they violate both the prevailing philosophy and current practice. Finally, there is no guarantee, or even supporting evidence, that the fulfilling of these functions would provide central leadership to adult education in the United States.

An Alternative Model for National Leadership

If the model of the federal government as the major leader in continuing education will not function effectively and might even interfere with the education of adults, are other options available? I believe that there are several, but to be consistent with the history of the adult education movement in the United States we must turn to the opposite end of the spectrum from federal governance. Adult education has succeeded to the extent it has because of the efforts of individual leaders; it will continue to grow to the extent that professional adult educators are willing to unite and furnish collaborative leadership in continuing education. This model of the individual working through his professional organization fits our democratic ideals. It also is more appropriate to the nature of education; for, as Hutchins (1968) pointed out when he described the "Learning Society," education is for manhood, not for manpower. Furthermore, it gives us a model much nearer the learner, the consumer, and thus puts us in a more logical position from which to begin our search for national leadership (Des-Champs, 1971).

An obvious prerequisite to such leadership is greater unity and cooperation among adult educators. On the occasion of the twenty-fifth anniversary of the Adult Education Association, Griffith (1976) analyzed the status of the adult education profession, particularly from the viewpoint of its potential political power. His thesis was: "If adult educators are to play a significant role in determining the nature and extent of adult learning activities, they must increase their involvement in the political process of shaping policy." After a thorough review—for the most part disheartening to the vision of a unified profession—Griffith (1976, pp. 294–295) concluded: "Imbued with the tradition of entrepreneurship, the individual adult educator has survived or failed largely on the basis of his own ability to function alone. Nevertheless, at the local, state, and national levels, there is an amazing array of organizations, institutions, and associations that are feeling some sense of frustration because of their seeming political impotence. There is a growing awareness of the need for and possible benefits of increased cooperation among the many segments of the adult education movement." Can this "growing awareness" be used as the catalyst to begin drawing together unified professional leadership for the field? Perhaps.

A major problem in unifying the profession of adult education is its developmental status as an "emerging profession." In the *Handbook of Adult Education*, Houle (1970, p. 112) wrote: "At present the adult educator can be considered a professional only in a loose and analogical fashion, such as that which distinguishes the trained from the amateur historian or the political scientist from the politician. By study and experience he has acquired a body of knowledge, a discipline, and an expertise which sets him apart from other people, but he is not yet a member of a consciously defined company of men who have achieved the socially recognized and legally protected stature of a profession." If we cannot envision ourselves as a unified association, we cannot provide national leadership to the field. But then neither can any outside agency, for any leader would first have to conceptualize and impose some unity before giving direction to the whole. In the final analysis, national leadership in adult education must await the further development of the profession.

In the decade that has passed since Houle questioned the professional status of the adult educator, some significant developments have occurred. Professional schools, or graduate programs, in adult education have grown in number and, presumably, in quality. Funding for adult programs has risen some on the federal level, more on state levels, and significantly in business, industry, and numerous professional organizations. Research peculiar to the field, together with a body of literature on the education of adults, is being amassed. As for programming, everyone—from hospitals to department stores to universities—seems to want to be part of the act.

But in developing a unified profession, we seem to have made little progress. A typical example can be seen in the short history of the Coalition of Adult Education Organizations (CAEO). Formed in 1969 to promote communication and cooperation among adult education organizations and to facilitate joint planning and solicitation of support, it attracted little notice, even among the members of its organizations (Griffith, 1976, p. 283). In many instances, we are unknown even to ourselves. But rather than bemoan a lack of unity we have never had, let us turn to several things that we who call ourselves adult educators could do, individually or together, to improve the leadership given adult education.

To claim the title of leaders in continuing education, we must improve our efforts in three areas: communication among adult educators and about adult education, general advocacy of adult education and involvement in policy formation, and development of professionally trained adult educators. These areas incorporate the common functions performed by most national

bodies of adult education as listed by J. R. Kidd and cited by James
(James, 1974, p. 62). Below are offered some suggestions for improving our accomplishment of these functions.

Some restructuring or redirection of our professional organizations seems necessary. Limited membership implies limited
political influence and restricted budgeting. At this point in our
development, we need professional staff persons with a major responsibility for lobbying or at least organizing members in some
consistent and comprehensive approach to public policymaking.
Another position needed is that of communications "chief" with
responsibility for journals, newsletters, and other forms of information. This person might also have the responsibility of compiling
mailing lists that would reach adult educators in all the diverse
agencies of our field. A third useful position would be that of
conference planner. The face-to-face contact possible at national
or regional conferences could be a powerful means of building
cohesiveness among adult educators. Today the major effort at
such events is directed toward serving diversity of interests among
attendees, thus aiding and encouraging the existing fragmentation.

The burden of professional development cannot solely be
laid on the staff of a national office; it resides with each member of
the group. During the past decade, adult educators have been
chided repeatedly (Crabtree, 1973; Griffith, 1976; Jensen, 1973;
Roschwalb, 1976b) about their lack of political involvement. The
call consistently has been for broad representation of adult educators in the many facets of social and political influence. For example, Griffith (1976, p. 295) maintains: "Although the public needs
for adult education, or at least a band of the spectrum of such
needs, may be visible to each of the special interest groups of adult
educators, no means exists now to bring these bands together and
to show them to the public and its elected representatives." It is
time we respond to such pleas both with state and nationally organized efforts and with less formal approaches. We might, for
example, develop a system for sharing such things as press releases
promoting adult learning; we might also develop models of interagency cooperation.

A special role in development of the profession could be
carried out by the Commission of Professors of Adult Education.
For example, present efforts at communicating a positive image of

the profession are frequently negated by a general vagueness regarding what that image entails. The professors, better than any other group, should be able to conceptualize the field without letting the temptation to be all things to all adults obscure what they are really about. To paraphrase Houle's words quoted earlier, we will not be a profession until we can distinguish "the trained from the amateur" adult educator. Following clarification of what they are, the Commission of Professors could give increased attention to the improvement of training and research, particularly in those areas most proper to adult education. Recent attempts by this group to improve courses commonly taught in graduate programs seem to be a move in the right direction, but if the field is in rapid development constant updating is needed. Even (1975), for example, has suggested that the field is moving out of a stage where all training in adult education was in-service to a time when significant numbers are seeking preservice training. Rossman and Bunning (1978, p. 153), in their analysis of knowledge and skills needed by the adult educator, recommend that in training we distinguish between "those who are professional educators who control, direct, evaluate, provide leadership, and enhance the adult education process, and . . . those who are facilitators of the process because of expertise in any given area." Professors of adult education are certainly not the sole trainers in the field, but they do have a major responsibility for the development of the profession.

Two issues that have arisen in other fields of continuing professional education may haunt adult educators during the 1980s. If adult education is to become a profession, it must find some answer to the question of licensure or certification which will promote career opportunities for competent adult educators yet not violate the very notion of continuing or lifelong education. No longer can we afford to have each entrant to the field discover the common principles and procedures of adult education anew. The second issue is that of mandatory education for continuing educators. Of all professions, this group should have the expertise to develop and implement new and effective systems for continued development.

The recommendation of the National Advisory Council on Adult Education (1977, p. 28) that funding burdens must be shared by federal, state, and local sources is also relevant to efforts

at communication and public relations. As long as major portions
of adult education activities are directed toward noncaptive audiences, excellence of programming will remain the major means of
promoting continuing education. Such excellence calls for continuous responsiveness to local needs and interests. Restrictions placed
on the use of federal funds tend to stifle such local responsiveness
and thus must be deliberately written so as to encourage creativity
yet respect regional and national priorities.

Conclusion

In looking at national bodies of adult education in various
countries, James (1974), secretary of the New Zealand National
Council of Adult Education, concludes that they fall into two
groups. One tends to be funded substantially by the national government. Staffs tend to be large and to be heavily involved in the
teaching and administration of programs. In general, the major
emphasis of such bodies is on building many programs and not on
training, research, development, interagency communication, or
public advocacy. The second type is more likely to be found in
developed countries with long involvement in adult education and
a multitude of agencies providing it. Usually it takes the form of a
national association which links together those who do the actual
programming. It is nongovernmental and is characterized by
limited funding and staffing, by efforts to communicate about
adult education and thus influence policy formation, and by an
interest in quality as well as quantity education. These comments
provide an international perspective to the questions we have been
considering: Should the federal government be given the major
leadership role in adult education? The answer is "no."

The national leadership role belongs in the hands of the
professional in the field and should be exercised through the
agencies and organizations with which he is associated and especially through his professional organizations. This is consistent with
the history of the adult education movement in the United States,
which indicates that the major accomplishments have come from
individuals who harnessed the powers of their agencies to serve the
pressing needs of society. To enhance the practice of such leader-

ship, major efforts are needed to improve professional organizations, involvement in policy formation, communications among ourselves and with others, and the preparation and continued education of adult educators.

If we are to be called professional adult educators, we cannot ask the federal government or anyone else to do the job for us—or it will no longer be our job. As Gardner (1961, p. 161) has declared: "Free men must set their own goals. There is no one to tell them what to do; they must do it for themselves. They must be quick to apprehend the kinds of effort and performance their society needs, and they must demand that kind of effort and performance of themselves and of their fellows."

Chapter Twelve

Adult Education: Issues of the Future

Roger W. Boshier

Adult education, as a social science discipline and field of practice, has traditionally reflected changing social and cultural conditions. Predicting the future of this field involves a dilemma: all knowledge is about the past, but all decisions are about the future. In adult education and elsewhere, the past has been a reasonably certain guide to the future. Although planning predicated on the past has yielded useful concepts and processes, the past is no longer a useful guide to the present and a distinctly uncertain guide to the future, because the planet Earth is becoming transformed from an industrial era to a state of planetary awareness characterized by equilibrium, an ecological ethos, and humanistic values.

The body of knowledge which invites us to conclude that assumptions guiding future functions of adult education may be different from those guiding contemporary purposes and processes is variously referred to as futures research, futuristics, futuribles, prognostics, and futurology. According to Joseph (1974), the future can be divided into five periods, over which humankind has varying degrees of control: (1) now—the immediate future (one year from now), which is frozen and largely dictated by the past and largely uncontrollable; (2) the near or short-term future (one to five years), which can be partially controlled because decisions made today can cause major shifts in this time frame; (3) the middle-range futures (five to twenty years), which are almost completely controllable and decidable today; (4) the long-range futures (twenty to fifty years), where many alternative opportunities are visible but largely uncontrollable from today; and (5) the far futures (fifty years and beyond), which are largely invisible and uncontrollable. Futures research usually involves the study of social, political, psychological, and technological environments far enough into the future to be beyond the range of normal projection tools.

Purposes of Adult Education

The purposes of adult education are best represented on two axes which lie in an orthogonal relationship to each other (Figure 1). These axes allow portrayal of the extent to which an adult education institution or activity is learner centered or societal

Figure 1.   Model Showing Desired and Likely Functions of Adult Education in the Future

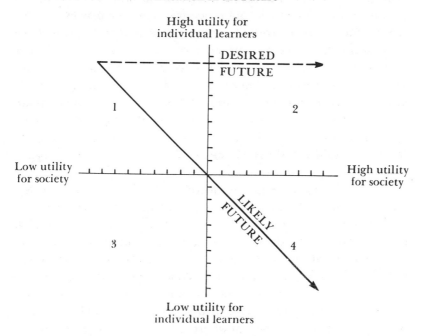

High utility for
individual learners

DESIRED
FUTURE

1   2

Low utility
for society

High utility
for society

LIKELY
FUTURE

3   4

Low utility for
individual learners

centered. Examples of adult education activities which fall within each of the quadrants shown in Figure 1 illustrate the utility of this model. Adult education fulfilling functions in Quadrant 1 has high and direct utility for individual learners but low utility for society. Craft, hobby, and personal development classes, such as those offered in many university extension programs, would be examples from this quadrant. They facilitate the self-actualization and development of the individual learner but yield only marginal or indirect social benefits. An example in Quadrant 2 would be the community education and action programs promulgated by Freire (1970). These programs fulfill functions having high utility for both individual learners and society as a whole. Examples of adult education falling in Quadrant 3 would be some of the programs conducted by "foreigners" in Third World countries. For example, during the heyday of colonialism, West Africans were provided with reading books describing the adventures of a middle-class white boy visiting the seaside at Sussex. This education had low

utility for African learners and for African society. Functions
falling in Quadrant 4 are exemplified by wartime educational programs. Armed forces education programs are not usually keyed to
the satisfaction of individual learner needs. Although the fortunes
of armed forces personnel in wartime are bound up with those of
society, their needs take second place to more macroscopic and
urgent societal considerations. Another example of Quadrant 4
adult education would be programs designed to facilitate recycling
of resources and "waste." Ultimately, these programs will satisfy
learner needs, but the short-term focus will be on programs with
high social utility. Individual needs will be subsumed below societal
needs.

     Adult education in the future will have high utility for both
individual learners and society, but, because of perils associated
with biospheric disequilibrium and transformation to a postindustrial society, the needs of collectivities (communities, societies, nations, the global family of nations) could come to transcend those of
individuals in the middle-range future. The anticipated shift in
the functions fulfilled by adult education in the Western world is
shown in Figure 2. The radical learner centeredness of the present
will be replaced by a situation where adult education programming
is more geared to the satisfaction of societal and global needs for
the attainment and maintenance of biospheric equilibrium. Instead
of individual needs "pressing" outward, the needs of collectivities
will press inward. In this press, democratic government and individual freedom could be eroded. Certainly the freedom to exploit
natural resources for private profit—in the manner of unfettered
capitalism—will disappear. There is also a danger that in times of
extreme distress and social chaos governments will fall into the
hands of reckless elements who threaten other governments with
attack because of the scramble for vanishing resources. Learner
centeredness is a luxury of affluence that may not endure much
longer. The situation is reminiscent of earlier times, when adult
educators had to reeducate large numbers of people. Examples are
the second-language training which followed the flow of Hun-
garians to host countries after the 1956 revolt, the training of
soldiers in wartime, the current need for second-language training
in Quebec, and the retraining of the entire populations of Australia

Figure 2.   Future Adult Education Need Levels

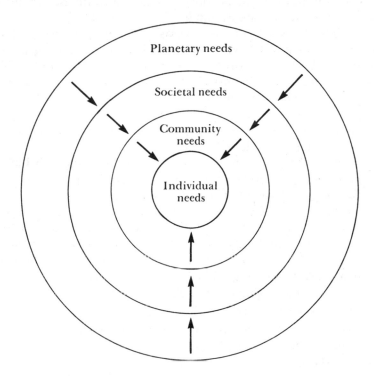

and New Zealand when they abandoned pounds, shillings, and pence and adopted a decimal currency system. Unlike these examples, future problems will be matters of life and death for the planet. The major difference between earlier examples and the future is the fact that biospheric disequilibrium is global, international, and the source of disaster more grave than anything faced before.

The following scenario is not meant to be predictive, but the hypothetical constructions employed are intended to be plausible and internally consistent and are designed to reflect certain implicit and explicit assumptions. The scenario is not embedded in one nation. Neither is it exhaustive. It does not contain all possibilities which flow from recognition that the planet is in transformation.

The scenario is moderate. Spectacular developments of the type envisaged in the "learning pill" (whereby, according to current research, it may become possible to "teach" an adult by administering a pill) are deliberately omitted.

The scenario outlines events pertaining to the purposes of and issues in adult education which occurred during periods described by Joseph (1974) as the near, short-term, and middle-range future (one to twenty years). The scenario assumes the existence of the following conditions:

1. A decrease in birthrates and attainment of zero population growth in the developed world.
2. A broadening definition of adult education and global acceptance and promotion of lifelong education as a master concept for the development of education systems.
3. Recognition of the finite nature of planetary resources and the worldwide acceptance of biospheric equilibrium as a fundamental principle guiding social, political, and economic behaviors.
4. Worldwide acceptance of the fact that learning occurs in a broad array of settings, of which the school is only one.
5. Continued development of both high- and low-technology information systems.
6. An absence of catastrophic events such as global nuclear war.
7. Maintenance or balkanization of existing nations and national boundaries.

A Scenario of Adult Education: 1982–1992

Extract from *Lifelong Learning: The Adult Years,*
September 1982

The fourth World Conference on Adult Education (on the theme "Education for Transformation") was held in Paris this month. About one third of the 900 governmental representatives and delegates from NGOs (nongovernmental organizations) were from Asia, Africa, and Latin America; another third were from Eastern and Western Europe; and the remaining third were from Australasia and North America. In his opening address, the director-general of UNESCO observed that since the third World Conference held in Tokyo almost ten years ago many nations have adopted lifelong education as a master concept. These last ten years, he said, have clearly demonstrated the need to provide education for the stubborn, ill-informed, selfish, and irresponsible people who still do not perceive the planet in global terms.

A spokesman for the Commission on Learner-Centered Adult Education revealed that in almost all the developed countries political authorities have begun to hasten withdrawal of support for hobby- and leisure-oriented adult education activities. Resources previously assigned to these activities are now largely devoted to the development of education linked to national goals. The British and Canadian delegations deplored this withdrawal of support as eroding the traditional purposes of adult education. Third World delegates were less perturbed.

The Commission on Adult Education Knowledge Creation, composed of adult education professors and scholars from disciplines represented in the national Lifelong Learning Consortiums, met for three days prior to the main conference. The major issue concerned uneasy relationships between knowledge producers and practitioners in the field of adult education. North American delegates said that, of the thirty-two graduate schools in Canada and the United States, only four or five are producing scholars whose research can be used by practitioners to meet the learning needs of individuals, their communities, and the planet. Delegates traced the problem back to the 1970s, when many universities—under pressure from the field of adult education—abandoned traditional functions in favor of community service. This so-called "service," they noted, was often trivial and designed to satisfy individual learner needs only marginally related to more macroscopic social and international problems. Several delegates applauded the fact that other groups and scholars have perceived the need to create knowledge about adult education and are stepping into the vacuum. Many delegates also applauded establishment last year of the *International Journal of Lifelong Learning and Adult Education,* which has published important materials on the conceptual foundations of adult education, educational responses to biospheric disequilibrium, and reviews of educational systems that harness the energies of existing social networks.

At the main conference, delegates discussed the government-inspired training programs in adult basic education, special education, and gerontology and listened with interest as delegates from Australia, Canada, and Botswana described pilot programs in environmental systems education.

Delegates listed the following as research priorities: the development of concepts to unify the dispersed field of adult education and all the disparate elements encompassed through adoption of lifelong education; the development and testing of strategies to ensure equal access to informal opportunities for learning; research into models appropriate for the training of adult educators working in formal and nonformal settings; research and development of systems for diffusing knowledge about adult education to field practitioners who cannot afford or do not want to engage in the academic study of adult education in university settings; research into the social, psychological, and economic benefits of paid educational leave; research and development of continuing education programs for elected and appointed officials in the highest parliaments and the lowest village council; continuation of research and development of strategies to eliminate illiteracy (which delegates saw as a major impediment to transformation into a postindustrial society); research and development of strategies to foster self-directed learning; research and development of "appropriate" or frugal technologies that can be employed for environmental systems education in all countries of the world; and comparative research which tests the cross-cultural generality of adult education methods, techniques, and devices.

Convergence, Newsline Supplement, Fall 1984

Passage of the Lifelong Learning Act in the United States and the Education Amendment Acts in Australia, New Zealand, Canada, and Britain, which established lifelong learning as the master concept for the development of educational systems, has resulted in vigorous arguments in national adult education associations. At the annual meeting of the Commission of Professors of Adult Education, held in conjunction with the conference of the Adult Education Association of the U.S.A. in Los Angeles earlier this year, it was contended that adult education is being taken over by elementary and high school teachers who have been laid off by the shortage of children in North America. One group from the Northeastern Self-Directed Learning Institute said that adult education should welcome all comers and that removal of artificial barriers between segments of the educational system will increase our ability to meet problems associated with biospheric disequilibrium. This group also argued that the issue of andragogy (now defined as the art and science of helping people learn) versus pedagogy is outmoded. A group of professors and graduate students from the Pacific Northwest argued that adult education must be considered within the context of lifelong learning. Back in 1977–1979, they noted, governments passed lifelong learning legislation, and some adults were induced to return to classes taught by teachers with blackboards and chalk. Although this was hailed as a breakthrough—illustrating lifelong learning and the erosion of the generation gap—most people now agree that it was not adult education at all but youth education for adults. According to the Northwest group, who largely hail from the Pacific Northwest Institute for Equilibrious Education, the problems facing the planet make it imperative that redundant elementary and secondary school teachers be retrained to work in adult education.

A spokesman for the Temporary System for Laid-Off Teachers said that teachers realize their need for retraining in adult education concepts and processes. However, since passage of the 1982 Informal Learning Opportunities Act, most of the desired information can be obtained through the ERIC interactive training systems. The spokesman, Dr. Harold Stellars, said that more than 150 adult education packages are being added to the system each year and that redundant teachers in urban areas with cable television have unrestricted access to the ERIC system. Twenty-eight core competencies can be obtained for only seventeen educredits. Stellars sounded conciliatory, but a sour note was struck when he rebuked the professors' organization for continuing to characterize elementary and secondary education as detached from the realities of life in the 1980s. During the 1970s, he said, adult educators and their organizations had been at the forefront of efforts to change the functions of elementary and secondary education. As a result, preadult education has changed from an "empty vessel" model (wherein children were filled up with knowledge that would be obsolete within a few years) to a "self-directed learning" model. Most preadult educators are now educating children and adolescents to become self-directed learners. In this way, they are developing positive attitudes toward learning, information seeking, and the technology of education and will be well equipped to assist campaigns for equilibrium. Toward the end of the speech, some UCLA graduate students jeered when Stellars suggested that preadult educators practice better principles of adult education than adult educators do. This issue clearly remains unresolved and will almost certainly be raised at the 1985 Annual Meeting.

UNESCO Notes & News, Issue 26, 1985
(Microdot file 4634/85)

In his annual televised address to people on six continents, the director-general of UNESCO deplored the loss of the Biospheric Systems Educational Resource Center. Earlier this year, the center was destroyed in circumstances that the Decentralist Party (DP) said pointed to the "captains of industry" who still resist calls to "clean up" their corporate consciousness. (The Decentralist Party opposes industrialism and advocates political and economic de-centralization at every level.) The president of the American Businessmen's Association described this as malicious gossip and said that an overwhelming majority of his members had supported the work of the center.

Prior to its destruction, the center—located on the Hudson River in New York and connected by satellite-mediated computer links with cable television systems in forty-two countries—had con-tained 28,543 educational packages. Citizens in the forty-two countries could gain unrestricted access to any educational package by using the "mediated selector" switch on their television sets or, in some countries, videophones. Each learner could interact with the package selected by employing any configuration of key words which could be scrutinized by dialing 999 on the selector.

The center opened in 1984 and was nicknamed the George Orwell thinktank by the president of Trans-World Consolidated Copper Ltd., who said it would threaten the company's operations in countries like Chile, Indonesia, and Somalia. It operated for thirteen months and in that period delivered programs to and interacted with 28 million citizens of the planet. The most popular packages requested by learners in Latin America, Africa, and Asia were those on "Finding and Maintaining Clean Water," "Emergency Housing," "Birth Control," "Solar Systems," "Crop Rotation," and "Parenting." Packages most frequently requested by learners in North America were entitled "The Side Effects of Jogging," "Solar Energy Installations," "Organizing for Environmental Action," "Preparing for Paid Educational Leave," "Alternatives to the Motor Vehicle," "Intimate Networks," "Interpersonal Characteristics Necessary for Temporary Systems," "Understanding Your Environmental Tax Laws," "Your Rights as a Victim of Crime," "The Transcendence of Interplanetary Travel," and "A Register of Opportunities for Learning."

Although some developed countries have yet to acquire cable television, the staff of the Criterion-Referenced Evaluation Unit said that the objectives set for the first year have all been met. The director-general thanked the translation staff for work done during installation of the packages and said that their skills will be needed when the center is reestablished in accord with the findings of the Commission on the Year 2050, which recommended decentralization of systems for transformation education. In a recent teleconference, the ministers of education and ministers of the environment and environmental systems informally agreed to adopt these recommendations. There will now be a delay of about four weeks while the implications of these changes are fed back and tested on the citizenry around the world. In Canada and the United States, the Cybernated Control Systems—originally set up to facilitate electronic voting on issues before Parliament or the House of Representatives—will be used to solicit feedback concerning the future of the Biospheric Systems Education Resource Center.

In a report issued to adult educators last week (available on home television by dialing MS 43562/23/1985/UNESCO), the director-general said that most developed countries have followed the lead of Australia and lowered the school-leaving age to 14 years. As a result, a great number of malcontents and others who prefer "open" learning or a sojourn in the work force have left secondary schools. Many are now gainfully employed, but a significant number have resumed learning through opportunities available under the various Informal Learning Opportunities Acts of member countries. Of those who have opted back into some form of learning, approximately 30 percent have returned to institutionally based education and 70 percent have chosen one of the mediated self-learning systems. With the proliferation of informal noninstitutional opportunities for learning and the continuing growth of community colleges and community learning centers (which in most countries are funded through the various ministries of education) there are now hundreds of new opportunities for learning.

In several countries, the arrival of thousands of out-of-school youth on the labor market brought a sudden increase in unemployment rates, but these were offset in Canada, the United States, and Australasia by widespread application of the paid educational leave (PEL) regulations gazetted last year. Employers pay 50 percent of the costs associated with PEL; the other 50 percent comes from government sources, who this year slashed defense budgets to help pay for PEL and other new "social contract" policies. A research study coordinated by the Adult Education Research Center at the University of British Columbia shows that for each dollar invested in PEL the employer receives in return a benefit equivalent to $4.25. Workers receiving PEL for nonwork-related learning showed improvements in the workplace equivalent to those manifested by employees engaged in work-related learning during PEL. Although automation has now eliminated many menial jobs, the existence of PEL for blue-collar workers has also created job opportunities for many out-of-school youth.

Elsewhere in the UNESCO report are descriptions of temporary systems created to deal with food shortages and pollution. In British Columbia, the government has created an oil spill clean-up group employing resources provided by oil and chemical companies, shippers, the federal agency Environment Canada, the Department of Corrections, the Out-of-School Youth Temporary System, police and harbor board authorities, and lumber companies. Each year, 800 tankers are navigating the waterways on the west coast of the United States and Canada; since the opening of the Alaska pipeline in 1977, there have been about six major spills per year. The Oil Spill Temporary System has issued a report saying that the situation should change toward the end of the decade, when widespread application of solar and wind technologies will decrease dependence on Alaskan and imported oil. In the meantime, the system continues to employ closed circuit television systems of coastal communities to educate people about how to behave in a spill. A severe test occurred last year, when the *Hercules Maru* foundered in the Straits of Juan de Fuca and spread a ten-inch slick of bunker oil across almost the entire British Columbia and Northern Washington coastlines. The government has been unable to obtain compensation or clean-up costs from the *Hercules Maru* owner, a paper company registered in Liberia. About half of the now unemployed salmon fishermen are being retrained at British Columbia community colleges for entry into the Alberta Food Diversification Program. But about 50 percent of the fishermen refuse to budge from British Columbia, and many are threatening violence against the owner of the *Hercules Maru*.

Newsletter of the Commission of Professors of
Adult Education, Spring 1986

This year the Adult Education Research Conference (AERC) breakaway group attracted more papers and participants than the "main" conference. The convenors of the main conference have now asked the leader of the alternative group to present the keynote address at the 1987 AERC.

When the breakaway group first met separately (in 1984), they heard twenty-eight papers that reported research conducted within multivariate paradigms. In 1983 the alternative group had held a symposium whose members contended that single-variable adult education research fails to represent reality and cannot capture the system qualities of most adult education phenomena. In the 1960s, adult education research consisted mainly of clientele or participation surveys that were rarely subjected to multivariate analysis. The same trend appeared in the 1970s, although at the 1977 AERC there had been a call for research within multivariate paradigms. Because adult educators are now more involved in research and development of strategies to facilitate transformation to an equilibrious society, researchers are aware of system qualities. Researchers born after 1960 who received a university education after 1980 are aware of the need for multivariate paradigms because they took compulsory courses such as "Environmental Systems," "Ecological Foundations of Planetary Transformation," "Futures 2050," and "The Interactive Nature of the Human Prospect."

Most of those presenting papers at this year's conference of the alternative AERC are recent graduates of adult education departments. Typical of the papers presented are "A Frugal Strategy for Literacy Education in Africa and Urban North America," "A Multivariate Analysis of Variables Influencing Adoption of the General Electric Home Solar Heating Unit," "Program Planning and Cybernation: A Systemic Analysis," "Adult Education Networks in the Rural Communities of the Slocan Valley: A Path Analysis," "Problems of Cybernation in Teleconferencing," "A Multivariate Paradigm for Evaluating Ripple Effects Associated with Dial-Phone Systems in West Africa," "The Effects of a Continuing Education Program on the Adoption of Wind Power Technologies Among the Farm Groups of South Dakota, Northern Vermont, Central Australia, and Northern Saskatchewan," and "The OISE Inner-Space Project: A Cosmic Voyage."

During the 1960s and 1970s, papers offered at AERC were largely concerned with aspects of program planning and instruction and various problems associated with what used to be known as ABE (adult basic education). The papers often dealt with institutional or administrative matters of local interest but with no major import for the rest of the field. It was rare for a paper to concern a concept or process that devolved from the need to transform to a postindustrial society, although papers on development of informal learning opportunities given earlier in this decade were perhaps congruent with transformation. This year, about half of the papers at the main conference and nearly all the papers at the alternative conference are directly tied to problems associated with transformation. When we met for the Vancouver AERC of 1980, who would have guessed that six years later there would be papers describing applications of adult education to problems associated with adoption of solar energy, wind power, personal transit systems, intimate networks, resource use, citizen participation, cybernation, home computing, altered states of consciousness, and the new frugal technologies? Who would have suspected that theory building and model development would account for such a major share of the space here? Would we have suspected that our paradigms would allow for broad and unified views of human experience which generate papers with titles that refer to "psychic consciousness," "imagery," and "transcendentalism"?

Extract from the *Sydney Morning Herald*,
August 27, 1988 (Microfiche Edition 8754/88)

The Solar Energy Education Project (SEEP)—established by the President of the United States; the Prime Ministers of Canada, Australia, and New Zealand; and representatives of most African and Latin American nations—today announced that the devastating Northern Hemisphere winter of last year has caused the project's members to speed up plans.

Addressing the project's fourth annual meeting, held this week in Sydney, Australia, Jennifer Sunnyford, executive director of the Adult Education Association of the United States and co-director of the Solar Energy Education Project, said that three events had caused a change in priorities. The first was the devastating winter of 1987, when Hydro-Quebec saved hundreds of thousands of residents in the northeastern United States from a freezing death. The second was the obliteration and irradiation of Portland, Oregon, by the explosion of the Trojan nuclear power plant last year. The third was the fact that the Greenpeace Foundation and fishermen on the west coast of Canada had effectively stalled all west coast oil tanker traffic after the 66 major and 288 minor spills following the opening of the Alaska pipeline.

Ms. Sunnyford said that all homeowners in North America will receive free instruction in the installation, operation, and maintenance of solar units under provisions of the 1982 Informal Learning Opportunities Act. In Australia the program will be operated under the aegis of the Lifelong Learning Act. Although instruction will be free, most governments have agreed to monitor the program by employing resources developed under the various Educredit Acts passed in most countries between 1978 and 1985. In Canada educredits are issued annually on March 1, along with the free Air Canada travel vouchers (originally issued in 1981 to encourage Canadians to vacation in their own country), and are credited to each individual's social insurance number. In the United States one hundred educredits are issued each January 1 and credited to each person's social security number. Governments will encourage participation in the Solar Energy Education Project by offering each participant fifty additional educredits if the learner can provide evidence of having manifested all ten competencies developed for the program. This administrative aspect was criticized at a recent meeting of the International Commission of Professors of Adult Education. Although the professors applauded the use of educredits as reinforcers for participation in the program, they contend that it will have greatest appeal to the upper socioeconomic groups and that those who most need the solar systems will remain untouched. They also contend that educredits will do little to erode the opposition of the power utility companies, who dislike the program because it destroys their monopoly on the generation and distribution of energy. As the director of Fossil Fuel Systems Ltd. said, "The trouble with the sun is that it is free and worldwide."

Extract from the International
Adult Education Infoservice Newsletter,
September 21, 1990

The fifth World Conference on Adult Education was held in Saudi Arabia last week. The conference was attended by nine hundred delegates from around the world. The theme was "Cybernation of Adult Education Processes." Opening the conference, the coordinator of the La Jolla Institute for Decentralized Interactive Education Systems said that the present theme can be traced back to the 1980s, when most organizations abandoned hierarchical models because they impede the upward and downward flow of information. In reviewing the history of cybernation, the team leader, William P. Schumacher, said that hierarchical organizations were appropriate for tackling the tasks of the industrial era; however, as infotechnology has grown more complex, the giant linear bureaucracies in both government and the private sector have grown increasingly dysfunctional.

Reviewing the functions fulfilled by adult education since the third World Conference, Schumacher noted that adult education is now meeting a broad array of societal, planetary, and learner needs. In the late 1970s and early 1980s, however, there was a yawning gap between the espousal of democratic rhetoric concerning adult education processes and what actually happened in the field. For example, said Schumacher, although democratization emerged as a major theme of the Montreal, Tokyo, and Paris world conferences, cybernetic systems were actually installed only in the developed and OPEC countries. In the 1960s and 1970s, democratization suggested two things: the removal of barriers that impede access to adult education, and the involvement of learners in the design and management of their own learning experiences. Many of the barriers to learning have been removed through the proliferation of informal opportunities for learning. But learners still are not fully involved in the design and management of their learning experiences. Although mandatory continuing education is now well established in most countries, it has been resisted in places where cybernation systems are inadequate.

Infoservice Supplement to Microdot Edition of
Canadian Journal of Adult Education,
September 1992

At a joint meeting of the Canadian Association for University Continuing Education and the National University Continuing Education Association of the United States (successor to the National University Extension Association), it was revealed that the continuing education function of the university now attracts more than 70 percent of university resources. In opening the joint conference, held in Antigonish, Nova Scotia, the president of McGill University said that university continuing education has "truly come of age" and is now assigned high priority along with research and teaching. The decline in internal student numbers during the 1980s was only partly offset by the arrival of the children of the persons born during or after World War II. As a result, continuing educators have moved from old houses on the fringes of the university to the heart of the university. The retraining of former graduates now constitutes the bulk of the work. Despite pressure created by recent disasters and crises, the traditional functions are also still prominent in the continuing education operation.

During discussion that followed the opening address (which was recorded and can be seen by dialing 5678654 OE/AG of the MS Selector on home television), the coordinator of the Temporary System for Adult Education Retraining at the University of Southern California said that the proliferation of informal opportunities for learning has created an enormous need to retrain adult education facilitators and temporary system coordinators. In the current drive for biospheric equilibrium, the education of professionals in services such as health, pollution monitoring and control, cybernetic systems, infotechnology systems, rapid transit, and solar space projects has been emphasized. In this press, the learning needs of adult educators have sometimes been overlooked. Although they can avail themselves of informal opportunities for learning, they are inclined to overlook their own needs for education. This training should involve more than a few short courses and interactive packages mounted in the Educational Resources Information Center (ERIC) or similar cybernated systems. The definition of adult education has grown broad and now encompasses people engaged in the Intergalactic Space Travel Project, the trainers from the various equilibrious systems institutes, and those from university continuing education, the voluntary associations, and the business and decentralized industry systems. It is again necessary to attempt a classification of adult education concepts and processes.

The vice-chancellor of Sydney University, himself a former director of continuing education, said that the present place of the continuing education function in the university can be traced to the willingness of universities to expand the academic study of adult education significantly during the early 1980s, when it became obvious that the need for primary and secondary educators was diminishing. By 1985, he said, every major university in the developed world had some form of adult education department, and before 1989 most of the major learning institutes in the lifelong education systems of Africa, Asia, and Latin America had established the academic study of adult education. In the mid 1980s, academics in Australia had fought back when adult educators in the field accused them of detachment from the reality of education for equilibrium. The situation was partly ameliorated when field-based adult educators were employed in temporary systems attached to the university departments. At first this led to a slight lowering of academic standards, which the Australian Criterion-Referenced Evaluation Unit said was a source of concern; but these problems have now been overcome with a constant interchange of academics and field people. Indeed, during the five-year Nullabor Plains Antifamine Project, academics from the Sydney University adult education department spent most of their time in the field or at computer and videophone consoles associated with the project. Similar patterns were revealed during the Saskatchewan Foodbowl Diversification Project, the Arizona Hot Climate Agricultural Project, and the Decentralized Farm Projects of British Columbia, Vermont, and New Hampshire.

The vice-chancellor also said that university continuing education has been both enhanced and inhibited by the abolition of additional stipends for continuing education teaching (now an archaic word). "Although continuing education 'teaching' has been a requirement associated with all university appointments in Canada, the United States, Britain, and Australasia since around 1986, it took several years for this function to be accepted by all university staff members. It has enhanced our ability to offer a broad range of courses, but since 1984 we have been faced with the problem of training university staffs. Although university continuing education is now a central component of national lifelong education systems, some professors still fail to realize that adults are not the same as the adolescents they taught in the 1970s and early 1980s. The dramatic rise in the mean age of university students observed worldwide in the 1980s was partial preparation for the present. Fortunately, most universities had overcome the problem through effective utilization of resources in their various graduate schools of adult education, through programmed instruction modules delivered on computer monitors found in most faculty offices,

and through provision of refreshment learning activities for professors on paid educational leave."

During the second part of this meeting, there was a teleconference involving participants in western Canada, the south-
western United States, Great Britain, and France. A highlight was
presentation of a report on lifelong education credentialing, which
is still controversial and did not win full acceptance. The gist of the
report is the fact that several major Canadian and United States
universities have stopped awarding conventional bachelor's and
master's degrees and have created a system whereby graduates
undertake recurrent education throughout their lives. The degree
is finally awarded at the end of the person's professional life. Thus,
a physician or a lawyer attends university for an initial three-year
period. With the sophisticated learning systems we have today, he
can acquire sufficient minimal knowledge to begin practicing after
three years. After two years in the field, the candidate returns
for one year of continuing education, returns to the field for another three years, and so on throughout life. At the end of the
initial three-year period, an interim certificate is issued. These continuing education universities have become very popular in the last
seven years and in provinces and states with sophisticated PEL
regulations appear to be working well. Research conducted at the
University of Alberta suggests that clients of persons attending
these universities feel safer and manifest higher levels of trust and
confidence in their physician, lawyer, and accountant than clients
served by persons with traditional degrees.

Candidates who move away from the university catchment
area continue their education and thus maintain professional
standing at other continuing education universities or through interaction with the self-learning packages available on home television or in learning centers. The system is competency based. The
objectives are revised constantly and make extensive use of feedback from the various fields of practice.

Conclusion

This scenario is only a partial attempt to describe potential
futures for and issues in adult education. If some ideas seem fanci-
ful and the time frame too compressed, it should be remembered
that the time lag between invention and application is diminishing.

Whereas 112 years separated the discovery and application of photography principles, only two years separated the discovery and widespread application of solar batteries.

From one perspective, this entire volume is about issues of the future. Although some previous chapters discuss mundane issues which in the future will be mere memories of times past, they all point to a need for future adult educators to take a more active and less reactive stance than at present. This chapter has highlighted a need to facilitate interventions which can be employed to divert individuals, communities, nations, and the planet from catastrophe. Although adult educators will not shoulder the entire burden of saving the planet, they will be at the center of attempts to avert catastrophe and will thus be more future oriented than at present. Any scenario for the future of adult education will not be actualized if adult educators continue the overreactive posture which currently characterizes their concepts and operations. In the future, adult education will be less reactive to sometimes trivial needs of the present; will manifest positive attitudes to research, particularly that conducted within multivariate paradigms which reflect system qualities; and will face an obligation to produce well-tested strategies to modify the attitudes and behaviors of tens of millions of adults all over the planet.

H. G. Wells once asserted that civilization is in a race between education and catastrophe. Although he may have overestimated the potential impact of education, it appears that the planet is on a life-threatening trajectory. If adult education cannot meet the challenges of the future and there continue to be lengthy delays between the onset of problems and the research and development of suitable solutions, the imposition of radical coercive strategies becomes likely. Adult educators must become connected to the realities of life in their communities, nations, and the planet. They should become more accountable, imaginative, future oriented, research oriented, risk taking, and willing to confront a future that is no longer an extension of the present. Educators cannot passively await the arrival of the future. Adult education is a powerful instrument to help shape the future. Although powerful forces threaten existence, planning horizons contain an array of desirable possibilities. In this context, every adult educator is an architect of the future.

References

Adler, M. *Modern Philosophies and Education*. Chicago: National Society for the Study of Education, 1955.

Adult Performance Level Study. Austin: APL Project Staff, University of Texas, 1973.

Aker, G. F. *Criteria for Evaluating Graduate Study in Adult Education*. Chicago: Center for Continuing Education, University of Chicago, 1963.

Aker, G. F. "Teacher Certification in Adult Education." In B. R. Lyle (Ed.), *Teacher Certification in Adult Education*. Austin, Tex.: Health, Education and Welfare Region VI Staff Development Project, 1975.

Angel, J. L. *Directory of Occupational Licensing in the United States*. New York: World Trade Academy Press, 1970.

Apps, J. W. *Toward a Working Philosophy of Adult Education*. Syracuse, N.Y.: Syracuse University Publications in Continuing Education, 1973.

Apps, J. W. "A Foundation for Action." In C. Klevins (Ed.), *Materials and Methods in Continuing Education*. New York: Klevins Publications, 1976.

Aspy, D. N. *Toward a Technology for Humanizing Education*. Champaign, Ill.: Research Press, 1972.

Bahm, A. J. "Science Is Not Value Free." *Policy Sciences*, 1971, *2*, 391–396.

Banathy, B. H. *Instructional Systems*. Belmont, Calif.: Fearon, 1968.

Bandura, A. *Principles of Behavior Modification*. New York: Holt, Rinehart and Winston, 1969.

Bandura, A., and Walters, R. P. *Social Learning and Personality Development*. New York: Holt, Rinehart and Winston, 1962.

Barron, W. E., and Kelso, C. R. *Adult Functional Competency: A Summary*. Austin: Extension Division, University of Texas, 1975.

Beale, C. L. *The Revival of Population Growth in Non-metropolitan America*. Washington, D.C.: Economic Development Division, Economic Research Service, U.S. Department of Agriculture, 1975.

Beck, C. *Educational Philosophy and Theory*. Boston: Little, Brown, 1974.

Becker, G. *Human Capital*. New York: National Bureau of Economic Research, 1964.

Benne, K. D. *Education for Tragedy: Essays in Disenchanted Hope for Modern Man*. Lexington: University of Kentucky Press, 1967.

Benne, K. D. "Technology and Community: Conflicting Bases of Educational Authority." In W. Feinberg and H. Rosemont (Eds.), *Work, Technology, and Education*. Urbana: University of Illinois Press, 1973.

Bennet, C. "Up the Hierarchy—A Staircase of Measuring Extension's Impact." *Journal of Education*, 1975, *13*, 7–12.

Berdahl, R. O. *Statewide Coordination of Higher Education*. Washington, D.C.: American Council on Education, 1971.

Bergevin, P. *A Philosophy for Adult Education*. New York: Seabury Press, 1967.

Best, F., and Stern, B. *Lifetime Distribution of Education, Work, and Leisure: Research, Speculations, and Policy Implications of Changing Life Patterns*. Washington, D.C.: Institute for Educational Leadership, George Washington University, 1976.

Biddle, W., and Biddle, L. J. *The Community Development Process*. New York: Holt, Rinehart and Winston, 1965.

Bird, C. *The Case Against College*. New York: Macmillan, 1975.

Blakely, R. J. "What Is Adult Education?" In M. S. Knowles (Ed.), *Handbook of Adult Education in the United States*. Washington, D.C.: Adult Education Association, 1960.

Blakely, R. J. "Conclusion." In A. N. Charters (Ed.), *Toward the Educative Society*. Syracuse, N.Y.: Syracuse University Publications in Continuing Education, 1971.

Blakely, R. J., and Lappin, I. M. *Knowledge Is Power to Control Power: New Institutional Arrangements and Organizational Patterns for Continuing Education*. Syracuse, N.Y.: Syracuse University Publications in Continuing Education, 1969.

Bolton, R. E. "The Economics and Public Financing of Higher Education: An Overview." In *The Economics and Financing of Higher Education in the U.S.* Washington, D.C.: U.S. Government Printing Office, 1969.

Boshier, R. W. "Motivational Orientations of Adult Education Participants: A Factor Analytic Exploration of Houle's Typology." *Adult Education*, 1971, *21* (2), 3–26.

Bradshaw, J. "The Concept of Social Need." *Ekistics*, March 1974, *37*, 184–188.

Brauner, C. J., and Burns, H. W. *Problems in Education and Philosophy*. Englewood Cliffs, N.J.: Prentice-Hall, 1965.

Broschart, J. R. *Lifelong Learning in the Nation's Third Century*. Washington, D.C.: U.S. Government Printing Office, 1976.

Broudy, H. S. "Three Perspectives on Competency-Based Education." In W. R. Houston (Ed.), *Exploring Competency-Based Education*. Berkeley, Calif.: McCutchan, 1974.

Browder, L. H., Jr. (Ed.). *Emerging Patterns of Administrative Accountability*. Berkeley, Calif.: McCutchan, 1971.

Brown, D. M. *Checklist for Humanistic Schools*. Washington, D.C.: Association for Supervision and Curriculum Development, Working Group on Humanistic Education, 1977.

Brown, L. M. *General Philosophy in Education*. New York: McGraw-Hill, 1966.

Bühler, C. *The Course of Human Life*. New York: Springer, 1968.

Bullmer, K. *The Art of Empathy*. New York: Human Sciences Press, 1975.

Callahan, D. "Health and Society: Some Ethical Imperatives." *Daedalus*, 1977, *106* (1), 23–34.

Cameron, C., Rockhill, K., and Wright, J. *Certification: An Examination of the Issue by and for Adult Educators*. Unpublished paper, Task Force on Certification, Commission of Professors of Adult Education, 1976. (Mimeographed.)

Carlson, R. A. *Professionalization of Adult Education: A Growing Issue in North America.* Saskatoon: University of Saskatchewan, 1975. (Mimeographed.)

Carlson, R. A. *Professionalization of Adult Education: A Historical Philosophical Analysis.* Saskatoon: University of Saskatchewan, 1976. (Mimeographed.)

Chamberlain, M. N. "The Competencies of the Adult Educator." *Adult Education,* 1961, *11* (2), 78–83.

Christoffel, P. *Federal Programs Supporting Lifelong Learning.* Washington, D.C.: Institute for Educational Leadership, George Washington University, 1976.

Clark, B. *Adult Education in Transition: A Study of Institutional Insecurity.* Berkeley: University of California Press, 1958.

Clark, W. W., Jr. "Ethical Considerations in the Anthropological Evaluation of Educational Programs." Paper presented at annual meeting of American Educational Research Association, San Francisco, April 1976.

Clegg, D. "Work as a Motivator." *Journal of Extension,* Fall 1963, *1* (3), 141–148.

Coch, L., and French, J. R., Jr. "Overcoming Resistance to Change." *Human Relations,* 1948, *11,* 512–532.

Cohen, H. S., and Miike, L. H. *Developments in Health Manpower Licensure.* Washington, D.C.: U.S. Department of Health, Education and Welfare, June 1973.

College Entrance Examination Board. *Lifelong Learning During Adulthood: An Agenda for Research.* New York: CEEB, 1978.

Committee on Evaluation, Adult Education Association of the U.S.A. *Program Evaluation in Adult Education.* Washington, D.C.: Adult Education Association, 1952.

Comptroller General of the United States. *The Adult Basic Education Program: Progress in Reducing Illiteracy and Improvements Needed.* Report to the Congress. Washington, D.C.: U.S. Office of Education, U.S. Department of Health, Education and Welfare, 1975.

Crabtree, A. "A Call to Action." *Adult Leadership,* May 1973, *22* (1), 2–4, 38–46.

Cross, K. P., Valley, J. R., and Associates. *Planning Non-Traditional Programs: An Analysis of the Issues for Postsecondary Education.* San Francisco: Jossey-Bass, 1974.

Cyphert, F. R., and Gant, W. L. "The Delphi Technique." In E. R. House (Ed.), *School Evaluation: The Politics and the Process.* Berkeley, Calif.: McCutchan, 1973.

Davitz, J., and Davitz, L. *Making It from 40 to 50.* New York: Random House, 1976.

Delker, P. "Governmental Roles in Lifelong Learning." *Journal of Research and Development in Education,* 1974, 7 (4), 24–33.

Derbyshire, R. C. "Relicensure, Mandatory Continuing Education and the State Regulatory Agency." In D. E. Moore, Jr. (Ed.), *Proceedings, Mandatory Continuing Education: Prospects and Dilemmas for Professionals.* Urbana: Office of Continuing Education and Public Service, University of Illinois, 1976.

Derthick, M. *The Influence of Federal Grants.* Cambridge, Mass.: Harvard University Press, 1970.

Derthick, M. *New Towns In-town: Why a Federal Program Failed.* Washington, D.C.: Urban Institute, 1972.

DesChamps, A. "Considerations for the Organization and Administration of Lifelong Education." *Continuous Learning,* 1971, *10* (4–5), 147–159.

Deshler, J. D., Farmer, J. A., Jr., and Sheats, P. H. *Developing Community Services in the Seventies: New Roles for Higher Education.* Sacramento: California Postsecondary Education Commission, 1975.

Dewey, J. *Democracy and Education.* New York: Macmillan, 1920.

Dewey, J. "Theory of Valuation." In *International Encyclopedia of Unified Sciences.* Vol. 2, Issue 4. Chicago: University of Chicago Press, 1939.

Dolinsky, D. "The Student in a Competency-Based Program: Does He Have an Active Role?" In W. R. Houston (Ed.), *Exploring Competency-Based Education.* Berkeley, Calif.: McCutchan, 1974.

Drucker, P. *The Effective Executive.* New York: Harper & Row, 1966.

Drucker, P. *The Age of Discontinuity: Guidelines to Our Changing Society.* New York: Harper & Row, 1969.

Dubin, S. S. "Updating and Mid-Career Development and Change." *Vocational Guidance Quarterly,* Dec. 1974, pp. 152–158.

Duval, M. K. "The Provider, the Government, and the Consumer." *Daedalus,* 1977, *106* (1), 185–190.

Edding, F. "Educational Leave and Sources of Funding." In *Recur-*

rent Education. Washington, D.C.: National Institute of Education, 1974.

Eisner, E. W. "Instructional and Expressive Educational Objectives: Their Formulation and Use in Curriculum." Unpublished paper, 1970.

Eisner, E. W. "The Perceptive Eye: Toward the Reformation of Educational Evaluation." Paper presented at annual meeting of American Educational Research Association, Washington, D.C., 1975.

Elias, J. L., and Merriam, S. *Philosophical Foundations of Adult Education.* Huntington, N.Y.: Krieger, 1980.

Erikson, E. H. *Identity: Youth and Crisis.* New York: Norton, 1968.

Erikson, E. H. "Reflections on Dr. Borg's Life Cycle." *Daedalus,* Spring 1976, *105* (2), 1–28.

Etzioni, A. *The Active Society.* New York: Free Press, 1968.

Even, M. "Trends and Issues in Graduate Programs in Adult Education." Paper presented at meeting of Commission of Professors of Adult Education, Chicago, Nov. 8, 1975.

Farmer, J. A., Jr., Deshler, J. D., and Williams, R. G. *Report on the Chartering Progress.* Sacramento: Chancellor's Office, California Community Colleges, 1974.

Farmer, J. A., Jr., and Knox, A. B. *Alternative Patterns for Strengthening Community Service Programs in Institutions of Higher Education.* Washington, D.C.: Community Service and Continuing Education Program, Bureau of Postsecondary Education, U.S. Office of Education, U.S. Department of Health, Education and Welfare, 1977.

Farmer, J. A., Jr., Sheats, P., and Deshler, J. D. *Developing Community Service and Continuing Education Programs in California Higher Education Institutions.* Sacramento: California Coordinating Council for Higher Education, 1972.

Federal Regional Council, Region II. *Citizen Participation Handbook.* New York: FRC Task Force on Citizen Participation, 1976.

Fenn, N. E. "The Identification of Competencies Pertinent to the Certification of Teachers in Adult Basic Education." Unpublished doctoral dissertation, Florida State University, Tallahassee, 1972.

Ford, D., and Houle, C. O. "Doctorates in Adult Education, 1978." *Adult Education,* 1980, *30* (2), 123–125.

Forest, L. B. "Using Value Types to Identify Need." *Journal of Extension,* Fall 1973, *15,* 24–34.

Forest, L. B. "Accent: The Damn Dog Wouldn't Quit Barking." *Adult Leadership,* 1976, *25* (4), 116.

Forest, L. B., and Marshall, M. G. *Impact of Extension in Shawano County: 1. Conclusions and Implications.* Madison: Division of Program and Staff Development, University of Wisconsin-Extension, 1977.

Frandson, P. E. "Continuing Education of the Professions: Issues, Ethics and Conflicts." Paper presented at meeting of National Association of State Universities and Land-Grant Colleges, July 1976.

Frankena, W. D. "A Model for Analyzing a Philosophy of Education." In J. Park (Ed.), *Selected Readings in the Philosophy of Education.* New York: Macmillan, 1974.

Franklin, R., and Franklin, P. *Tomorrow's Track.* Columbia, Md.: New Community Press, 1976.

Freire, P. *Pedagogy of the Oppressed.* New York: Herder and Herder, 1970.

Gage, N. L. *Teacher Effectiveness and Teacher Education: The Search for a Scientific Basis.* Palo Alto, Calif.: Pacific Books, 1972.

Gagné, R. M. *The Conditions of Learning.* (2nd ed.) New York: Holt, Rinehart and Winston, 1962a.

Gagné, R. M. *Psychological Principles in System Development.* New York: Holt, Rinehart and Winston, 1962b.

Gardner, J. *Excellence.* New York: Harper & Row, 1961.

Geake, R. "Professional Services and Quality." In D. E. Moore, Jr. (Ed.), *Proceedings, Mandatory Continuing Education: Prospects and Dilemmas for Professionals.* Urbana: Office of Continuing Education and Public Service, University of Illinois, 1976.

Glaser, R. (Ed.). *Training Research and Education.* Pittsburgh: University of Pittsburgh Press, 1962.

Grattan, C. H. *In Quest of Knowledge.* New York: Association Press, 1955.

Grattan, C. H. (Ed.). *American Ideas About Adult Education.* New York: Teachers College Press, Columbia University, 1959.

Graubard, S. R. Preface to special issue on adulthood. *Daedalus,* 1976, *105* (2), v–viii.

Graves, W. B. *Intergovernmental Relations.* New York: Scribner's, 1964.

Griffith, W. S. "Adult Educators and Politics." *Adult Education*, Summer 1976, *26* (4), 270–297.

Grigsby, T. "A Study to Develop a Competency-Based Program for the Preparation of Community Education Personnel." Unpublished doctoral dissertation, Oregon State University, Corvallis, 1972.

Grodzins, M. *The American System.* Chicago: Rand McNally, 1966.

Grogan, P. "Education for the Professions with the Help of Continuing Education Unit." In *1974 Proceedings* of meetings of Association for Continuing Higher Education. DeKalb, Ill.: ERIC Clearinghouse in Career Education, 1974.

Hahn, H. (Ed.). *People and Politics in Urban Society.* Beverly Hills, Calif.: Sage, 1972.

Hall, L. "Participatory Research: An Approach for Change." *Convergence*, 1975, *8*, 24–32.

Hallenbeck, W. "The Function and Place of Adult Education in American Society." In M. Knowles (Ed.), *Handbook of Adult Education in the United States.* Washington, D.C.: Adult Education Association, 1960.

Hallenbeck, W. "The Role of Adult Education in Society." In G. Jensen, A. A. Liveright, and W. Hallenbeck (Eds.), *Adult Education: Outlines of an Emerging Field of University Study.* Washington, D.C.: Adult Education Association, 1964.

Hansen, W. L. "Total and Private Rates of Return to Investment in Schooling." *Journal of Political Economy*, April 1963, *70* (1), 128–140.

Hansen, W. L. "The Financial Implications of Student Independence." In *Who Pays? Who Benefits?* New York: College Entrance Examination Board, 1974.

Harman, D. "Illiteracy: An Overview." *Harvard Educational Review*, 1970, *4*, 226–243.

Harrington, F. H. *The Future of Adult Education: New Responsibilities of Colleges and Universities.* San Francisco: Jossey-Bass, 1977.

Havelock, R. *Planning for Innovation.* Ann Arbor: Center for Research on Utilization of Scientific Knowledge, Institute for Social Research, University of Michigan, 1971.

Havighurst, R. J. "Education Through Life Span." *Educational Gerontology*, 1976, *1*, 41–51.

Hefferman-Cabrera, P. "The Potential for Humanistic Endeavor."

In W. R. Houston (Ed.), *Exploring Competency-Based Education.* Berkeley, Calif.: McCutchan, 1974.

Herzberg, F. *Work and the Nature of Man.* New York: World, 1966.

Herzberg, F., Mausner, B., and Snyderman, B. B. *The Motivation of Work.* New York: Wiley, 1959.

Hesburgh, T. M., Miller, P. A., and Wharton, C. R., Jr. *Patterns for Lifelong Learning.* San Francisco: Jossey-Bass, 1973.

Hiemstra, R. *Lifelong Learning.* Lincoln, Neb.: Professional Educators Publications, 1976.

Hill, A. W. "Career Development: Who Is Responsible?" *Training and Development Journal,* May 1976, pp. 14–15.

Hirschman, A. O. *Development Projects Observed.* Washington, D.C.: Brookings Institution, 1967.

Hodgkinson, H. "Improving Education and Work Linkages." *Training and Development Journal,* July 1976, pp. 40–51.

Houle, C. O. "The Education of Adult Educational Leaders." In M. Knowles (Ed.), *Handbook of Adult Education in the United States.* Washington, D.C.: Adult Education Association, 1960.

Houle, C. O. *The Inquiring Mind.* Madison: University of Wisconsin Press, 1961.

Houle, C. O. "The Educators of Adults." In R. M. Smith, G. F. Aker, and J. R. Kidd (Eds.), *Handbook of Adult Education.* New York: Macmillan, 1970.

Houle, C. O. *The Design of Education.* San Francisco: Jossey-Bass, 1972.

Houle, C. O. "The Changing Goals of Education in the Perspective of Life-Long Learning." *International Review of Education, 1974, 20,* 430–445.

Houle, C. O. "Adult Education." In *Encyclopedia Britannica.* Vol. 1. Chicago: Encyclopedia Britannica, 1975.

Houle, C. O. *Continuing Learning in the Professions.* San Francisco: Jossey-Bass, 1980.

House, E. R. (Ed.). *School Evaluation: The Politics and the Process.* Berkeley, Calif.: McCutchan, 1973.

House, E. R. *The Politics of Innovation.* Berkeley, Calif.: McCutchan, 1974.

House, E. R. "Transferability and Equity in Innovation Policy." Paper presented at National Conference on Innovation and Change, Detroit, Sept. 1975.

Houston, W. R. (Ed.). *Exploring Competency-Based Education.* Berkeley, Calif.: McCutchan, 1974.

Huberman, M. "Looking at Adult Education from the Perspective of the Adult Life Cycle." *International Review of Education,* 1974, *20,* 117–136.

Huff, S. "Education, Work, and Competence." *Society,* 1976, *13* (2), 44–51.

Hunter, C., and Harman, D. *Adult Illiteracy in the United States: A Report to the Ford Foundation.* New York: McGraw-Hill, 1979.

Hutchins, R. *The Learning Society.* New York: Praeger, 1968.

Hutchins, R. "Toward a Learning Society." *The Center Magazine,* 1971, *4* (4).

Illich, I. *Deschooling Society.* New York: Harper & Row, 1970.

Illich, I. *After Deschooling, What?* A. Gartner, C. Greer, and F. Reissman (Eds.). New York: Harper & Row, 1973.

Institute for Educational Leadership. *Perspectives on Federal Educational Policy.* Washington, D.C.: Institute for Educational Leadership, George Washington University, 1976.

International Bureau of Education, Geneva. *Educational Planning.* 25th International Conference on Public Education. Publication No. 242. Paris: UNESCO, 1962.

Issues Facing Kentucky. Lexington: Department of Sociology, University of Kentucky, Dec. 1975.

Jackson, P. *Life in Classrooms.* New York: Holt, Rinehart and Winston, 1968.

James, D. "Conference of National Organizations for Cooperation in Adult Education." *Convergence,* 1974, *7* (3), 61–68.

James, H. T. "The New Cult of Efficiency and Education." In L. H. Browder, Jr. (Ed.), *Emerging Patterns of Administrative Accountability.* Berkeley, Calif.: McCutchan, 1971.

James, W. B. "What APL [Adult Performance Level] Is—and Is Not." *Adult Literacy and Basic Education,* 1977, *1* (1), 13–20.

Jencks, C., and others. *Inequality: A Reassessment of the Effect of Family and Schooling in America.* New York: Basic Books, 1972.

Jensen, G. "Education for Self-Fulfillment." In R. M. Smith, G. F. Aker, and J. R. Kidd (Eds.), *Handbook of Adult Education.* New York: Macmillan, 1970.

Jensen, G. "Certification of Adult Educators." *Mountain Plains Journal of Adult Education,* 1972, *1* (1), 22–26.

Jensen, G. "Who's Calling Whom What?" *Adult Leadership*, 1973, *22* (3), 97–99.

Jensen, G. "Concerns at Cuernavaca." *Adult Leadership*, 1974, *23*, 166.

Johnson, B. "The Impact of Certification on Local Programs." In B. R. Lyle (Ed.), *Teacher Certification in Adult Education.* Austin, Tex.: HEW Region VI Staff Development Project, 1975.

Johnstone, J., and Rivera, R. *Volunteers for Learning.* Chicago, Aldine, 1965.

Joseph, E. C. "What Is Future Time?" *The Futurist*, 1974, *8* (4), 178.

Katz, E. "The Social Itinerary of Technical Change: Two Studies on the Diffusion of Innovation." *Human Organization*, 1961, *20*, 70–82.

Kaufman, H., and Couzens, M. *Administrative Feedback.* Washington, D.C.: Brookings Institution, 1973.

Keats, J. *The Sheepskin Psychosis.* Philadelphia: Lippincott, 1965.

Keeton, M. T., and Associates. *Experiential Learning: Rationale, Characteristics, and Assessment.* San Francisco: Jossey-Bass, 1976.

Kirchner, E. "Philosophy of Education—Directive Doctrine of Liberal Discipline." In J. Park (Ed.), *Selected Readings in the Philosophy of Education.* New York: Macmillan, 1974.

Knowles, J. H. "The Responsibility of the Individual." *Daedalus*, 1977, *106* (1), 57–80.

Knowles, M. "Historical Development of the Adult Education Movement." In M. Knowles (Ed.), *Handbook of Adult Education in the United States.* Washington, D.C.: Adult Education Association, 1960.

Knowles, M. *The Adult Education Movement in the United States.* New York: Holt, Rinehart and Winston, 1962.

Knowles, M. "The Field of Operations in Adult Education." In G. Jensen, A. A. Liveright, and W. Hallenbeck (Eds.), *Adult Education: Outlines of an Emerging Field of University Study.* Washington, D.C.: Adult Education Association, 1964.

Knowles, M. *The Modern Practice of Adult Education: Andragogy Versus Pedagogy.* New York: Association Press, 1970.

Knowles, M., and Klevins, C. "Résumé of Adult Education." In C. Klevins (Ed.), *Materials and Methods in Adult Education.* New York: Klevins Publications, 1972.

Knox, A. B. "Continuing Professional Education: Need, Scope, and Setting." *Illinois Education Review,* 1972, *1* (1), 9–18.

Knox, A. B. "Mandatory Continuing Education for Professionals: Implications for the Future." In D. Moore, Jr. (Ed.), *Proceedings, Mandatory Continuing Education: Prospects and Dilemmas for Professionals.* Urbana: Office of Continuing Education and Public Service, University of Illinois, 1976.

Knox, A. B., and others. *An Evaluation Guide for Adult Basic Education Programs.* New York: Center for Adult Education, Teachers College, Columbia University, 1974.

Krathwohl, D. R., Bloom, B. S., and Masia, B. B. *Taxonomy of Educational Objectives.* Handbook II: *Affective Domain.* New York: McKay, 1964.

Kreitlow, B. W. *Educating the Adult Educator. Part 2: Taxonomy of Needed Research.* Madison: Wisconsin Research and Development Center, University of Wisconsin, 1968.

Kreitlow, B. W. "Federal Support to Adult Education: Boon or Boondoggle?" *Adult Education,* 1975, *25* (4), 231–237.

Kurland, N. *Financing Life-Long Learning: An Approach to an Age-Neutral Educational Entitlement.* Albany: State Department of Education Study of Adult Education, State University of New York, 1975.

Kurtz, E. G. "Help Stamp Out Non-behavioral Objectives." *Science Teacher,* Jan. 1965, pp. 31–32.

Lane, W., Corwin, R., and Monahan, W. *Foundations of Educational Administration: A Behavioral Analysis.* New York: Macmillan, 1966.

Langdon, S. *Citizen Participation in America.* Lexington, Mass.: Lexington Books, 1978.

Lapidus, I. M. "Adulthood in Islam: Religious Maturity in the Islamic Tradition." *Daedalus,* 1976, *105* (2), 93–108.

Lawson, K. H. *Philosophical Concepts and Values in Adult Education.* Nottingham, England: Barnes and Humby, 1975.

Leagans, J. P. "Continuing Education: A Fourth Dimension." In J. R. Squire (Ed.), *A New Look at Progressive Education.* Washington, D.C.: Association for Supervision and Curriculum Development, 1972.

Leider, R. J. "Mid-Career Renewal." *Training and Development Journal,* May 1976, pp. 16–30.

Lessinger, L. M. "The Powerful Notion of Accountability in Education." In L. H. Browder, Jr. (Ed.), *Emerging Patterns of Administrative Accountability.* Berkeley, Calif.: McCutchan, 1971.

Lewin, K. "Group Decision and Social Change." In G. Swanson and others (Eds.), *Readings in Social Psychology.* New York: Holt, Rinehart and Winston, 1952.

Lindeman, E. *The Meaning of Adult Education.* Montreal: Harvest House, 1961. (Originally published 1926.)

Lindeman, E. "Classrooms Without Walls." In R. Gessner (Ed.), *The Democratic Man.* Boston: Beacon Press, 1956.

Lionberger, H. *Adoption of New Ideas and Practices.* Ames: Iowa State University Press, 1960.

Lippmann, W. *The Public Philosophy.* London: Hamish Hamilton, 1955.

Little, K. J. *The Education and Training of Racial Minorities.* Madison: Center for Studies in Vocational and Technical Education, University of Wisconsin, 1968.

Litwak, E., and Rothman, J. "Towards the Theory and Practice of Coordinating Agencies." In W. R. Rosengren and M. Lefton (Eds.), *Organizations and Clients.* Columbus: Merrill, 1970.

Liveright, A. A. "The Nature and Aims of Adult Education as a Field of Graduate Study." In G. Jensen, A. A. Liveright, and W. Hallenbeck (Eds.), *Adult Education: Outlines of an Emerging Field of University Study.* Washington, D.C.: Adult Education Association, 1964.

Liveright, A. A. *A Study of Adult Education in the United States.* Boston: Center for the Study of Liberal Education for Adults, 1968.

London, J. "Adult Education for the 1970's: Promise or Illusion?" *Adult Education,* 1973a, *24* (1), 60–69.

London, J. "Reflections upon the Relevance of Paulo Freire for American Adult Education." *Convergence,* 1973b, *6* (1), 48–60.

Lopez, F. M. "Accountability in Education." *Phi Delta Kappan,* Dec. 1970, pp. 231–235.

Lowe, J. (Ed.). *Adult Education and Nation Building: A Symposium on Adult Education in Developing Countries.* Edinburgh, Scotland: Edinburgh University Press, 1970.

Lowe, J. *The Education of Adults: A World Perspective.* Paris: UNESCO Press, 1975.

McClusky, H. Y. "The Adult as Learner." In S. E. Seashore and R. J. McNeill (Eds.), *Management of the Urban Crisis.* New York: Free Press, 1971.

McDonald, F. J. "The Rationale for Competency-Based Programs." In W. R. Houston (Ed.), *Exploring Competency-Based Education.* Berkeley, Calif.: McCutchan, 1974.

McGowan, J. "The Impact of Certification on Local Programs." In B. R. Lyle (Ed.), *Teacher Certification in Adult Education.* Austin, Tex.: HEW Region VI Staff Development Project, 1975.

Maier, N. R. F. *Problem Solving Discussions and Conferences: Leadership Methods and Skills.* New York: McGraw-Hill, 1963.

Mandel, T. F. "Alternative Futures and Adult Education." *Convergence,* 1975, *8* (3), 53–62.

March, J. G. "Model Bias in Social Action." *Review of Educational Research,* 1972, *42* (4), 413–429.

Maritain, J. *Modern Philosophies and Education.* Chicago: National Society for the Study of Education, 1955.

Maslow, A. H. *Motivation and Personality.* New York: Harper & Row, 1954.

Meyer, P. *Awarding College Credit for Non-College Learning: A Guide to Current Practice.* San Francisco: Jossey-Bass, 1975.

Mezirow, J., Darkenwald, G. G., and Knox, A. B. *Last Gamble on Education: Dynamics of Adult Basic Education.* Washington, D.C.: Adult Education Association, 1975.

Miller, J. W. "Expanded Role of the Commission of Educational Credit of the American Council on Education." *Adult Leadership,* 1975, *23* (8), 251–255.

Mocker, D. W. "The Identification, Classification, and Ranking of Knowledges, Behaviors, and Attitudes Appropriate for Adult Basic Education Teachers." Unpublished doctoral dissertation, State University of New York at Albany, 1974.

Moore, W. E. *The Professions: Roles and Rules.* New York: Russell Sage Foundation, 1970.

Moses, S. *The Learning Force: A More Comprehensive Framework for Education Policy.* Syracuse, N.Y.: Syracuse University Press, 1971.

Mullen, E. J., and Associates. *Evaluation of Social Intervention.* San Francisco: Jossey-Bass, 1972.

Mushkin, S. J. (Ed.). *Recurrent Education.* Washington, D.C.: National Institute of Education, U.S. Government Printing Office, 1973.

Nagel, T. S., and Richman, P. T. *Competency-Based Instruction: A Strategy to Eliminate Failure.* Columbus: Merrill, 1972.

National Advisory Council on Adult Education. *Federal Activities in Support of Adult Education.* Washington, D.C.: National Advisory Council on Adult Education, 1972.

National Advisory Council on Adult Education. *An Historical Perspective: The Adult Education Act, 1964–1974.* Washington, D.C.: U.S. Government Printing Office, 1976a.

National Advisory Council on Adult Education. *A Target Population in Adult Education.* Washington, D.C.: U.S. Government Printing Office, 1976b.

National Advisory Council on Adult Education. *Adult Education: Futures and Amendments.* Washington, D.C.: U.S. Government Printing Office, 1977.

National Commission on the Financing of Postsecondary Education. *Financing Postsecondary Education in the United States.* Washington, D.C.: U.S. Government Printing Office, 1973.

Neugarten, B. (Ed.). *Middle Age and Aging.* Chicago: University of Chicago Press, 1968.

Northcutt, N. *Adult Functional Competency.* Austin: Division of Extension, University of Texas, 1975.

O'Toole, J. "On-the-Job Learning." *Worklife,* Jan. 1976, pp. 2–6.

O'Toole, J. *Energy and Social Change.* Cambridge, Mass.: M.I.T. Press, 1978.

Ohliger, J. "Is Lifelong Adult Education a Guarantee of Permanent Inadequacy?" Public lecture at the University of Saskatchewan, 1974a.

Ohliger, J. "Is Lifelong Adult Education a Guarantee of Permanent Inadequacy?" *Convergence,* 1974b, 7 (2), 47–58.

Orfield, G. *The Reconstruction of Southern Education: The Schools and the Civil Rights Act.* New York: Wiley-Interscience, 1969.

Organization for Economic Cooperation and Development. *Review of National Policies for Education: United States.* Vol. 7. Paris: OECD, 1971.

Otte, E. *Retirement Rehearsal Guidebook.* Indianapolis: Pictorial, Inc., 1971.

Overstreet, H. A. *The Mature Mind.* New York: Norton, 1949.

Penfield, K. R. "Academic Excellence vs. Public Service: Conflict and Accommodation Within the University as Manifest in the Development of the University of California Extension Division." Unpublished doctoral dissertation, University of California, Berkeley, 1972.

Penfield, K. R. "Prospects for a Learning Society." *Adult Leadership*, Sept. 1975, *24* (1), 40–44.

Pfeiffer, J. W., and Jones, J. E. *A Handbook of Structured Experiences for Human Relations Training.* Vol. 4. Iowa City: University Associates, 1974.

Pirsig, R. *Zen and the Art of Motorcycle Maintenance.* New York: Random House, 1974.

Powell, J. W., and Benne, K. D. "Philosophies of Adult Education." In M. Knowles (Ed.), *Handbook of Adult Education in the United States.* Washington, D.C.: Adult Education Association, 1960.

Reagan, M. D. *The New Federalism.* New York: Oxford University Press, 1972.

Rhyne, R. F. "Communicating Holistic Insights," *Fields Within Fields . . . Within Fields,* 1972, *5* (1), 93–104.

Rippey, R. M. *Studies in Transactional Evaluation.* Berkeley, Calif.: McCutchan, 1973.

Rivera, W. "The Basics Missing in ABE." In C. Klevins (Ed.), *Methods and Materials in Continuing Education.* New York: Klevins Publications, 1976.

Rivlin, A. M. *Systematic Thinking for Social Action.* Washington, D.C.: Brookings Institution, 1971.

Rockhill, K. "The Past as Prologue: Toward an Expanded View of Adult Education." *Adult Education*, 1976, *26* (4), 196–207.

Rogers, C. R. *Freedom to Learn.* Columbus, Ohio: Merrill, 1969.

Rogers, E. *Diffusion of Innovations.* New York: Free Press, 1962.

Rohlen, T. P. "The Promise of Adulthood in Japanese Spiritualism." *Daedalus*, 1976, *105* (2), 125–143.

Roomkin, M. "Evaluating Basic Education Programs: Some Conceptual and Methodological Problems." Paper presented at Adult Education Research Conference, Chicago, April 1972.

Roschwalb, J. "Continuing Education and the Reluctant Magicians." *Continuum,* Dec. 1976a, *41* (2).

Roschwalb, J. "The Federal Government and Higher Education: A View from Washington." *UCLA Educator*, 1976b, *18* (1), 15–21.

Rossman, M., and Bunning, R. "Knowledge and Skills for the Adult Educator: A Delphi Study." *Adult Education*, 1978, *28* (3), 139–155.

Rosten, L. *The Education of H*Y*M*A*N K*A*P*L*A*N*. New York: Harcourt Brace Jovanovich, 1937.

Schroeder, W. L. "Adult Education Defined and Described." In R. M. Smith, G. F. Aker, and J. R. Kidd (Eds.), *Handbook of Adult Education*. New York: Macmillan, 1970.

Schroeder, W. L. "Typology of Adult Learning Systems." In J. M. Peters and Associates, *Building an Effective Adult Education Enterprise*. San Francisco: Jossey-Bass, 1980.

Schultze, C. L. *The Role of Incentives, Penalties, and Rewards in Attaining Effective Policy*. Indianapolis: Bobbs-Merrill, 1969.

Schwertman, J. B. *I Want Many Lodestars*. Chicago: Center for the Study of Liberal Education for Adults, 1958.

Schwille, J., and Porter, A. "The Use of Fieldwork in Educational Evaluation: From the Perspective of Two Nonanthropologists." Paper presented at annual meeting of American Educational Research Association, San Francisco, April 1976.

Scriven, M. "The Methodology of Evaluation." In *Perspectives of Curriculum Evaluation*. AERA Monograph 1. Chicago: Rand McNally, 1967.

Sergiovanni, J., and Carver, F. *The New School Executive: A Theory of Administration*. New York: Dodd, Mead, 1973.

Seymour, W. D. "A Skills Analysis: Wrapper Stemming (GTW) for Spun Pipe Tobacco." In *Skills Analysis Training*. London: Pitman, 1966.

Sheehy, G. *Passages*. New York: Dutton, 1976.

Sheffield, S. B. "The Orientations of Adult Continuing Learners." In D. Solomon (Ed.), *The Continuing Learner*. Chicago: Center for the Study of Liberal Education for Adults, 1964.

Sigfried, R. "Science and Technology: Hero of the Past, Villain of the Future." *Wisconsin Academy Review*, 1975, *21* (3), 4–9.

Skinner, B. F. *The Technology of Teaching*. New York: Appleton-Century-Crofts, 1968.

Smith, R. L. "A Study to Determine the Perceptions of Competencies Needed by Adult Basic Education Teachers." Unpublished doctoral dissertation, Oregon State University, Corvallis, 1972.

Smith, T. V., and Lindeman, E. C. *The Democratic Way of Life.* New York: New American Library, 1951.

Stake, R. E. "The Countenance of Educational Evaluation." *Teachers College Record,* 1967, *68,* 523–540.

Stake, R. E. "Objectives, Priorities, and Other Judgment Data." *Review of Educational Research,* 1970, *40* (2), 181–212.

Stake, R. E. "Issues About Objectives." Paper prepared for AFT Quest Consortium, Washington, D.C., April 1972.

Steele, S. M. "Concept of Macro Evaluation." Paper presented at workshop on program effectiveness, Extension Service, U.S. Department of Agriculture, 1977.

Stolz, O. G. *Revenue Sharing: Legal and Policy Analysis.* New York: Praeger, 1974.

Strother, G., and Swinford, D. N. "Recertification and Relicensure: Implications for the University." NUEA *Spectator,* 1975, *38,* (19), 5–9.

Stubblefield, H. "Adult Education for Civic Intelligence in the Post World War I Period." *Adult Education,* 1976, *26* (4), 253–269.

Sufrin, S. C. *Issues in Federal Aid to Education.* Syracuse, N.Y.: Syracuse University Press, 1962.

Taylor, H. *On Education and Freedom.* New York: Abelard-Schuman, 1954.

Taylor, H. *How to Change Colleges: Notes on Radical Reform.* New York: Holt, Rinehart and Winston, 1971.

Taylor, P. *Normative Discourse.* Englewood Cliffs, N.J.: Prentice-Hall, 1961.

Texas Education Agency. *Adult and Continuing Education Class Reports for the State of Texas.* Austin: Division of Adult and Continuing Education, Texas Education Agency, 1975.

Thompson, D. F. *The Democratic Citizen.* Cambridge, England: Cambridge University Press, 1970.

Thompson, J. D., and McEwen, W. J. "Organization Goals and Environment." In A. Etzioni (Ed.), *Complex Organizations: A Sociological Reader.* New York: Holt, Rinehart and Winston, 1961.

Tough, A. *The Adult's Learning Projects.* Toronto: Ontario Institute for Studies in Education, 1971.

Tu, W.-M. "The Confucian Perception of Adulthood." *Daedalus,* 1976, *105* (2), 109–123.

Turner, T., and Williams, R. "International Education: A Political Action." *Convergence*, 1971, *4* (1), 75–79.

Tyler, R. *Basic Principles of Curriculum and Instruction Syllabus.* Chicago: University of Chicago Press, 1950.

Udell, G. "Yes, a Change Agent Can Evaluate." *Journal of Extension,* Sept.–Oct. 1975, *13*, 14–21.

Ulmer, C., Blakely, R. J., and Kuhn, S. "Prospects for a Learning Society Symposium." *Adult Leadership*, Sept. 1975, *24*, 35–37.

UNESCO. *Second International Conference on Adult Education: Final Report.* Paris: UNESCO, 1960.

UNESCO. *Third International Conference on Adult Education: Final Report.* Paris: UNESCO, 1972.

United States Bureau of the Census. *Statistical Abstract of the United States, 1974.* Washington, D.C.: U.S. Government Printing Office, 1975.

United States Department of Health, Education and Welfare. *Perspectives of Adult Education in the United States and a Projection for the Future.* Washington, D.C.: U.S. Government Printing Office, 1972.

United States Department of Health, Education and Welfare. *Digest of Educational Statistics: 1973 Edition.* Washington, D.C.: U.S. Government Printing Office, 1974.

Veri, C. *Competencies Assessment Survey for Adult Educators.* DeKalb, Ill.: Northern Illinois University, 1974.

Vermilye, D. W. (Ed.). *Lifelong Learners—A New Clientele for Higher Education.* San Francisco: Jossey-Bass, 1974.

Vescolani, F. "Teacher Certification in Adult Education." In B. R. Lyle (Ed.), *Teacher Certification in Adult Education.* Austin, Tex.: HEW Region VI Staff Development Project, 1975.

Ward, F. C. (Ed.). *Education and Development Reconsidered: The Belagio Conference Papers.* New York: Praeger, 1974.

Warren, R. L. *Truth, Love, and Social Change.* Chicago: Rand McNally, 1971.

Weisbrod, B. *External Benefits of Public Education: An Economic Analysis.* Princeton, N.J.: Industrial Relations Section, Department of Economics, Princeton University, 1964.

Weiss, C. H. *Evaluating Action Programs.* Boston: Allyn and Bacon, 1972.

Weizenbaum, J. *Computer Power and Human Reason: From Judgment to Calculation.* San Francisco: Freeman, 1976.

Whale, W. B. "Appraisal of a Process of Planning for Total Resource Development in a Wisconsin County." Unpublished doctoral dissertation, University of Wisconsin, Madison, 1966.

White, T. J. "Philosophical Considerations." In R. M. Smith, G. F. Aker, and J. R. Kidd (Eds.), *Handbook of Adult Education.* New York: Macmillan, 1970.

Wilkening, E. *Acceptance of Improved Farm Practices.* Technical Bulletin 98-RS. Raleigh: North Carolina Agriculture Experiment Station, 1958.

Wirtz, W. *The Boundless Resource: A Prospectus for an Education-Work Policy.* Washington, D.C.: New Republic Book Company, 1975.

Zeigarnik, B. "Das Behalten erledigter und unerledigter Handlungen" [The Memory of Completed and Uncompleted Actions]. *Psychologische Forschung,* 1927, *9,* 1–85.

Ziegler, W. *On Civic Literacy.* Syracuse, N.Y.: Educational Policy Center, 1974.

Ziegler, W. "The Life of the Public and the Life of Learning: Notes Toward a Social Philosophy for Adult Learning." *Adult Leadership,* April 1976, *24* (8), 254–256, 281–284.

Ziegler, W., Healy, G., and Ellsworth, J. "Futures-Invention: An Approach to Civil Literacy." In C. Klevins (Ed.), *Methods and Materials in Continuing Education.* New York: Klevins Publications, 1976.

Name Index

277

Subject Index